Summer Lightning
Distant Thunder

Summer Lightning Distant Thunder
is the first in The Wagon Road Trilogy.

Other books by Tony Kinton:

Outside and Other Reflections

Fishing Mississippi

For an updated list of new releases go to
www.tonykinton.com.

Summer Lightning
Distant Thunder

TONY KINTON

Cedar Arrow
PUBLISHING

ISBN 978-0-9836829-0-5

LCCN 2011910879

Tony Kinton
Cedar Arrow Publishing
P.O. Box 88
Carthage, MS 39051

Glossary

Flintlock (Flinter): A firearm of either rifled or smooth-bore configuration that uses a piece of flint struck against a metal plate (frizzen) when the hammer falls to ignite the powder charge.

Center Seams: Simple foot wear (moccasins) with a single seam running from toe to ankle on top center. Common to Native Americans, center seams were quickly adopted by long hunters.

Fowler: A flintlock firearm with a smooth bore, generally loaded with small shot for hunting birds, waterfowl and small game.

Half Face: A makeshift shelter made with whatever materials are on hand—usually small poles, brush and leaves. Much the same shelter as a lean-to.

Jager: A hunting rifle with a relatively short barrel of 30 inches and in big bores, such as .62 and above. German origin.

Poccon: An ancient remedy made from natural substances and used to treat infection.

Tump Line: A leather strap with a leather or linen string running through from each end onto which a blanket or similar item was rolled and tied. The tump line was thrown across the shoulder for carrying.

Quilled: Native Americans of the East used porcupine quills colored with dyes made from plants to decorate items such as leggings, moccasins and knife sheaths. This practice was later adopted by those arriving in the colonies and moving to the frontier.

Acknowledgments

A book is not the product of one individual. That one may actually write the manuscript, but the finished publication contains the efforts of a great many people. This one is no exception. So, it is with much sincerity that I offer my deep gratitude to the following:

Charles Sutherland of E.T. Lowe, Nashville; the team at Lightning Source, Nashville; Farrah Howell, Sandra Jones, Kathy Sanders, Debbie Stringer, Sherry Thornton, Lori Wilcher, and Nancy Williams—all close-by friends, neighbors, and associates. And a special thanks to my wife Susan. The encouragement kept me going.

To all, thank you.

Tony Kinton

CHAPTER 1

London - Autumn 1773

 Sun Bain watched a cold fog roll over London. Afternoon shadows were conquering the day; wind bit his face. His brown hair, pulled back into a queue and tied off with a finger-wide leather thong, was buffeted by the gusts, and he tugged a woolen greatcoat and scarf about his neck. He shivered there alone.

A sturdy young man standing five-feet ten, Sun had fair skin that tanned to a rich hue at the first hint of exposure to sunlight. His blue eyes darted about with inquiry at practically everything he encountered. His thirst for knowing was insatiable; his intellect was keen. He had come to the Mother Country to complete his education and had done so with dignity. Jackson Bain now possessed credentials that went unquestioned, here or in the New World.

More than three months had passed since he had written his father to tell of his intentions upon returning home. He knew what Squire Bain's reaction would be, but Sun had hoped for at least a response. None had come. From childhood Sun had understood that he was expected to get a formal education and move into a strategic position within his father's business. Boston was to be his home; business was to be his life. And he was to marry properly. Even before he left three years earlier there were rumblings from his father regarding the union of Jackson Bain and Rebecca Bomar. These were to be Boston's elite, and their marriage would assure the merger of the two most powerful business interests in Boston. Sun's decision and subsequent letter precluded such activity.

How can I do this to my family? The thought brought agony. Family was important to Sun and his had done nothing but support this only son. Now he was willingly and intentionally going against their expectations, at least the expectations of his father. He was not certain about his mother's feelings in the matter, but he suspected she would be more understanding than Squire. Sun was certain, however, that his father had broached the subject with his wife more times than a few since the letter had arrived. And he was certain that his father was not always gentle in those presentations.

But how can I not do this? This is who I am. I must be and do what I must be and do. True thoughts and ones that should bring some resolution, but they simply added to the struggle that was tearing Sun apart.

How far does my responsibility go? To whom am I responsible? Am I obligated to do what I am expected to do? There were no answers. The world seemed out of harmony. Jackson Bain, at a time that most would anticipate being a high point in his life, saw only gloom and rejection. He had been in England for three years and wanted very much to return home, to see those he loved, to offer highlights of his life in the Mother Country, to have his mother listen and marvel at what a fine man he had grown into and remind him that he was still her little boy and her speck of sunshine. Mature now and desiring to get about the business of his future, Sun still possessed that need for mothering, a need for that sense of all rightness that had been always familiar when he was in the presence of Martha Bain. It had been too long. But he feared that a joyful meeting was not waiting for him when he left the ship in Boston Harbor.

Candles and lamps began to flicker along the streets of London as Sun moved about, the chill gnawing. A quickened pace was evidenced as residents and guests, some in their finery and some in their squalor, started their parades to various venues—eating establishments, pubs, theaters,

2

even locales where a handout might be garnered or some item of value might be filched. Sun watched and wandered, but mostly he contemplated his life and what he would face when he returned home.

A rowdy crowd sang drinking songs that trickled through the door of a local pub. He smiled briefly at some of the words that met his ears but cut that smile and its resultant thoughts short when he considered how he had been brought up. His mother would not be pleased if she knew he entertained such bawdy behavior. Laughter resonated from the room and spilled into the street. Sun moved closer.

"Jackson Bain. How goes it with you this fine evening my boy?" Sun recognized the voice even before he saw Cedric. Standing there with Sun just outside the door of the pub was an acquaintance from the university. Cedric was an amiable fellow who had befriended Sun early on and was fully Brit, possessing that Old World resolve and protocol that made him an agreeable sort. He avoided any discussion that would hinder their relationship and considered Sun a superb example of what the New World represented, a subject that would make England proud. He and Sun were both aware of rumored tensions between King George and the colonies, but both were gentlemen enough not to let these dissuade their friendship.

"A fine evening? I hadn't noticed," Sun replied with a shrug. "I'm not completely sure anything would fit the designation of fine at this moment." Cedric proffered a hearty handshake that was reciprocated by Sun. "I have a mountain of troubles with no easy answers."

"Now my boy, it can't be all that bad. Come on in here and let me buy a round. We'll talk about the life we have just completed at the university and your return home and yes, your troubles. Come on now; drinks are on me."

"I . . . I don't know Cedric," Sun stammered. "Perhaps I should just go on to my room. I'm hardly in a mood for what I hear going on inside there. Please excuse me and I'll be on my way."

"I'll have nothing of it," Cedric countered. "You'll come in here and let me help you figure out some answers, or at least let me help you forget your troubles. Now in you go, my boy." Cedric pushed the door open and marched Sun   3 ahead of him. The room was dim and noisy and filled with pipe smoke and the smell of alcohol. Young and old men alike lined the bar and sat at tables scattered about the pub. The atmosphere had the appearance of joviality, but Sun wondered about the depth of that joy. A lute player sat in one corner, his entourage singing along and swinging half-filled mugs to the rhythm of the song.

"One round," Cedric shouted over the din. Almost immediately a pair of huge steins containing a frothy brew appeared. "Now drink up, my boy." Cedric lifted his and wolfed down a sizable portion of the dark liquid before removing it from his lips. Sun did similarly, but with much less gusto than that exhibited by his comrade.

"When do you leave?" Cedric asked of Sun.

"Just about two weeks now. I sail in 12 days. Cedric, I'm ready to go home, but I am extremely worried about what I will find. My father is displeased with me. He is not the forgiving sort, and I am filled with a dark dread of what awaits me back in Boston.

"My father expects me to step into his business, to even take over a large measure of that business. He sent me here to be fully educated in such matters. But at least for now, that is not what I want to do. I want to explore the frontier. I need to know who I am before taking such a monstrous responsibility as following my father's plan. He even has my wife selected for me, another business move."

Cedric had pretended to listen intently and perhaps he did, but his response told Sun that Cedric was not as sympathetic or concerned as Sun would have liked. "Tough break, my boy, but let's talk about all that a bit later. Right now let's talk about the hunting trip."

"The hunting trip?" Sun asked in amazement.

"Yes, of course. You will join my family and me on a hunting trip. Red stag and boar. We will travel by coach; it is only a long day's journey. We will hunt the forests north of here for five days and you will still be back with ample time to meet your ship. Additionally, you need the experience to help you prepare for that frontier you want to conquer in the New World."

"I don't want to *conquer* the frontier," Sun chided, a touch of sarcasm in his voice. "I simply want to explore it and see what it has to offer. The Indians have it and that is the way it will remain. I have no interest in conquest."

"Well, perhaps, my boy," Cedric opined. "But sometimes survival demands conquest."

"Perhaps you are right, but I remind you that I have no need for dominating anyone or anything, much unlike my father I might add. I simply want . . . no, I need to see what lies westward." Sun spoke with conviction. The thought of possibly having to take the life of a fellow human being sickened him. It wasn't fear particularly; it was a deep dread, an unnerving grief over tragic loss and how he would deal with such travesty that he himself had meted out should the occasion require. He thought he knew, but he could not be sure, having never faced such an obstacle.

"Shakespeare was right," Sun offered.

"Aye, he was, my boy, but to what do you refer in that observation?"

"*Hamlet*," Sun answered. "Do you recall when Laertes was leaving home and his father Polonius was giving him that last bit of advice? *To thine own self be true, and it must follow, as the night the day. . . .*"

"*Thou canst not then be false to any man*," Cedric interrupted. "Of course I remember that, my boy. I am a Brit. Shakespeare is one of our great treasures. And he was an astute student of human nature. How could I help but know?" Sun, always impressed with Cedric's knowledge of poetry and theater and all things of quality, smiled and nodded.

"I must do as Laertes was instructed," Sun said. "I must be true to myself."

Boston 1773

"Foolish." The word exploded from Squire Bain's scowling face with a force that reverberated around the room. During the 35 years of their marriage, Martha had witnessed her husband's rigidity countless times, but this episode had been particularly long lived.

"What does the boy want?"

The library in which Squire Bain unleashed his tirade was opulently furnished. So was the entire house, a sym- 5 bol of prestige that he had promised Martha early on in their marriage, and one which he frequently reminded her of during his too-regular journeys into dour moodiness. Leather-bound books of philosophy, religion, poetry, and law lined shelves made from the finest mahogany. Velvet and brocade drapes, their valances trimmed in rococo scroll, graced long windows that looked out over a manicured garden of roses and fountains. Queen Anne furniture was set strategically about the room. A William Hogarth painting held prominence over a decorative fireplace at the center of one wall.

Squire Bain sank into an upholstered chair near a window. He lifted a blown-glass container of brandy from the table and poured half full a gold-rimmed snifter. Lips pursed and brow wrinkled, he sighed in disgust.

"Squire," Martha said in a gentle tone of understanding that no one possessed in regards to her husband but she, "perhaps you are not viewing this as you should. Let's look at the facts of this situation."

"Facts? You want to talk facts? The facts are that Jackson has disregarded everything we hold precious. The facts are that he is unworthy to be called our son."

"Squire, you don't mean that. Listen to what you are saying. Sun is a treasure, an essential part of the future. I fail to see how he in any way is intentionally disregarding you or your wishes for him." Named Jackson Squire at birth, Sun's name had gone through the derivation to *Sun* because in his childhood Martha reminded him regularly that he was her gift of sunshine in an often dismal world.

"The future? Our son?" Squire hissed, the snifter now empty. "He has no concept of the future. I have set his future before him and he won't take advantage of it. No son of mine would do such a thing. My son would have the insight to grasp what I offer and not have to struggle as I have to get to this point. The name Bain holds status; it will open every door of opportunity he could hope for. Don't talk to me of *our* son."

"But Squire; God is in control and He has a plan," Martha countered.

6   "And there you go with your *God* business again."

Squire's emphasis on the word held poison, cutting deeply into Martha's heart and bringing a flush to her face and tears to her eyes.

"Squire, please," Martha whispered. "You believe. I know you do. You know God has guided and blessed us. We would never have accomplished and obtained as we have without His hand in it all."

"Oh, I believe I suppose. I was brought up to believe. But I know that what I have accomplished is due to my hard work and wise choices. What does God have to do with that?"

"Everything," Martha answered with assurance. "God gave you the ability and intellect. He has kept you safe and healthy and allowed you to be in the right places to further your business and life. And I don't know about you, but I have prayed every day that He would give you the direction you needed in every situation. God has everything to do with it."

"Enough of this God talk. I hold firm that I have done what I have done because of me. I have made myself successful. You have been there and I appreciate that, but I have made this business and our lives. Now I want to pass it along to an ungrateful boy who is filled with wanderlust and void of wisdom. This letter proves it." Squire pulled the crumpled paper from an inside pocket of his greatcoat. The message had arrived from England two months prior and had instigated Squire's resent discontent.

"You call him a boy, Squire," Martha said in a quiet voice. "He is 23, hardly a boy."

"He is a boy, Martha. And not a very wise one at that."

"Do you remember our wedding?"

"Of course I remember our wedding," Squire answered, his sarcasm obvious in the condescending tone. "How could I forget? But what does that have to do with this conversation? How does that relate to this betrayal now facing me?"

"The little church there on the outskirts of Boston was simple and sparsely decorated," Martha recalled. "We had nothing. No fancy bouquets. You even had to borrow a greatcoat from Mr. Johnson, but oh how handsome you looked in that borrowed coat. And the buggy we used to go out to the inn

7

that night was borrowed as well. I remember every detail. The wedding kiss. The large crowd of friends and well wishers. Rev. Bevin's squeaky voice and pointed nose and too-tight shoes straight from England.

"The smell of the night air as we rode away that evening. The moon rising over Boston Harbor. Every detail."

Squire indulged his wife by maintaining silence, but his heart remained stoic, unmoved, his spirit unforgiving.

"But among all those vivid memories the one that I most remember was your passion," Martha continued. "Not just your passion regarding this new institution we had just entered, although that was most apparent!" Martha smiled coyly and was a bit embarrassed when recalling the sheer abandon with which she had conducted herself that night 35 years past. "I remember your passion for life.

"You then were two years younger than Sun is now. You possessed nothing more than a desire to achieve. Our parents couldn't help; they had not long been free of their indenture. They had laid a foundation, but the type building to go up on that foundation was our choice. You wanted nothing more. You were a free spirit that could not be tamed. You were not then nor now one to fit some mold. My hero you were. You still are. I loved you then; I love you now."

Squire Bain was quiet, reflective. Martha's words had touched him, but bitterness had grown toward his son as well as most of the world because of arduous years of work and the false satisfaction of immense success. Life had become a superficial game of winning and gaining and controlling. Gone was the gentleness of those early years. Gone was his practice of looking to God and giving Him thanks. The passion of which Martha spoke was a dim recall. He had not realized it had somehow slipped away and would not now allow that realization to gain a hold. He was Squire Bain, a powerful, influential man who would not give in to this depth of truth.

Squire set the snifter down with authority, pulled an ornate English pipe from his weskit pocket, and stuffed it with tobacco. The sweet smell of smoke soon filled the room. Martha felt estranged as Squire began walking from the library. "I have no son," he said with decisive contempt.

8

CHAPTER 2

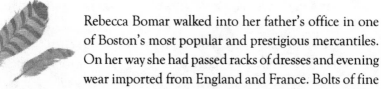

Rebecca Bomar walked into her father's office in one of Boston's most popular and prestigious mercantiles. On her way she had passed racks of dresses and evening wear imported from England and France. Bolts of fine linen lay on tables in one section. In another were knee breeches and silk stockings and weskits and greatcoats. Shirts with ruffled collars. Black leather shoes with brass buckles. Rebecca smelled the leather and dye and fluffed her fingers through the broad assortment of clothing as she passed. She smiled, her own dress swirling about small feet in shoes from an English cobbler. She felt smug as she climbed the stairs, entering her father's office without a knock.

"Hello Papa." She rushed to his side and hugged him. Richard Bomar, a heavy-set gentleman with a head full of thick grey hair and a pronounced belly that bulged his weskit looked up from his paperwork and with his right arm returned Rebecca's hug. His oversized oak desk held an ink well, quill pen, letters, a huge ledger and those ever-present business documents. Stacks of them everywhere. The office smelled of pipe smoke, leather, and business. That latter was not something Rebecca could clearly designate, but from the time she was a little girl her father's office had a specific odor that she equated with business. It spoke of success, of a comfortable house and luxuries. It was a smell of security that this daughter had never questioned.

Rebecca possessed natural beauty. Golden curls that

hung below her shoulders; a mouth that quickly broke into a wide smile accentuated by full lips; eyes that danced with pleasure. She was the envy of other girls her age and the target of countless Boston bachelors who hoped to gain her favor. She flirted and toyed with them, taking great pleasure in the attention she received.

And that attention was not limited to the would-be suitors. It had been heaped upon her by Richard Bomar from the day she was born. Richard's only child, Rebecca had her dad's ear at any time she wanted. Business and Rebecca—these were the driving forces of Richard Bomar's life.

"What are you doing, Papa?" Rebecca quizzed. "You work too hard."

"Not at all," Richard responded. "I do work hard, but that is a great part of my life. Besides, I want to do this for you and your mother." He hesitated. "And yes, for me. I enjoy being successful." Rebecca thumbed through some notes Richard had scratched out.

"Are you considering another business?" she asked after looking over the things that Richard had written.

"Perhaps. I am thinking of expanding into hardware. There is a solid market, and it appears that a westward movement is on the horizon. The frontier will need hardware much more than fine dresses and ruffled shirts, and I think I will begin developing business interests in that area."

"The frontier? Oh Papa, that is just a land of savages. Who would want to go there in the first place, and why would you want to try and do business there? I would never want to visit the frontier. In fact, I would never consider leaving Boston."

"Of course not," Richard opined. "You were born for Boston. This is your city. You will never have to endure the hardships of the frontier. And I'm not going, either. I'm just looking into some business endeavors that could provide needed goods for those who do choose to go there. And I predict that England's influence, through those hardy settlers who move west, will reach as far as Kan-te-Kee before you know it. I want to be prepared."

10   "The Indians?" Rebecca injected.

"Well, there can be trouble. Particularly with the Shawnees. There is talk from out there along Beautiful River. We can expect some unrest there and throughout Kan-te-Kee."

"You really can't blame them," Rebecca said. "That is their home." Always quick to speak her mind on such things, Rebecca almost felt as if she should not address this matter. It was against the prevailing thought of most. But it was troubling to her.

"Now Rebecca," Richard countered, "that is not something of concern for us. We are business people and provide supplies that people need and enjoy a handsome profit in so doing. I have nothing to do with treaties or intrusion. I just do business where business needs doing."

A decent man who held others in high regard and respected his associates, Richard Bomar believed only part of what he was saying. He had seen the abuse of treaties and was aware of what had happened in earlier years as French and English immigrants came to this New World, but he was so involved in his business life that he pushed such thoughts from his mind and refused to dwell on them.

"Is your mother home?" The house was not far from the business district in which Richard's primary store and office were located. This dwelling was designed to impress—a towering Georgian edifice with winding staircases intricately carved and ornate mantels surrounding four fireplaces. It was, in lumber and stone and ironwork, an emblem of wealth, of ease, of class. Rebecca often walked the shady streets from home to visit her father at his business establishment.

"She had just called for a carriage when I left. She said she was going to the Westmorland mansion for tea with some neighborhood women. I'll do the same when I am married and fall into the social life of Boston. I'll boast of my doting husband and our travels to England and his many business adventures—just like yours. I'll sip tea as I tell of my wonderful children. It will be delightful." Rebecca was giddy with her sense of entitlement. She was, after all, the daughter of Richard Bomar.

"As I said earlier, you were born for Boston!" Richard nodded as he smiled at his daughter.

Again Rebecca fumbled somewhat tentatively with   11

some of the correspondence on Richard's desk. One was an envelope addressed to him that carried a familiar return —Squire Bain. She gestured toward it and asked, "Are you in regular contact with Mr. Bain?"

"Yes, we talk often. Business most of the time. He tells me his son will be returning from England soon. What do you think of Jackson? He is well educated, Boston born, and I'm sure he will be immediately involved in his father's business once he gets home. That, I believe, is the answer to that doting husband you plan to boast about."

Rebecca, just three months past 19, became even more animated than before and was obviously intrigued by the possibilities, but she was also uncomfortable with the direction of the conversation. She had thought of marriage and had known Jackson Bain all her life. They were friends, companions from childhood. And even though she was aware of family hopes that the two would marry, she was filled with uncertainty at the suddenness of her father's proclamation.

"Sun?" she questioned hesitantly. Gone was that magnetic smile and those bouncing eyes, these replaced by a troubled frown.

"Well of course, Sun," Richard said. "He is a perfect young man for you. He knows Boston and business. You two would be the talk of the town."

Rebecca's emotions were now in a whirl. She envisioned life with Sun Bain here in Boston—the children they would have, the social and political events in which they would be involved, the handsome couple with no worries and viewed with envy. She would indeed be what she wanted to be, as her dad said, "the talk of the town." This all appealed to her and filled her with grandiose notions of how everything would be: Perfect. *And perfection is what I deserve* she thought as her mind continued to race and paint splendid portraits of the future.

"Are you sure Papa?" Rebecca asked with some trepidation. "I like Sun; he is my friend. But I am not in love with him."

"In love? Heavens daughter. Being in love is a fantasy. Love is something that grows as you live life. A good match is the best you can hope for, and the match of you and Jackson Bain is good."

"Oh Papa, you sound so certain. I trust you and believe that you want the very best for me, but I want to marry the man I love. I am not in love with Sun Bain."

"Nonsense. You take my word for it. I know what is best and I know what you need. Jackson Bain is a good choice. And that will lead to the Bain & Bomar Company, the most influential business endeavor in the New World. You will see; you will be happy. Now off with you. I have to get back to the business of business. Your mother and you would think poorly of me if I did otherwise."

Rebecca Bomar turned and walked away. She wanted to share the conclusion of her father. She even smiled tentatively at the thought of her marriage to a childhood friend and how she could ever adjust to an intimate physical connection with one she had seen grow up, one with whom she had laughed and talked in childish fashion. This troubled her, but then she admitted to herself that Sun Bain was handsome and gentle and desirable. She even admitted that thoughts of physical contact with Sun had many times been present as she lay awake and held her pillow in the quiet sanctuary of her room, her breathing accelerated and heart fluttering like the pigeons she studied in amazement as they rose from their perches and ascended toward Heaven. Still, she had given little serious consideration to Sun becoming her husband. But she would think of little else now. She was no longer that child Sun had kissed on the cheek.

As she left Richard Bomar's establishment somewhat downcast yet willing to follow her father's directives, she hardly noticed the finery of the articles she had so fondly admired upon that earlier entrance.

•   •   •

Twilight found Martha Bain sitting silently at the dining table, her Bible open to Matthew 5. As she read she paused at the end of verse 9: *"Blessed are the peacemakers: for they shall be called the children of God."*

Oh Lord, she prayed silently, *let me be a peacemaker. Peace is not present in this household. I know I can't do it alone*   13 *and I know I can't take the responsibility for Squire or Sun. The choices they make are theirs alone. But allow me in some way to help them come to terms; allow me to be a peacemaker. It will be You who does the healing, not I. Give me wisdom in this matter. I pray for peace in this divided family. I love Squire. I love Sun. But my love for You is greater than my love for them. Don't let me stand in the way of Your working to bring peace.*

Tears flowed freely now. Martha had known conflict with Squire, and she had seen conflict grow between him and Sun as Sun grew older. Most of those conflicts were minor, at least when weighed against this most recent one. This one was filled with threat. This one could wreck the structure Martha had grown to treasure more than anything in this world.

Peace, Lord. I pray for peace. Touch hearts. Open eyes. Heal hurts. Bring peace to this family.

CHAPTER 3

Elizabeth Bomar arrived home as Rebecca was returning from Richard's office. The two spoke in a perfunctory fashion and entered the house.

"Have you been to see your father?" Elizabeth quizzed.

"Yes. He was busy of course. Always is. But he and I talked."

"Yes, I'm sure he was busy. He is a successful man and successful men are busy men. He does it for us, you know."

"Perhaps, but he also does it for himself," Rebecca added. "He even admitted it. He enjoys success"

"And why should he not enjoy it?" Elizabeth said, a sharp tone to her voice. "Success is something to be proud of, something to be desired. He is right to enjoy it."

"Does he enjoy you, mother? Have you pushed him to this work schedule that demands his time and consumes practically every minute of his life?"

"Rebecca Bomar! How dare you? When did you come to such absurd conclusions? And you of all people. You are the recipient of that work and status and prestige. You will inherit the fortune your father has amassed. That is you and your husband will. You must have a husband to make decisions of how you will handle the money and property. And it must be the right husband, one who will assure your continued acceptance into Boston's finest. You do want a husband, don't you?"

"Well of course I do mother, but. . . ." Before Rebecca could say more Elizabeth interrupted.

"We were just talking about such things today over tea at the Westmorland Mansion. Rebecca, it was a most wonderful event. All the right women of Boston were there, the elite whose husbands are the leaders of this grand city. Mrs. Westmorland, of course, and there was Mrs. Cresap, Mrs. Braddock, Mrs. Johnson, Mrs. Franklin and many others. All wives of influential men. All proper material for Boston. All representing what this country should be.

"We talked endlessly. Some of the women discussed the upcoming marriages of their daughters to young men destined for important positions in Boston and New York and Charleston, though I can't see why anyone would want to move as far away as Charleston.

"And some talked of married sons and daughters who had already moved into roles of importance, the daughters now becoming mothers of children who will do as their parents and grandparents did and become people of significance. It was all just wonderful. And while I blushed with pride about you as you are now, I can hardly wait to announce your engagement to one of Boston's elite."

"People of significance, mother? Are not all people significant?"

"Well, I suppose they are. But don't let some sentiment get in the way and blind you to facts. It is the people to whom I refer who are of greatest importance. Those poor indentured ones among us will never amount to more than some rude farmer or woods runner or long hunter. They have not the breeding to be anything more. You were born into class and elegance. That is where you will live your life, happily."

"Happy, mother? Are those women you mentioned happy? Is my father happy? Are you happy, mother? Consider that; are you happy?"

"Rebecca! Why would you talk of such things? I am astounded that you would ask foolish questions that go beyond the scope of your understanding. Happy? What do I have to be unhappy about? We have wealth, status. Your father is a highly successful businessman and civic leader. People look up to us. Of course I am happy."

16

"What about your relationship to your husband, my father? Is that happy?

"Stop that. You have no right to inquire into such matters. Your father and I move in proper circles. I stand proudly by his side. He provides abundantly for the two of us. And you speak of happiness. That is happiness."

"I'm not so sure mother. Oh, I want to be a part of Boston's finest, but I think my happiness will be centered on a loving relationship with my husband, and if I am blessed with children they must be the focus of our lives. I want to be able to brag of my perfect life when I attend those teas and social gatherings, and when I stand beside my husband my heart will be filled with love for him, not what he can provide."

"Oh my dear, you are naïve. What is going to happen to this new generation? Now, no more of this talk. Your father will be home soon and we must be ready to go to the Griffiths' gala. There will be a great many young men there trying to gain your attention. Look your best."

CHAPTER 4

The Frontier 1773

Isaac Walker recoiled in shock. He had, only seconds before, reached to extract a peeled pole from a stack that had been curing in the sun. This would be one of many used to make a pole barn on his homestead east of Cumberland Gap. The rattler had given no warning; it had simply lashed out and sunk its fangs into the muscle between Isaac's thumb and index finger on his right hand.

Isaac's entire life flashed before him in the instant he realized what had just happened. He thought of the voyage from England and then his seven-year indenture in eastern Pennsylvania. He thought of his move from there, along with his wife Patience and 16-year-old daughter Anna. He thought about that long walk to the Yadkin Valley and the two years the three of them had spent there. He thought of the decision to leave there and travel farther westward to new land, of the joy he and Patience shared at the discovery that after 18 years with only one daughter, another child would be added to the family. And he certainly thought of Patience and how he still missed her dreadfully a year after sickness took her and the unborn child. This land he so desperately sought and struggled for held the body of his true love, and Isaac feared that within hours it would hold his as well.

"Anna! Anna; come quick." Isaac stumbled to the porch of the rough log cabin, his hand already grotesque and his head pounding in agony. "A rattler," he managed to choke from a burning throat and swollen tongue. He raised his hand and slumped to the oak porch boards beside a split-log bench.

"Oh my God, Papa! Papa! Isaac, what happened? Dear Lord, help us."

"And only He can, girl. God, don't let me leave Anna here alone." Isaac was now gasping and heaving and struggling to breathe. The swelling was already marching up his arm, his vision distorted. He was quickly passing the point of having the ability to move on his own, and he was already feeling the threat of unconsciousness.

"Stay with me Papa; Isaac, stay with me. Try to lean on me and let me get you to the bed. Stay with me, now." Anna's heart was aching and her mind whirling with dread. What could she do?

Anna Walker was a unique young woman. Small and trim with raven hair that hung freely to her waist, she had brown eyes that sparkled with a mischievous glow. Looking deeply into those eyes could cause a man to lose himself, to see wonderment and intrigue. Even in a loose homemade dress of unbleached muslin and a calico apron brought all the way from Yadkin Valley, Anna's femininity was most apparent. She was fully woman, her passion always evident in her quick wit and laughter and love for her family. She even worked with passion, carving a home from the wilderness alongside Isaac. And in her quiet moments, that passion pushed her to think of the possibility of meeting a man and experiencing a life she had not yet known. She shuddered with the magic of it all, but for now she was content.

"Poccoon; I must have poccoon and green moss," Anna concluded through a fog of thoughts and a rush of fear that threatened to disorient her and put her in a state of panic. But she must not panic. She had not panicked when that bear attacked the only calf she and Isaac had. She had held the big flintlock steadily and threaded the ball past the bawling calf and into the bear. Its skin was now a bed covering; she and Isaac had eaten bear bacon for two months. She would not panic now.

19

With Isaac in his bed, Anna rushed from the cabin and into the yard, a long-blade hunting knife tucked into her apron strap. She grabbed a copper bucket from the porch. Her thin center-seam moccasins were little protection from rough ground, but she hardly noticed. She pulled the muslin dress above her knees so that she could better and more quickly negotiate the terrain, revealing smooth legs that were perfectly proportioned to her fit and equally perfect body, made more so by physical labor and much walking. Anna had not traveled far before finding the ingredients she sought. With resolve, she filled the bucket with the red root and handfuls of green moss.

Back at the cabin she struck fire with flint and steel and coaxed the spark to life in char cloth and birch bark kept handy for that purpose, her breath, now coming in pants from a heaving chest, giving rise to the flame she so desperately needed. With the fire roaring, Anna placed the root into a bucket of water and hung it over the heat. The container boiled in due time, and Anna took the root bath inside to apply to the snake bite. She then wrapped patches of green moss around it and secured the poultice with a linen rag. There was now nothing to do but pray and wait.

As Anna bathed her father's face and talked softly to him, he writhed and moaned, lapsing momentarily into unconsciousness, only to wake in a state of anguish. He would each time try to speak, but Anna could not understand his lethargic, thick-tongued words. She concluded once that he attempted, *I love you*, but she was aware of that without his saying it. They needed meat; she needed to shoot a deer or buffalo. But that would have to wait. As she would have to wait—and pray constantly. "God help us."

London 1773

"Here is the Jaeger I told you about my boy," Cedric said as he handed Sun a true piece of art. The 30-inch barrel was bored .62 caliber. Silver inlays decorated the side plate. The cock and frizzen were filled with ornate engraving, as was the full-length stock of thick, heavy walnut. This was a simple tool built in Old World excellence. "You can shoot, can't you?"

"Yes, I can shoot," Sun answered with a smile. He was feeling a sense of freedom and awe after arriving at the hunting lodge, his worries about returning home to his father's probable explosiveness not a matter of concern at the moment. The lodge itself was art, a castle really. More evidence of Old World grandeur. "There are not a great many hunting opportunities in the business section of Boston, but I have learned to shoot. Don't trouble yourself over that." Sun allowed his mind to wander and speculate on the freedom those long hunters of his own country must feel on the frontier. He, too, must feel that when he returned.

Hunting as Cedric knew it was a social event reserved for the privileged. Each dressed in his finest woolens and Balmoral. Horns and bags, like the elegant English and German rifles and fowlers, were most decorative. Cedric supplied all these so that Sun would feel a part of the celebration and not distract from protocol required in such endeavors.

Action came quickly on that first day of the hunt. Hounds bawling in dark forest indicated game had been located, and almost immediately a magnificent stag, his antlers towering over his back like nothing Sun had ever seen, dashed across an opening some 50 yards from Sun's station. He tracked the front bead of the Jaeger with the stag, and when the flint fell a putrid cloud of blue-grey smoke erupted from the muzzle and pan like storm clouds rolling over a mountain, momentarily obscuring Sun's view. The woods fell silent, almost as if an earthquake had just shaken the surrounding country side. But when that black-powder smoke drifted off on the breeze, a great stag lay in the grass in front of Sun. He was filled with varying emotions—exhilaration and joy tempered with sobering sadness.

"A beauty, my boy," Cedric offered when he walked to Sun's side. "And the steaks will be superb. Your first stag?"

"Yes," Sun replied, his breathing still sporadic and measured. "I have never even taken a deer or buffalo. There are plenty in my country, but a scattering of waterfowl and pigeons is about all I have hunted. This. . . . 21

this is purely magnificent." He stroked the thick hair of the stag and smelled the musty odor typical of rutting males of the species. Cedric plucked a shoot of grass and placed it in the stag's mouth.

"The last bite ceremony," Cedric said to Sun's non-verbal question. "This is to honor the animal. We Brits think the animal is an honorable creature and not to be taken for granted. We offer this last bite as a matter of respect."

"You do well to honor life," Sun opined. "Life is special, whether animal or human. I admire your practice."

The hunt followed a similar pattern for the remainder of the days at the lodge. Five stags fell, as did 12 boars. Sun took one of those. And each time he admired an animal he felt that joyful sadness. He was as free and unencumbered by life's trials as he had ever been, and he knew he had found more direction regarding his own future. *I am now ready to go home,* he thought, with no need to express that thought to anyone.

CHAPTER 5

The Frontier 1773

 On the sixth day after Isaac Walker's encounter with the rattlesnake, there was evidence that he was healing; survival was no longer in question. Isaac was still weak and swollen and the flesh around the bite had begun to peel away in layers, but the poison had done all the damage it was going to do. He was no longer fighting to breathe; he was no longer lapsing into unconsciousness. Isaac would wear a hideous scar and have only partial use of his right hand, but he was on the way to recovery.

Anna, relieved and in a perpetual state of gratitude to God for His care through this ordeal, was exhausted. She had stayed by Isaac's side and changed the dressing and poultice twice daily, hardly even moving except to accomplish essential tasks. Collecting and boiling the red root and applying it to Isaac's hand had consumed her. The two of them were now desperate for food.

"We need meat," Isaac said weakly. "But I can't hunt; I can't even leave the cabin."

"No, of course not. I'll take care of all that. You just rest and get better."

"But you need rest, too."

"Yes, but I'll rest after I have taken care of the things that must be done," Anna said, not sure how she would do what she had to do. "I'll go see if I can get us some meat. That is what we need most."

"I hate that you have to do this, but it seems necessary. I'm sorry I have let you down."

"Oh, you have never let me down, Papa. Put that out of your mind. I will be fine, and I will be back as soon as I can. I may have to stay on the trail tonight; all depends on how far I have to go to make meat. Are you sure you will be all right while I am gone?"

"Yes. Just help me get a bucket of water inside. That dried fruit and parch corn will keep me going. There are two strips of jerk left in that bag." Isaac gestured toward a cloth bag lying on a small shelf. "You take it and some parch corn."

Anna collected a bucket of water and brought it inside. She then pulled the bags of dried fruit and parch corn from a shelf and put them close to Isaac. "You can get to these now without having to get up and move around much," she said as she put the meager collection of supplies on the table. "I'll get ready and go hunting. But I do need to wear something other than this dress and apron."

Isaac lay down on the bed and closed his eyes. He was asleep almost immediately, while Anna went about the business of making ready to get on the trail in an effort to find game. The situation was dire; they must have food.

As Anna reached for the long, graceful .52-caliber flintlock and shooting pouch, Isaac roused. He squinted his eyes and said with a start, "Anna, girl you look different! Can't say I remember seeing you like that."

"Necessity Papa; necessity." Anna no longer wore the muslin dress that she used around home. Instead, she had on buckskin leggings cinched tightly just below the knees with strips of quilled leather, these leggings pulled over too-big knee breeches. She wore a linen shirt split up the middle in front, its outside edges frayed. She had pulled her hair back at her neck and tied it with a leather thong. On top of the shirt—and the long hair hanging down her back—she had a canvas hunter's frock, this pulled together and tied with a wide wool sash. The sash held a hunter's knife and small camp ax. A heavy wool point blanket was rolled tightly on a tump line, this hanging from one shoulder. On the other was a haversack containing a corn boiler, a tin cup, a horn spoon, flint and steel and char, two small horns of salt and pepper, a tube-shaped bag of parch corn and jerk, and a small, tattered Bible. A ragged tricorn sat on her head.

"Oh, girl, you are a real long hunter," Isaac noted. "If any of those men see you they'll think you are one of them."

And the Indians will think I am a poacher, she thought silently. But she quickly put that out of her mind. She needed to concentrate on collecting game, not some fear that was only a remote possibility. She would, with all that was within her, attempt to avoid conflict with others along the way.

"Well, let's hope I don't meet any long hunters," Anna chided. "I'd hate to have to show them up!" Her brown eyes flashed and her full lips curled into a smile that would melt ice off winter cliffs of the Blue Ridge. Even in this pastoral garb of the vagabonds who lived off the land, it was obvious that Anna was a woman. There could never be any doubt about that.

"Girl, be careful out there, you hear." Isaac's voice trailed off as he sank back onto the bed. Fatigue from his injury and the lack of nourishment held him captive.

Anna made good time westward, despite her heavy load. Still, late afternoon was upon her and she had spotted no game she could stalk and shoot. She would have to stay on the trail and take up the hunt the following morning. She had done so before, but always in the company of Isaac—and her mother a few years back as they walked from Pennsylvania to Yadkin Country. Tonight, however, she was quite alone.

• • •

The small fire cast dancing shadows off overhanging branches. Its warmth was inviting, and Anna sat close, the   25 two strips of jerked meat and most of the parch corn gone by now. A wolf howled from a ridge in the distance.

Suddenly Anna found herself laughing—out loud and almost hysterically. She determined such action out of place for the moment, but it was uncontrollable. "A long hunter," she said to no one, between bouts of boisterous giggles. "And here I am thinking about a man, a husband." Those desires of womanhood had enveloped her of late, and she, even in the midst of gladly doing whatever it was she had to do to maintain the home she and Isaac shared, let the thought and need of having someone to hold and love creep into her being.

What man would want me? I even look like a long hunter. The laughter came anew, but the absurdity of it all gradually lost its comic appeal and laughter was replaced with tears. She was alone—not just here tonight, but alone in her emotions and thoughts at all times. *Empty.* The word crept through Anna's mind. *A heart full of passion with no one to share it is worse than no passion at all.* She moved as close to the fire's warmth as possible and sobbed.

Just before the light from her fire faded, Anna took out her Bible and read from The Proverbs: *Hope deferred maketh the heart sick; but when the desire cometh, it is a tree of life*—13:12. She rolled into the blanket, tucked herself in tightly in the brush half-face she had constructed, and closed her eyes in a simple prayer: *You know, Lord. You know.* Dawn would come early.

CHAPTER 6

Boston 1773

"William Clarkson is his name," Richard Bomar said in response to Rebecca's question. "Why do you ask?"

"Oh, he just has a pleasant smile. And he is hand-some!" Rebecca said with a coy grin.

"So, is that the reason you have been to see me every day for three weeks now?" Richard quizzed. "To see this boy who is working for me?"

"Well, shame on you," Rebecca chided. "You know there is no one I had rather see than my dear, sweet father. I can't think of anyone I would walk downtown for but you." Rebecca's eyes sparkled as she put on that smile that could charm clouds from a rainy sky. She hugged Richard and kissed him on the cheek. "There is only one man in my life."

"Oh daughter, flattery will get you everywhere with me! But you know that already."

"Not flattery, sir; just the honest truth. You are the best."

"My, where did you get that charm? It is certainly not from your father. Look at me—gruff, plain spoken, a man driven to achieve. But not my daughter. She is one of the very few."

"Papa, you don't see in yourself what I see. You are perhaps those things, but you are also gentle, kind. Proba- 27 bly too accommodating most of the time. And Mr. Clarkson out there, why did you hire him? Could it be to give him a chance? Could it be because down deep you see him as I see you? You may try to hide it, but there is a gracious man lurking in the depths of your heart."

"Why did I hire him? I needed a good man; that is why. He is becoming an excellent employee. Quick to learn, willing to work, an agreeable sort of fellow. Why would I not hire someone like that? But more importantly, why do you ask about him? Do you have some interest in this young man?"

"How could that be Papa? I have never met him."

"You were the one who asked about him, so you tell me how that can be. You said he had a pleasant smile and was handsome. Are you still concerned with this falling in love you mentioned awhile back?"

"Oh Papa, every young girl is concerned with falling in love. It is just in our nature. Don't let that alarm you."

"Well you best keep that nature under control young lady," Richard added, this time with a more serious tone than he had used earlier in the conversation. "You were born for the good life that I have provided. You were born with status and class. You are a Bomar. You need to put your thoughts on marrying well, and you need to heed my advice in such matters. Jackson Bain will be home before the week is out. Turn your attention in that direction. Mr. Clarkson is a fine fellow and a hard worker; he will probably do well. But he is common. His family is common. They are hardly in the class of Rebecca Bomar."

"But Papa, you say he will probably do well. He just may become the successful businessman that you are. I know you were born into class and mother was as well, but people can obtain class. And remember, class has very little to do with dignity and honesty and integrity. These can be traits of common folk."

"Is that so?"

"It is. Look at Mr. Bain. He was not born into wealth. You often mention his arrival in the business district here in Boston and how he struggled to launch his shipping firm. You have even said how much you admire him. But he was not born into it; he did it himself. And now his family is as wealthy and influential as ours. You even want me to marry his son."

"But Rebecca, you don't. . . ." Rebecca began talking before Richard finished.

"Then what about Mr. Clarkson, or any other young man for that matter? Can it not be that some or all these will prove reliable, successful, and yes, become wealthy? Is it such a tragedy if I do fall in love with one of them and the two of us struggle to accomplish just as you and Mr. Bain have? Papa, what could be wrong with that?"

"Rebecca, I know you can't understand my position on this, but you will in time. Now please, I can't continue this conversation at the moment. It distracts me from what I must do. Please, let this rest for now. Distance yourself from it. Everything will work out, I promise."

"Whatever you say Papa. But I can't see that you are right in this matter. And I can't say that I can distance myself from it. It is too deep. You can't expect me to deny what I know deep inside is right for me." Rebecca composed herself briefly before leaving her father's office. "I will see you at home this evening, Papa."

• • •

"Mr. Clarkson, is it?" Rebecca said as she walked down the isle where William was working.

"Uh, yes ma'am; William Clarkson."

"I'm Rebecca Bomar," she said, her eyes dancing. She twirled a strand of hair that dangled beside her ear, far more self conscious of her boldness than she thought she would be.

"Yes ma'am; I definitely know who you are!"

"And just why would you know such a thing? Why would you know the name of just this one girl when there are hundreds of others who come in here? Or could it be, Mr. Clarkson, that you know the names of all the pretty girls of Boston?" William was taken aback.

"Oh yes ma'am; I mean no ma'am. I mean. . . ." He was speechless. This beautiful young woman had taken 29 him by surprise. She had beaten him at a game he had often played with the girls of his social class. He had always held his own as one of suavity, but this encounter had been his undoing. Rebecca laughed with abandon at his awkwardness.

"It's all right," Mr. Clarkson. "Relax."

"Yes ma'am; I'll try."

"And my name is Rebecca, not ma'am."

"Yes ma'am, but I was taught to show respect. I was brought up in proper form."

"Oh, I'm sure you were, Mr. Clarkson."

"And it's William, not Mr. Clarkson!" Still uncomfortable with the forwardness of this perfect example of young womanhood, he was beginning to regain some of his poise. He was slowly beginning to consider what was happening and was enjoying the possibilities. "Rebecca it will be."

"Good William. I'm glad that obstacle is out of the way."

William Clarkson's eyes embraced Rebecca's beauty, his mouth as dry as a summer afternoon.

Clarkson was, as Rebecca had noted, a handsome young man. Twenty years old, he was tall and slender, his face a bit boyish. With sandy hair and deep, rich eyes, William exuded confidence and determination—except in these last few minutes when any confidence he might have had slipped from him, leaving him vulnerable. He was from good stock, common in the view of the elite, but good stock. William Clarkson would succeed in the business world of Boston.

"How do you like working for my father?"

"Oh, I like it very much. I am interested in business, and this is the start I need. I was fortunate that I found your father. He is a caring man. Demanding and opinionated at times, but caring." Rebecca smiled and nodded in agreement.

"Please, excuse me. I didn't mean. . . ."

"Think nothing of it," Rebecca interrupted. "I know him far better than you do, and he is indeed all those things."

30

"Yes ma'am." William was once again swept into Rebecca's spell. Her eyes drew and engulfed him in wonderment. "Sorry. Not ma'am; your name is Rebecca."

"Now you have it!" she smiled, deepening the trance that captured William Clarkson in a grip he had never known.

"Walk me home some time," Rebecca invited with an element of innocence that was spiced with mystique. "Where do you live?"

"Out away from here, in the opposite direction from your house. And I'm sure that would not be proper, my walking you home and all. And without a chaperon? No, that would not be proper."

"Because I am the boss's daughter?"

"That, and the fact that I don't really know you."

"Well, you could eliminate that last thing by walking me home. You could get to know me."

"Yes, but I just don't think it proper. But I thank you just the same. Maybe we. . . ."

"William Clarkson! You are a gentleman. I am pleased."

"And I am flattered, Rebecca. Thank you again, but you must excuse me. I have to get back to work. Your father might change his opinion of me if he saw me idle. Now if you will excuse me."

"Yes, of course. I enjoyed talking with you. And take good care of my father down here. Don't let him work too hard."

"Yes ma'am. Uh, yes Rebecca." William watched Rebecca glide down the long row of merchandise and disappear out the door. He could not take his eyes off her, and he found himself smiling. He soared with exhilaration and the remote possibility of seeing her again. Rebecca, too, felt exhilaration. She curtsied to a law official and tickled a baby under the chin as she stepped into the street in front of her father's business, her smile a permanent fixture on a dainty face as she almost floated along toward home.

• • •

"Sun will be sailing soon," Martha reminded Squire as he prepared for his day's activities. "I was hoping you would join me in welcoming him home."

"Welcoming him?" Squire scorned. "Why would I be welcoming him?"

"Can't you let this go, at least temporarily? This is your son whom you haven't seen in three years. Can't you just be glad he is home and safe?"

"Oh, I suppose I am glad he is safe, but he can never come home—to the home I know. And I'm glad for you. You don't seem to share my opinion of this situation, and I know how very much you love Jackson. But unless he is coming home to apologize and get down to the business of working with me, he is not *coming home*." Squire spoke these two words in a hard, distasteful manner, almost spitting them from his lips in a pronounced form that spoke of disgust and an unwillingness to budge. "You know exactly where I stand on this. You go to the dock; you take the carriage; you organize a parade if you like. But me? I'll be working as I have for more than 30 years. If he wants to see things my way, send him over and we will talk."

Martha was not surprised, but the depth of Squire's resolve stunned her. She had prayed daily that her husband would modify his behavior and receive Sun as a father should receive a child coming home. But Squire Bain had become a resolute man, a man filled with bitterness that was growing out of control, one who saw things one way—his way.

CHAPTER 7

The Frontier 1773

Anna awoke with a start, her eyes still matted with dried tears. The woods around her half-face were yet dim and haunting, but dawn had begun its struggle with darkness and shapes and shadows were becoming recognizable. And there before her was a young doe, fat and sleek, big eyes attempting to figure out what this strange being was, nose sampling the air, ears twitching, first one way and then the other. Anna could not believe her good fortune, and she prayed silently *Lord, we need this gift of food.*

Anna began in slow motion to move the big flintlock into position. She expected the doe to bolt and disappear into thick tangles that encroached in every direction. Anna was nearing desperation; she and Isaac needed meat. It appeared at the moment that God had provided.

The *clack* of flint on steel and its resultant *whoosh boom* took Anna by surprise—as any proper shot should. It was only then that she threw back the blanket and scrambled from the half-face. The doe lay still. "Thank you Lord," Anna said aloud.

Acutely aware that a shot or voices could invite trouble, Anna realized that she must care for the meat and leave 33 the area as quickly as possible. With a practiced skill most commonly reserved for the long hunters, Anna rolled the doe over and opened the body cavity. She then coaxed the hide off to form a ground covering and boned out the sweet venison. In little more than an hour, Anna had 40 pounds of much needed protein packed and tied inside a perfect hide. The latter would make moccasins and rawhide; the meat would provide sustenance. With as much haste as she could manage, Anna slung the heavy load of meat, haversack, tump line, shooting pouch and flintlock over her shoulders and headed back the way she had come the previous afternoon. She needed the safety of home.

• • •

"Isaac. Papa, you in there?" Anna called as she approached the cabin. "I'm back. I have meat."

"Girl, is that you? I was worried about you. Surely am glad to see you."

"It's me, Papa. And I'm glad to see you. That was a hard night on the trail, but God has provided."

"He always does girl. You get a deer?"

"Yes, a fat doe. I have the meat boned and wrapped in this hide. How are you feeling?"

"Tolerable, but I'll be better with a belly full of that venison." Isaac smiled, obviously proud of his daughter and the difficult task she had completed. "We'll have enough to make a good passel of jerk from that load you have."

"That we will. But first we are going to cook some of this and let you have your fill. You need meat to help you get your strength back." Anna was, as her father, proud. She was a young woman, full grown and desiring emotional and physical connection with a man, but she was, at least for the moment, also a provider. "You rest while I cook. We'll make jerk racks and strip the meat after we have eaten. Reckon you might be able to help me cut some poles and build the rack?"

34 "I can't do much one handed, but I'll do what I can.

I can at least hold the poles while you put the rack together." Isaac smiled, content and hopeful. But he looked at his daughter with a touch of regret. *A fine young woman*, he thought. *But she deserves better than this. God, don't let me stand in the way of her happiness.*

• • •

The meal was basic—venison back strap fried in bear lard. Salted cornmeal cooked into a mush in that same lard completed the menu. Simple, but nourishing.

"Don't think I've eaten that much in a month," Isaac said with a smile. The spark had come back to his eyes and his face, though creased and weathered, had taken on more color.

He is a good man, Anna thought as she watched him, pleased with his recovery. *I would do well to have one just like him.*

"You haven't eaten like that in a month because we haven't had this much to eat in a month," Anna added, a touch of laughter emitting from the naturally beautiful face.

"Now, if you feel up to it, let's cut some poles and start making jerk. But let me change into something a bit more ladylike." Anna was pained by her own statement. Though she was content with what she had, she owned only two dresses—one the simple muslin she wore around the house, the other a calico with gathered bust and full skirt she used for church—when she and Isaac could go. There were no churches in the immediate vicinity, and to attend they faced a long ride in a wagon back to the settlement.

And Isaac was no better clothed than his daughter. His everyday outfit was that of the frontier, that common to long hunters and Indians—moccasins, leggings, knee breeches, a long shirt. He had made them all, save the breeches. He, like Anna, kept one set of clothes for more up-town affairs such as church: A pair of black buckle shoes, a pair of stockings, one pair of canvas knee breeches that he refused to use under the leggings, a linen shirt, and a greatcoat, this showing marked signs of age and wear.

"Hold this for me, Isaac," Anna said after they col-   35

lected the poles and branches needed for smoking the meat. He took the forked pole in his left hand and held fast while Anna pounded it into the ground. They put four such poles roughly into a square, and then laid smaller poles in the "Y's" of the forked poles. Across these smaller ones they placed others, forming a rack approximately three-feet from the ground. A slow fire would be kept under the rack until the meat was thoroughly dried. "Now, let's strip that meat," Isaac advised. "We'll have plenty of jerk for a month or more. I can tend the fire while you rest."

Anna was exhausted. She went to the stream and stripped, flexing aching muscles but also conscious of her womanly body. The chill of autumn air bit at her skin, offering an unfamiliar element of sensuous exhilaration. *How would it feel to have a gentle and loving man rub this tired back?* she wondered as she waded into the stream. Anna washed the grime of the trail away as the refreshing water caressed her. The afternoon sky was azure, with a hint of orange on the western horizon. It was glorious, distant, surreal. It was the artistry of God. Anna slept soundly that night.

CHAPTER 8

Boston 1773

 The ship was docked and passengers offloading when the carriage pulled to a halt near Boston Harbor. Winter threatened the city. Martha Bain strained for a look at her son. *God, thank you,* she prayed silently. *Thank you for protecting Sun and bringing him home safely. And thank you for giving him to me. He is special. Not more special than his sisters; I thank you for them, too. But Sun has always had my heart in a way that is different. And Lord, work a miracle in Squire's life. Let him recognize what he has in Jackson and let him be at peace with whatever decision Sun makes. Only you can change this hard heart that is now within my husband. It is in your hands, Lord. Work as you will. Thank you.*

Martha Bain's lips curled into a wide grin and her eyes filled with tears as she recognized her son walking down the gangplank. *Oh, how handsome he is,* she thought. The tears were now profuse, and she could hardly wait to reach out and hold Jackson as she had so many times in the years past.

"Mother," Sun shouted when he saw Martha. He dropped his bag and scooped her up into his arms. The two stood motionless, staring at one another.

"Sun; Sun. Oh, how I have missed you terribly. My life is not the same when you are not here."

37

"Nor mine, when I am away from you, Mother," Sun said, his deep eyes peering into her very being. "And I have missed you, too. Are you well? Cora and Cassie and their families; are they well?"

"Yes, everyone is well. God has blessed us," Martha said, her eyes still spangled with tears. "They will be looking forward to seeing you as quickly as possible. And you simply must see your nieces and nephew. They have grown like weeds. You will hardly recognize them." The two embraced again and stared a bit longer. "Let's get your luggage. The carriage is waiting." As they walked from the dock to the carriage, Martha couldn't help but notice that Sun had not mentioned his father. She, however, was willing to wait for Sun to bring that subject up himself. They put the luggage aboard and stepped into the comfort of the carriage, settling themselves on leather-covered seats.

"Mother, do you mind if we don't rush? I'd like to see some of Boston before we go on home. There is plenty of time; it is just early afternoon."

"I think that would be all right," Martha added, knowing deep inside that Sun was avoiding the inevitable as long as he could. Sun instructed the driver to take a serpentine route that would reacquaint him with Boston: the Old North Church, Granary Burying Ground, King's Chapel, Copp's Hill Burying Ground. The surroundings were familiar to Sun, but they held that sense of strangeness one feels after a long absence.

"How was England? Tell me everything."

"Oh, I can't tell you everything in this short time, Mother," Sun advised, smiling. "But I can tell you it was spectacular. The university was an opportunity for growth. It was perfect. And I love the country-side—open, lush, handsome farms scattered about.

"And I left some very good friends behind; Cedric and I became particularly close. He and I went hunting just before I left. It was all incredible."

Martha cringed a bit at that statement about Cedric and the hunting trip. She was fully aware of Sun's propensity toward wanderlust and his plans to explore the frontier when he returned. A hunting experience proba-

38

bly helped stoke the flames of his desire to see what lay west of the settlements.

"What about Father?" Martha detected the hesitancy in Sun's voice when he asked, and she struggled with the appropriate response.

"Your father is well."

"That's good. Why didn't he come with you?

"Oh, you know your father. Always working."

"Yes, of course. Busy, I am sure. But is that the real reason he didn't come?" Sun continued, knowing well what his father must think after the letter arrived. "I would guess that he is not going to be too pleased with me."

"Sun, your father loves you."

"I am aware of that, Mother, but I think this matter has little to do with love. I fear that I have created a situation Father is not dealing with well. But Mother, I. . . ."

"Sun, your father has become a bitter man," Martha said in a reticent voice filled with regret. "He is not the man I once knew. And your decision to travel the frontier rather than enter his business is not sitting well with him. According to him you will go off and waste your life becoming, as he often puts it, *one of those useless long hunters*. He is frightened, Sun. He is a proud man who sees this as an affront to all he has planned and hoped for. He sees it as an insult, as a blatant rejection of what is rightfully yours. But he is firm in his stubbornness. I have been unable to reach him.

"And I am afraid as well," Martha continued. "I am afraid that our family will be divided, torn apart because we can't agree and reach a compromise."

"And part of that is my fault. I can't agree to go into business with Father, and I can't compromise my deep need to go to the frontier—at least not now, Mother. I can't. Doing so would crush my spirit. I must see what is there, what opportunities are available west of the settlements. Boston is home, but I just can't be sure at this time that I want to settle into some prescribed business endeavor that is not of my doing. I'm not saying that I won't come back and do that and I'm not saying that I won't find some need 39 out there, some opportunity for business that will fit perfectly into what Father has already, but I can say that I must go and see for myself. Can Father not understand that?"

"Can't or won't," Martha answered. "As I have already said, he is a bitter man. I don't know if he doesn't have the ability to see that you could still figure into his plans or if he is just too obstinate in this matter to see. I just don't know. But he is holding firm. Nothing seems to move him in this. You are going to see a hard man, Sun."

"Does he even want to see me?" Martha couldn't bring herself to tell Sun that Squire had said *I have no son*, so she didn't answer Jackson's question.

"He is glad you are safe," she opined. "We will all visit over dinner tonight. Your sisters and their families will come."

"I suppose Robert and Jonathan have fallen into the business regimen Father has set."

"They are involved in the business, if that is what you mean," Martha said.

"Yes, I guess that is what I mean," Sun responded. "It just seems that they too willingly fell under Father's spell"

"Sun, they have families now. They must have stability. Your father offered them the opportunity and they accepted. They are happy and work diligently to make Bain Enterprises a success."

"But they will never know what they could have done on their own," Sun noted. "How can a man hold his head high when his accomplishments are not his own? How can he look his wife and family in the eyes, knowing that it was not he who struggled and survived and provided and emerged victorious in life? I just don't see how a man can fully be a man without such knowledge."

"Jackson, this talk is alarming. Is this some nonsense you encountered in your studies, some philosophy you adopted as a result of too much thinking?

"Now Mother, you know me better than that. Sure, I studied philosophy and literature and a great many other things. But you have known since I was a child that I saw things differently, that I was drawn to experiment and question. None of this should come as a surprise to you, of all people."

"And it doesn't, Sun. I have down deep always known that you would not fit a mold someone else made for you. Your father didn't either. He was head strong and determined to make his own way. I remember well those early years of struggle and his sense of accomplishment as his business began to grow. I admired him so. And I admire you. You are now much as he was then. You two are just alike. You are definitely your father's son."

"Well then if he was like that and I am like him, why can he not understand what I must do?"

"Success and power, I suppose, are not always good. The struggle passes; influence and status take its place. Too many people come to do what is required of them by that one who has the influence and status, and perhaps that one begins to think that he can command all and that he knows what is best—at least in this case with your father. That could be it. Perhaps your father has just been conditioned to think that he doesn't have to think. That he already knows. That the course he has set is the only one with logic. As I have said, I just really don't know. I do know that I miss the man he was and I have missed you. I am thankful to have at least one of you back."

•   •   •

Cora and Robert, Cassie and Jonathan, their children in tow, arrived at the scheduled time. The sisters rushed to their brother and embraced him.

"It's about time you came home little brother," Cora said, wiping tears as she spoke. "I guess you are all educated and wise to the world."

"I have a document that says as much," Sun returned. "But I'm not certain that any printed proclamation makes a man wise."

"And just look at you," Cassie added. "All grown up and handsome."

41

"Handsome? I should have come home much earlier. And you two are more beautiful than ever," Sun said as he smiled at his sisters. He then extended a firm handshake to Robert and Jonathan, both amiable enough, but both possessing that stoic reserve of Squire Bain. *They are where he wants them,* Sun thought as he considered these brothers-in-law and his own father.

"And look at you three," Sun beamed as he acknowledged the two daughters of Cora and Robert and the son of Cassie and Jonathan. "Mother told me you were growing like weeds. She was right. Do you even remember your Uncle Jackson?" The children looked on, teased. Three years had been a long space in their young lives.

"Where is Father?" Cora asked. "He works too much."

"He will be here," Martha said. "He had to stop by the warehouse to check on a shipment that arrived today."

"Shipments and warehouses and business," Cassie added. "These take Father away from you, Robert away from Cora, and Jonathan away from me. Isn't there more to life than business?"

"Now Cassie," Jonathan said quietly, obviously troubled by the truth of her question. "Business is important. It demands much of us."

"And Father demands much of you," Cora added. No one spoke to this though all knew what she said was valid.

"You all go on into the parlor and visit," Martha said as the silence seemed to cave in and threaten all of them. "I'll wait here and meet Squire when he gets home."

"How was London?" Robert asked of Sun in an effort to turn the conversation toward a more comfortable subject.

"Interesting," was Sun's immediate response. He continued, "It is, as you would imagine, big, crowded, the center of commerce and culture. I enjoyed it, but I was ready to leave the confines it offered. I need space, and that is hard to find in a city such as London. I did, however, get out just before I left to come back here and went hunting with a friend from the university. It was a grand experience, one I plan to repeat soon." The mood once again became tense. All were aware of Sun's desire for the frontier and of Squire's bitter opposition.

42

"Oh, we will do that," Jonathan added. "As quickly as the fall flights begin, we'll go out to the marshes and hunt geese. Robert and I both just got new English fowlers, beautiful things in 11 bore, the best the Mother Country can provide. And your father has one. I'm sure he will let you use it if you can't get one before then." Jonathan's comments were pleasant enough, and there was no doubt regarding his sincerity toward his brother-in-law. He wanted peace in the family, and he wanted to get to know Sun better, to develop a relationship of trust and respect with this family member some considered foolish and rebellious.

"I thank you, and if I am here then we will do just that. But I want to be on or very near the frontier by the time autumn arrives. I don't want to miss the glorious color show of orange and yellow and gold. It will be incredible. And I want to get a rifle, not a fowler."

"What about a Jaeger?" Robert questioned. "That is Old World craftsmanship at its best. There are some available here I'm sure, and a few come over in shipments time and again. That would be a good choice if it is game bigger than geese and ducks you are after."

"Yes, the Jaeger is useful and well built. I used one on the trip with my friend Cedric there in England. But I want something more closely associated with the colonies. I want a long rifle. I'll probably look into the work of George Shroyer down in York County. Word comes on good authority that he is crafting some fine pieces. Still a little flair for his German heritage, but purely American—long, slim, smaller bores. That is what I plan to get."

"You going down that way to get this rifle?" Cora asked.

"Of course. I plan to go to the frontier as quickly as I can," Sun responded, increasing the dreadful chill that already hung over the gathering. Sun's insistence to abandon his father's wishes for Sun to enter business there in Boston was sure to culminate in a storm that would not be easily calmed.

"But Sun," Cassie countered. "What about Father?"

"What about Father, Cassie? How he reacts to me and my decisions is his choice. I can't choose for him, and I can't live my life according to his dictates."

"You know how he feels about this matter." Cassie's strained voice held the hint of a plea.

"Yes, I know how he feels. I was hoping for something else, but that is not to be. From what I know of our father, he was at one time just as I am now—determined to find his own way and shape life as he felt best. And I guess he is still that way. He certainly wants to shape our lives so that we all fit into what he chooses. Mother has told us about his single-mindedness in those early years. He wanted to carve out a life that was of his making. That is all I want to do. Seems that if anyone would understand it would be Father. Cassie, Cora, all of you, I'm not intentionally trying to create a problem. I love this family; I don't want to disrupt it. But to be anything other than absolutely honest with you and with myself would be a grave error. I hope each of you can understand and will support me, but if you choose to do otherwise I will still respect your opinions and love you."

"But Jackson, your father is offering you an opportunity that most your age will never have," Robert injected. "You will regret turning that down."

"Perhaps, but I will more regret not discovering who and what I truly am. Every man must do that, I believe." Cora bit her lower lip and hung her head. She had seen this need in her husband as Robert slumped into a soft chair on winter evenings after a difficult day at work with her father. "We must know ourselves and sort out our places in this world before we can be of much benefit to anyone else. I must do this." Other than the children scuffling about in the room, silence prevailed. It fell with a deafening, suffocating suddenness.

•　•　•

"Squire, Jackson's home," Martha said gently as her husband came up the long walk and entered the house. She took his greatcoat and hung it in the wardrobe just inside the entrance.

"I know. Is he well?"

"Yes, fine. And oh so grown up and handsome. He is no longer a boy, Squire. He is a man, a man of whom you can be proud. He is just like you."

"And I guess he is still determined to defy me," Squire said, his anger already growing toward his son.

"Oh Squire, please; he is not defying you. Can we not have a pleasant evening and welcome our son home?"

"Well what is he doing if not defying me, Martha? He is disregarding our wishes for him. It is defiance."

"Your wishes for him, Squire. Not *our* wishes for him."

"What? What are you saying woman? Are you abandoning me as well, casting me to the wolves as it were? Am I to be alone in this matter, my own family in opposition to me, to the one who has given them all this?" Squire's voice was now raised and spiteful, its rumble reaching the parlor where the others were gathered.

"Squire, no; I have tried to talk to you about this already, but you won't listen. I am not abandoning you; I never have—not when you were struggling in our early days together and not now. I supported you in your decisions and always wanted the best for you. I have stood by you and don't you say otherwise. You know that is not true. But Squire, you are now forcing me into a situation to which there is no answer. You are forcing me to choose between you and our son. I can't do that; I won't do that. I just think that the support I gave you as you fumbled and fell and got up again in your effort to be what you had to be should also be extended to Jackson. He deserves no less, and if you insist that he comply and force me to choose, you are the one who is doing harm to this family."

"Enough, woman; I'll have no more of this. I am being set aside by those who should be grateful. But instead of gratitude, I get disrespect. No, I'll have none of it. When you all come to your senses let me know. I'll be having my evening meal in liquid form down at the Green Dragon." The wardrobe rattled and the door slammed as Squire Bain stormed out. There would be no pleasant evening over a bountiful meal, imported wines, and stories from the past few years.

CHAPTER 9

Spring 1774 The Frontier

"Ho, Isaac. You in there? Ho."

"Well, Jule Chillington," Isaac said to no one. "I suspected it was about time for him."

"Howdy there Isaac," Jule said as Isaac walked to the porch of the cabin. "How's it been with you folks of late?"

"Hello Jule. Good to see you. I guess it *is* time for you to come around again. Looks like you got a good load of furs there." The pack animal tied behind Chillington's mount was laden with bear and deer hides. "I imagine they'll fetch a handsome sum over in Yadkin country."

"Hope so. I need 'em to fetch all they can. Been tough. Lots of long hunters and lots of Indians. The Shawnees stole 'bout these many more offn me a month or so back. 'Cept for the Good Lord they'd 'a stole my scalp, too. Mind iffn I git off and set a spell? Been a long ride outta' the Middle Ground."

"Oh, of course not, Jule. You are always welcome here. And you might as well plan to spend the night. Anna and I will fix up some supper for you. If you are in a rush on back toward the settlements, you can get moving at first light tomorrow."

46

"I'm much obliged to you, Isaac." Typical of long hunters, Jule wore moccasins, buckskin leggings, a knee-length hunting shirt, and a greatcoat. His .50-caliber Lancaster rested across the horn of a battered and worn saddle. And like all long hunters, save those who had just crawled from a forced bath in the river, Jule was filthy. He dismounted and began unloading the pack animal.

"Lots of game out that way?" Isaac asked. He was intrigued by the life of the long hunter but recognized that it was one of great risks, not one of stability and certainty. And it was likely a trade that would not carry long into the future. It was passing—romantic and appealing, but passing with the expansion westward.

"Plenty of it. Bears, deer, turkeys, wapiti, lots of bufflers. But I don't have a pack string to handle them buffler hides and meat. Them critters too big. Just mostly leave 'em alone, 'cept for shootin' one and gettin' the tongue and hump now and again. Best meat anywhur. A del'casy."

"That's true. Anna and I take one occasionally if we are where we can get it cut up and packed back here to dry. It is delicious, as you say a delicacy. Let me help you as best I can with the load and animals. Had a run in with a rattler back a while and my right hand will never be the same." Isaac held up a hand that was only partially functional. "Would you like to go down to the creek and wash some of that grime off you before we sit and visit? Is it too cold for you to do that?"

"Reckon that wouldn't be such a bad idear, and 'hit 'hain't too cold. I could do with bein' a little more presentful for Anna. And whur is that daughter of yorn, anyhow?"

"She went to the Jacobsons' cabin over the way about a mile. Mrs. Jacobson had a new baby and Anna cooked them a dried-apple pie and walked over that way to give it to them. And if I know her she will stay there to ooh and ah over the young one till dark pushes her toward home."

"'Spect you right, Isaac. That girl'll make a fine mama some day." Jule stood his Lancaster by a post on the porch and hung his shooting pouch on a peg. "Don't s'pose I'll need this widder maker down there on the creek," Jule said as he gestured his stubble-covered chin toward the Lancaster.   47

"Not likely," Isaac noted. "Things peaceable this far back from the frontier. Quite a bit of traffic now out this way."

"Yeah, 'magine so." Jule quickly disappeared around the house and walked toward the creek, the woolen sash already loosened from his waist. With his buckskins and hunter's shirt dangling from a bush, he stood in the shallows of the cold water and allowed his mind to wander. *Yessirree, that Anna Walker is one purtty woman. And needs a man, too. A real man. Not some high-fallutin' dandy from the settle-ments. Shorely would be cozy in a half-face with that woman. Reckon I best git 'bout to courtin'. Fall'll be here 'fore you know it.*

·　·　·

"I see Jule must be around," Anna said as she stepped onto the porch. She pushed back a strand of silky hair that had fallen from under the confines of her bonnet and loosed the woolen cape that hung from her shoulders. The afternoon air was clean, the sun already casting long shadows about the woods and cabin yard. Sunset was near, and the hint of its romance and grandeur was evident. Tentacles of orange and light yellow kissed the mountaintops to the west and trickled to the ground in dappled patterns that caused Anna's spirit to soar. "What a glorious day God has given us," she added.

"That He has," Isaac concurred. "And yes, it is Jule. Headed for the settlements on east. I asked him to join us for supper and stay the night. He's down there in the creek trying to get some of that frontier dirt off."

"If I know Jule, it will take more than the creek to get the dirt off," Anna said with a smile. "He'll probably kill all the fish for a mile downstream. We won't catch a blue cat till next summer. I thought you could get dirty Isaac Walker, but compared to Jule Chillington you're as clean as a newborn." Anna jabbed Isaac's shoulder in jest, her eyes alive with mischief and her heart giddy.

"And speaking of newborns, how's the little one?"

"Oh, fine; just fine. He is beautiful. That makes three

48   boys and two girls for the Jacobsons. Mrs. Jacobson said

she was going to take a stick to Mr. Jacobson if he even patted her behind from now on!"

"Anna Walker!" Isaac said with some embarrassment. "I've never heard you talk like that."

"Oh, Papa. I'm a grown woman now. I know all about that. Besides, I think it is truly romantic for a husband and wife to toy around about such things. I know I would want to tease my husband like that. And I would want him to do the same. That is a real part, an important part, of being a couple. The physical joys should be at the very heart of a good relationship. Don't you think?" Isaac looked away and didn't answer. His thoughts were on his own wife and his tragic loss of her. And his thoughts were on this daughter, now a woman with desires and needs like any other woman. No longer a little girl.

· · ·

"Well howdy, Miss Anna," Jule said as he walked up to the cabin, his leggings and shirt stained from weeks on the trail. "Hope you don't mind iffin I set a spell with you and Isaac. I'll git back on the way to the settle-ments at first light tomarr."

"Not at all, Jule. You are welcome. I'm not sure what we'll have for supper, but I don't think you'll go to bed hungry. Have you been on the trail long?"

"Yes'mm; nigh on two months now. Been out'n the Middle Ground huntin' and trappin'. Got a load of hides to market when I git to the settle-ments. Hope they's some sutlers there wantin' to pay a good price."

"I wish you well with that, Jule. I know the work is hard."

"Yes'mm. That it is. But it's jest what a man gits usein' to. 'Taint no hardern' than this here farmin' you and Isaac try to do."

"Well maybe not, but I don't think we have it as bad as the long hunters. And besides, there are people around. And more are on the way. The country is becoming settled out here. The Jacobsons' cabin is about a mile north, and I saw a new clearing between here and there today. Somebody's   49 getting ready to put up a cabin and probably a barn, maybe even a shed for grain storage and such. This is a pleasant place to live."

"Can git too many folks 'bout. Don't hardly never see nobody on out past here. Maybe another long hunter from time to time. And the Indians. They's plenty of 'em. Have to watch yore scalp out there."

"I don't think I would want to always be on the lookout for someone or something that is a threat, Jule. I want a bit more peace than that."

"Awh, you jest have to be careful. Jest keep yore eyes open and don't do nothin' foolish. I reckon my life is the frontier. Don't know much a' nothin' else. Don't really know that I care to know much a' nothin' else."

"I best get supper going, Jule. If I don't we'll *all* go to bed hungry."

• • •

"As always Anna, you outdid yourself," Isaac Walker said as he pushed back from the table.

"Thanks, Papa. It was nothing special. Those dessert cakes were just flour, corn meal, and honey. And the stew was jerk meat in broth with dried beans. But thank you; I'm glad you enjoyed it."

"Shorely was fine, Miss Anna," Jule added. "I ain't et that much since I left the settle-ments."

"Now you men go about your business while I clean up. I don't want you underfoot," Anna scolded in a good-natured fashion. Isaac and Jule put on their coats and made their way to the porch, while Anna picked up from supper. Soon the sweet smell of pipe smoke rode the night air and Anna, finished with chores, lighted a candle and opened a book. Though she was a voracious reader as a child and still enjoyed it a great deal, there were only a few books available to her this far from the settlements. The Bible was always close at hand, and tonight she opened *Pilgrim's Progress* to read it for the fourth time.

"Jule, how is the long hunter business these days?" Isaac quizzed. "I'd guess things are still brisk with a fair demand for hides and furs."

50

"It's good, Isaac. Them English folks like these here

deer skins and pelts. And even in the settle-ments, they can't git 'nough of that buckskin. Makes some fine, soft leather. Biggest problem is git-tin' all them hides back to sell. Iffin I had more horses, I could bring in more. Might even start workin' on them bufflers, but you gotta' have a way to move them hides. They's heavy and big."

"That they are. Even a freight wagon would be loaded quickly with buffalo hides. And the frontier is not the place yet for a freight wagon. That will all change I'm sure, but for now it is just afoot or horseback. When will you be back through here on your way out after you sell this load?

"'Bout a month or so I'd reckon," Jule said as he puffed his pipe contentedly. "I'll sell, study over my profit, look for another horse I can afford, and then rest up a spell. Gonna' go back out then and try a short spring run and come back in. Then I want to be back out there a'gin 'fore fall takes over. Won't try to stay the winter. I wanna' git a good load and come back east here 'fore the winter bites hard. Purtty dangr'us out that way with the snow flyin' and all.

"Isaac, I been specalatin' on talkin' to you 'bout somethin' for a while now. Hope you don't mind me jest bein' plumb up front."

"Well, I don't suppose I do, Jule. I guess it all depends on what it is you're *specalatin'* about."

"That girl of yorn. I'm specalatin' 'bout her. Specalate a lot 'bout her. She 'hain't no girl no more. She is a growed up woman, and a growed up woman needs a man. I'm gonna' ask you 'bout courtin' Anna. Shorely would like to take her with me come fall when I head out."

"Well now Jule, I'm not sure you are asking the right person. I appreciate your considering me in this and I would expect you to ask, but a decision like that belongs to Anna. She is grown and I know she is thinking about marriage at some point, but I don't think she is ready to make a hasty decision on such a serious matter. What, are you thinking that you can just mention this to her and pick her up on your way back out to the frontier in a few months?"

"Oh, I reckon that is what I was s'posin'. I figgered I'd   51 talk to her tonight after I talked to you and me and her could make some plans for fall. Gonna' be chilly in the Middle Ground come fall. Me and her could keep each other a mite warm I'd 'magine." Jule's eyes had a devilish flicker and he curled his whiskered face into a toothy grin. Isaac failed to find amusement in Jule's demeanor.

"Now Jule. That talk is a bit inappropriate. I understand; I've been in love and have been loved in return and have known the pleasure and comfort of a good woman. Believe me, I understand. But you are talking about my daughter here. This conversation is uncomfortable and out of place. Anna will make her decision when and with whom she chooses. I'll give my blessing then, but I'll have no part in choosing for her."

"T'weren't no harm intended Isaac. This here's just two men talkin'."

"And one of those men is the father of the woman you are talking about. You would be wise in the future to keep that in mind. Maybe your approach is acceptable among long hunters and some frontier folk, but it is not here. Now, you and Anna are grown; you can do what you want. I can't prevent her from talking with you and I can't prevent you from broaching the subject, but I will in no way enter into any decision making. Let me make that clear to you."

"Shore; shore. No harm meant Isaac."

"Jule, as far as I know you are a good man. I've never heard anything to the contrary. But there are a great many things to consider, and I know Anna is already considering those things. Don't be surprised if you get a reception even cooler than those autumn evenings in the Middle Ground you mentioned when you approach Anna about this. Now if you'll excuse me Jule, I'm going to turn in. I'll be up before daylight to help you pack. You can sleep in there by the fireplace. It will be cold tonight. Throw your ground cloth down there by the hearth. Good night, Jule"

"Night Isaac. And I shorely didn't mean nothin' unseemly 'while ago. Just talkin' man talk. I'll see iffin Anna wants to visit with me a spell here on the porch."

CHAPTER 10

Boston 1774

"Elizabeth, that daughter of ours can be absolutely insufferable at times," Richard Bomar told his wife as he walked into the parlor. "Hard headed, won't listen. If she weren't the grandest thing in Boston, I'd bend her over my knee and give her a good spanking."

"Just like her father!" Elizabeth noted.

""What are you talking about, like her father?"

"Well, he has been known to be single minded and intent, dead set on working things out to his advantage. And sometimes he won't listen."

"Well I never, Elizabeth."

"Oh Richard, I'm teasing you. But there is some truth in what I say. If you really look you will recognize in yourself some of those traits you find in Rebecca. They are not all bad, but they are not all good, either. Now, what is it in particular that has you convinced that our daughter is insufferable?"

"Well, for two months or so now she has been to my office almost every day. Some time back she was asking me about William Clarkson, a young man who works for me. I even saw her stop and talk to him before she left

53

that day. And every time since then she has managed to bump into Clarkson while visiting me. I think her head is filled with fantasy and romance."

"Could be. She has mentioned Mr. Clarkson to me. She says he is handsome. She tells me he comes from common stock but is intelligent and wants to succeed. A hard worker."

"That he is, a hard worker. And a good worker. I wouldn't want to do without him. He has done everything assigned, and he does it well. He will go far. And he *is* from common stock. Not the kind of material for Rebecca."

"Well now, don't be so sure about that, Richard. Rebecca knows quality when she sees it; even you say this young man is going to do well. He could be exactly what Rebecca wants and needs."

"Yes, but Elizabeth, he is not from Boston's elite. His parents were poor immigrants, just common laborers now. He has a long way to go, and even then he won't be all Boston expects."

"And so was Squire Bain—common. You have mentioned that often. And now you hold him in the highest regard. In fact, Boston holds him in the highest regard. No one else in this New World is more powerful in shipping, ship building, and lumber than Bain Enterprises. So powerful and influential is he that you have chosen his son Jackson to be our daughter's husband. And Jackson's father was common, just like William Clarkson."

"But Rebecca and Jackson are the right match, don't you think?"

"If the match is right for them, yes I do. But if it is not, then it won't be right for them and I think they will know it."

"But it will lead to a merger and tremendous expansion in business for all of us."

"And there is that *hard-headed-and-won't-listen* factor you are upset with Rebecca about. You are being hard headed and you won't listen."

"No Elizabeth. I just want what is best for Rebecca."

"Now are you sure of that? Are you sure it is Rebecca you are thinking of and not yourself?"

"Well, I thought you wanted the same."

"Oh the best; I want the best. But I'm not sure in

this matter what is best. Yes, I enjoy Boston society, and I admit that I have let appearance get the better of me in these past few years. I have become far too preoccupied with what others think and how our lives appear to them than I should. Rebecca and I have talked quite a bit, and I am convinced more than ever that she is a solid, intelligent, and thoughtful young woman. She can decide for herself.

"Richard, she even asked me a painful question recently. She asked me if I was happy, if you were happy. Are you happy, Richard?"

"That's outrageous. Of course I'm happy. I have everything I need."

"True; we need nothing else. But are you letting what you want interfere with what you need?"

"What on earth are you talking about Elizabeth?"

"Do you need a merger with Bain Enterprises? Do you need to expand? Do you need to let business consume your every minute? And more important, are you happy with me?" Elizabeth's words stung. Richard had hardly thought of this matter for years, and if he were pushed for an honest answer he feared that answer would bring hurt.

"I . . . I. . . ."

"That's all right Richard. You don't need to answer. I think I know. And I think I feel the same way. We are comfortable; we are busy; we are where we want to be in Boston society. But I'm not at all sure we are happy.

"Richard, I know we began much as you now want Rebecca and Jackson to begin. Our parents basically chose for us. It was the proper thing to do in society's eyes. We weren't afforded that opportunity to fall in love. I don't regret it, but that is the way it happened. But Richard, something else happened in the days that followed. I did fall in love, with you Richard. I felt passion and desire and concern I didn't know I had. But we didn't nurture that. We too quickly and too easily let our busy lives and societal expectations suffocate us. It robbed us Richard, and we allowed it to happen. I want that back. I want to begin anew and let the important elements of a relationship be our focus. I think God wants that as well. And Rebecca has helped me see that."

"God?"

"Yes, God. He has provided and blessed. He has given us more than we deserve. And He has given us, as you put it, *the grandest thing in Boston* in our daughter Rebecca. Not society; not business. These are not the grand things. Love and family are. I want these things that matter."

"Now Elizabeth, wait a minute here. Are you saying that all this I have worked for is of no importance to you? Are you saying that the business I have built is of no value?"

"Of course not. The business is extremely important. It has given us opportunities we would never have had otherwise. But I fear it has come to own us, to dictate who and what we are. That shouldn't be."

"But Elizabeth. . . ."

"Richard, think back on our early years. The miscarriages, the death of our baby, the eventual birth of Rebecca. It was family, not business that was most important. It was the tie that bound us together. And do you recall when we talked about using our wealth to benefit others? We even planned some projects that we simply never got around to doing."

"Sure, I remember. We wanted to begin a shelter to help Boston's destitute. We even talked about giving to some of the Indian families who were displaced. We had dreams of all sorts related to our money."

"We did," Elizabeth continued. "We were well intentioned but we never did it. We are wealthy and the credit goes to you. I haven't forgotten that. But maybe we should step back and look at life. Our days are getting shorter, and dying with nothing but being considered among Boston's top society is a poor epitaph. God has been dealing with me, and some of His dealing has come through our daughter. I have seen in her that youthful idealism that too quickly trickles away from those immersed in the world, business, the every day. Inevitable, I suppose, but it doesn't have to be. Some idealism is good; it can spur us on to things of value."

"But I. . . . uh, we have contributed," Richard added.

"Look at the jobs I have provided to others. Several have gone on to start their own businesses, and they would not have done that without me."

"Perhaps they wouldn't, but perhaps they would. It is impossible to know. You have indeed contributed and given opportunity to others. That is good; I admire you for it."

"And that is what I want to do for Rebecca and Jackson, give them a chance to succeed."

"And that is good. But Jackson doesn't need our money, doesn't need us to point him in the direction of success. And neither does Rebecca. She will be fine, even if she doesn't fall headlong into what those outside looking in consider Boston's best. That girl has spunk, Richard. She got it from you!" Richard Bomar smiled, the first such expression his wife had seen in a long time.

"But Elizabeth, I. . . ."

"Oh, no need to answer all this now. I've thrown a great many things out to you at once. And I'm sure they come as a big surprise. This condition we are now in was not all your doing. I am at fault. I have demanded and expected much from you and you always de-livered. But my eyes have been opened in the past month. God has dealt with me. Rebecca has dealt with me. And this has all caused me to deal with myself. I want more, but the more I want is not more money or more business or more social and political status. I want family. I want to be of value to this world. I want God to direct our lives."

"So you want to start a charity and give away my money?" Richard countered, with a questioning expression on his face.

"No, not in the way you seem to be thinking. But yes, some charity could be a step in the right direction. It is more complex than that. I want to be of service, and in being of service I believe we will find something inside ourselves that has been missing."

"The business?"

"Keep it. Make it grow. Expand so that others have jobs and opportunities. But don't let business for business sake be life. Let life be more. Your family; your friends; 57 your community. With no thought of what they can do for you. Let your business be a tool for doing good. I want God to be in control of business and everything else about us. And church."

"Church?" Richard quizzed.

"Yes. How long has it been since we have attended regularly?"

"Oh, I don't know. A few years I guess. But I haven't liked any of the preachers we have had in a long time. And some of the people there are not the ones I want to associate with."

"It is not about the preachers or the other people there. It is about us, about our relationship with God. Nothing should get in the way of that. There is no class distinction in Jesus. He died for all, and it is each individual's place to make a personal decision regarding Him. Please don't stumble over others in that journey."

"Well, I suppose you are right," Richard concluded. "But there are just so many other things to consider. I have to work these out in my own mind."

"And if your mind is set on God and on what He wants for you, you will work those out in due time. God is patient with us. He understands. And most important, He loves us unconditionally."

"And I guess you and Rebecca love me unconditionally."

"I'd like to say that I have always loved you unconditionally. But recently I have begun to see that I did have conditions on love. I have admitted already to placing high demands and expectations on you. So I can't honestly say that I have loved you unconditionally. But I can honestly say that from this point forward my love will be unconditional. And be assured that Rebecca loves you fully, without condition. She is even willing to allow you to choose a husband for her. She will argue and express her opinion, but she will follow your leading. Yes, you are loved completely by our child."

"Elizabeth, this pains me. I had no idea. I can't believe that I have let this happen. It seemed so logical and prescribed that I never questioned it. I can't imagine the kind of love you are talking about. And I can't imagine life without you. Can you forgive me?"

"And can you forgive me, Richard? I too fell into this

superficial trap of concern for appearance. But now I want to dwell on depth. You and Rebecca are what I want and need. Not teas and social gatherings. I love you, Richard."

"And I love you, Elizabeth." Richard Bomar held his wife for the first time in far too long. Held her in a way he had never held her before.

CHAPTER 11

The Frontier 1774

"It seems that Jule Chillington is sweet on me," Anna said as she and Isaac sat on the porch the day Jule left for the settlements. "He said last night that he wanted to court me, to marry me and take me with him to the frontier when he goes back out in early fall. I can't say this surprised me, but I can say that I don't really know how to react right now."

"Yes, he talked with me about it, too. Got a little out of hand, I tell you. I let him know I was not pleased with the direction of his conversation."

"You don't approve of Jule Chillington?" Anna quizzed.

"No, that's not it. He is a decent enough man. I just didn't approve of his approach and his references to you. Talked about keeping him warm and such."

"Well Isaac Walker. You are jealous. You are jealous about losing me to another man. And jealous that your little girl is now a grown-up woman, a woman who has entertained the idea of having a man in her life—having a man physically, I mean. Shame on you."

Anna's eyes again sparkled with that mischievous, teasing glint that Isaac had come to know so well, eyes that could look into a man's very soul and kindle a roaring flame.

"Oh Anna, that's not it."

"That's part of it, Papa. And that is natural. I'd guess it is difficult for a man to give his daughter to another man and know that the relationship will have a physical aspect that the father finds uncomfortable. I understand, and I love you even more for it."

"Well yes, that is part of it. And it is a natural feeling. A father can't help it. That is his little girl going off with another man and being a woman. She is not the little girl anymore."

"That's sweet, Isaac. But you are right. That woman is no longer that little girl. I guess you must now know how my mother's papa felt when she left to begin life with you."

"I suppose I do. I remember it well. It was a special time that I think about often. He gave us his blessing, but his heart was breaking even though he was glad for us. He even cried, Anna. Tried to hide the tears, but he couldn't. I felt terrible. But I was so in love with your mother that I was willing to break a few hearts—and noses too if they got stuck in our business!" The two laughed with abandon.

"He called me to one side the day your mother and I married and said in that thick Irish brogue, 'I tell you laddie, if I find out you ever mistreat this lass you'll have one hot Irishman to deal with. I'll skin you alive and chase your carcass all the way to Baltimore. Now off with ya' lad. Give me a cart load of grandbabies. I love you lad, and you got the best woman in the New World. God bless the two a' ya'.' It was a speech I never forgot; I knew he meant it!"

"I'm sure he did, and I'll just bet you would do the same for me."

"No question," Isaac noted. "Even in the best of situations life can be hard. But willful mistreatment is absolutely inexcusable. Mr. O'Mally cared for your mother as much as I care for you. He intended for her to have the best. I fear I didn't give her that."

"Now Papa, that is not true and you know it. The best is not determined by money. I know we have never had much materially and I know you wanted to give your family more, but we never lacked the things we truly needed. You gave us devotion, love. You protected us. And you led us to love others. You taught us of God's love for us. I'd say we were, we are,   61 wealthy far beyond what most would consider wealth. Mother recognized this and felt the same way. You loved her and she loved you. You gave her the best."

"Kind of you to say that. And yes, we loved each other deeply, intensely. I don't think there could ever be any love like that again."

"Oh, don't be so sure. You may meet a woman some day who sets your head in a spin just like my mother did."

"Anna, hush up. There will never be another like your mother."

"Not like her in some ways, but love is broad. I don't think we expend all we have on just one person or one thing. We can love and love and love."

"A pleasant thought, but I can tell you I am not looking for another wife. If I ever met another woman she would have to shake my world for me to take notice."

"Well Isaac Walker, you ole romantic. Shake your world. That is love talk if I ever heard it. You already have somebody in mind who is shaking your world?"

"Goodness no, girl. Just keeping up with you and this place is shaking enough. At my age I need my world to stay still, not rattle around."

"Your age? There is nothing wrong with your age. Men just get better with age. You are just about perfect at *your age.*"

"Come now Anna. You're beginning to get into that same line of talk as Jule Chillington. It's unnerving me. Hush up."

"Okay, but when we go to church or the settlements I'll keep my eye out in the direction that you are keeping your eye out. I suspect it may be that the pretty Widow Wallace is already rattling around in that handsome head and tender heart of yours. I best watch out for you and keep you in tow."

"Shaah, girl. Stop it.. Now tell me. What do you think of Jule Chillington? You said he was sweet on you and he told me the same. You considering him seriously?"

"Oh, I can't say for sure. I think Jule is a good man. I'm sure he would be good to me. But I don't think we are very well matched. Don't take this to mean that he

62

is not good enough. Far from it. It's just that you taught us about books and learning and thinking. Can Jule even read? That doesn't make him any less worthy, but I will have to give some long, hard thought before I agree to have Jule as a husband. I fear I would wither up and die without intelligent conversation, without discussion more involved than how to skin a buffalo.

"And passion, Isaac. You heard his talk. Is that all passion is to him—my keeping him warm on a frontier night? That could be part of it, but it should go deeper. I'm not sure I could live with that. Not really live. I could stay alive, but I would not be living. I don't want to settle."

"And you don't need to settle, Anna. You are right; there is more to life and love than you keeping some man warm. The physical can be a beautiful part, but it can't be one sided. It can't be some obligation. It must be a shared emotion, and for it to be shared it has to be nurtured and cared for. I guess you'd say earned. I'm not sure Jule could ever grasp that. Maybe, but he has a long way to go."

"But as you said, he is a decent man. A girl could do worse than get a decent man. There are many who are not."

"That's true. But there are some who are both decent and insightful. A better match for you, I'd think."

"Yes, better. But I won't omit Jule. And I won't make a decision yet. Time is passing, but it is not passing that fast! But if I am to be the wife of a long hunter, I can. Jule would have been proud of me that time I had to go hunt when you were down with the snake bite. I was a long hunter. I did well."

"That you did, and he would have been proud. I am proud. You are the best and deserve the best."

"Mutual, Papa. Now excuse me. I'm going inside and start supper."

CHAPTER 12

Boston 1774

Winter was reticent to loose its hold on Boston. Since Sun's return snow had been common, its cold adding to the chill already present in the Bain household. From his room at the Gage, Sun could see streets shoveled and scraped clean, only to see them time and again packed beneath a new blanket of white. Ordinarily beautiful and refreshing, this snow spoke of the suffocating silence between Jackson and Squire.

What can I do? Sun thought as he watched a carriage push through the slush below, the horses' nostrils shooting great plumes of fog into frigid air. *I can't even get Father to talk to me. There is no hope of getting him to understand. Maybe I have betrayed him, wronged him in some way. But I can't be anything other than what I am. Why will he not listen, not at least try to hear me on this? He was at one time exactly where I am now. He should understand. What can I do?*

Sun was so deep in thought that the knock on the door startled him. "Yes. Who is it?"

"Messenger. I am here to deliver a letter."

"I'll be right there." Sun walked sullenly to the door and turned its big handle. The heavy oak shutter creaked on ornate hinges.

"Jackson Bain?"

"The same. What do you have there?"

"A young lady asked that I deliver this note." The messenger handed Sun a piece of gold-trimmed stationary embossed with the Bomar *B*.

"Thank you." Sun handed the man a coin.

"Thank you, and good day sir."

"And to you sir." Sun gestured idly with his left hand, his eyes focused on and his mind curious about the letter he now held. *Bomar. Could this be from Rebecca?* Sun broke the seal and opened the letter. He sat back in a thickly-padded chair, his half-empty bottle of rum close at hand. He immediately recognized the handwriting.

> *Dear Sun,*
>
> *Welcome home. I have missed you terribly. It has been far too long, and a letter is no way to tell you all the things on my mind. Please, if you can, come by my house tomorrow at 2:00. We have a great many things to talk about. I will be waiting for you. I'm glad you are back.*
>
> *Love,*
> *Rebecca*

Oh Rebecca. The thoughts running through Sun's mind shifted focus. *What can I say to you? Will I crush you as I have my father? Will you understand? Is my selfishness going to destroy all those I care about? Oh Rebecca. Dear, sweet Rebecca.* "But I must keep this appointment," Sun added aloud. "I must see Rebecca and explain myself. Tomorrow, 2:00. I will be there."

· · ·

"Jackson Bain; please come in." Elizabeth Bomar opened the door at Sun's knock. "We have been expecting you. Rebecca will be down directly. Please come into the parlor and take a seat."

"Thank you Mrs. Bomar. How have you been?

"I am fine, thank you. Life has been good to us. God has been good to us. And you?"

65

"Fine as well; thank you for asking. England was most pleasant, and the university was an experience of great value. My time was well spent."

"That is good to know. And your parents and sisters, are they well?"

"Cora and Cassie and their husbands and children are fine. The nieces and nephew are, as my mother says, 'growing like a weed.' And my mother is well. Still the most loving and gentle woman I have ever known." Silence fell. Elizabeth Bomar was aware of the estrangement between Jackson and Squire and she didn't mention the matter. Neither did Sun.

"You haven't changed a bit in these past three years, Mrs. Bomar."

"Oh goodness Jackson. You flatter me. But then, you always did have a way with words. Knew exactly what to say to make a woman feel good about herself."

"Not flattery at all. You look just as I remember you. Still as young and vibrant as ever."

"Oh, go on now. I know better. But I do appreciate your saying so. You must come by more often! Please, excuse me and let me be sure Rebecca knows you are here. You know how that girl is. She will make the entire world wait for her if she can manage it. Wants to always make some dramatic appearance. I'll find her and hurry her along. Then I'll leave you two alone so that you can visit. But I do want to talk with you more. Want to hear of all your plans for the future."

"Yes ma'am. That will be fine. And don't trouble Rebecca. I have plenty of time."

"Thank you Jackson, and good day."

"And to you as well, Mrs. Bomar."

• • •

"Sun, Sun. My dear Sun. I can't believe you are here."
Sun stood upon Rebecca's entrance, his mouth partly open and his eyes staring at a truly beautiful woman. Re-

66 becca wore a ruffled dress that tapered with her perfectly-

formed body. The dress's hem flared into a big circle that swayed with her measured steps. The sleeve cuffs were trimmed in lace and the neck surprisingly low cut. The lace there accentuated Rebecca's soft skin. Sun could do little more than watch this lovely lady before him.

"Rebecca, you. . . . you are simply breathtaking!" Sun stammered, for the first time near speechless in the presence of a woman. "Breathtaking." Rebecca rushed to Sun and threw her arms around him. The two held one another tightly.

"*'Shall I compare thee to a summer's day?'*" Sun said as he pushed her back to arm's length to once again admire Rebecca, his eyes afire and his face beaming with a smile.

"There you are with your Shakespeare again, Sun. But please, go on. Flattery will get you everywhere!"

"Only truth, Rebecca. For *'I have seen a medicine that's able to breathe life into a stone. . . .'* That medicine is standing here before me. Did I say that you are incredible?"

"Enough, Jackson Bain. But oh how I have missed you and your Shakespeare and your smile. I have missed you my dear Sun. Far too much. Come; let's sit and talk." Rebecca directed Sun to a long sofa and she sat, gesturing to the spot beside her.

"Let's see; three years since you last sat here with me? Rebecca continued.

"Three years, two weeks, four days, and six hours," Sun replied.

"Oh, you do know how to impress a woman. Knowing the exact details of such matters lets her know that she was on your mind and that you anticipated the reunion. Indeed, I am fully impressed."

"I'm pleased, and I have definitely anticipated the reunion. I saw no woman in England as beautiful as you. And I thought of you with great regularity. It is good to finally be back in your presence."

"Oh my, my." Rebecca twirled a strand of hair beside her ear. "If more men were like you, more women would be giddy and smiling! Charm is blatantly absent in much of Boston society. Oh, there are the business deals and political maneuvers that demand pats on the back and prescribed recognition, but true charm is simply not present."

67

"That is tragic," Sun opined. "Charm is needed. The world is too full of those business deals and perfunctory behavior. A little grace along the way is essential. So tell me, how have you been?"

"Wonderful. Father's business continues to grow and we are all healthy. I am full grown now and beginning to explore directions for the future. Of course, my parents may have a different direction set for me than I have set for myself. You know what they have always hoped for."

"I do. Your parents as well as my parents—at least my father. They see Boston's premier couple in the two of us, and my father has always planned for me to step into his business, perhaps even negotiate with your father to meld the two into a giant conglomerate. Impressive, this thinking."

"Impressive, indeed. But is it what we want and need?" Rebecca frowned as she said this.

"Well, we have cut immediately to the core of the matter, haven't we, Rebecca? Do I hear you saying that you would be disappointed with marrying me and settling here in Boston, becoming a part of the business regimen and living happily ever after?"

"Oh Sun, please. Don't misunderstand me. I could never be disappointed with you. And I would never do anything to disappoint you. I love you, but. . . .

"And I love you, but what?"

"I have thought of you every day since you left for England. You have been the center of many conversations I have had with my mother and father. They hold you in highest regards. I do as well. And I admit, with sincere apology, that I have held my pillow in my bed at night and thought of you. My friend, my champion, my hero from childhood."

"And why would you apologize for that, Rebecca? You, as you just said, are full grown. Anything you may have thought and felt is completely natural. You should feel no shame."

"Maybe not, but this is awkward—admitting that I am fully human in my emotions."

"As am I. And don't you think I have experienced the same thoughts and feelings? You have never been far from me. In distance, yes, but in my heart, no. You have been right there. I have held my pillow with Rebecca floating in my imagination night after night. Please, no more apologies."

"There are none like you Sun. I have always been comfortable with you; you have always put me at peace. I don't deserve someone like you."

"Not true. You deserve the best life can offer. And you shall have it. You will settle for nothing less; you must settle for nothing else.

"One thing that always amazed me on my voyage to and from England was the ability of the captain to navigate. He kept his instruments close at hand and always followed the compass expertly. Even on those dismally dark nights at sea, he was always aware of his location and destination. Some passengers would even occasionally voice concern that we were lost. But we were not. The captain had the compass; he knew exactly where we were going and delivered us easily.

"You have a compass to follow, Rebecca. It is your heart. Trust it. It will point you in the right direction. Keep it close at hand and you will not go wrong."

"How very eloquent. And how very logical. Your wisdom is admirable; your kindness is exceptional. None like you for sure."

"Now, now. Don't get carried away with accolades. You know me too well for that. You know my faults. Number one among them is stubbornness. I set my mind and it won't be easily changed."

"Faults are common to us all. That is why we have forgiveness, grace. We need both regularly."

"That we do."

"Have you known forgiveness and grace? Have you had some particular experience that has made these real to you?"

"Life, Rebecca. Life has been the experience. Not one particular happening; just life with its twists and turns. I don't perceive myself as especially religious, at least not in the terms of how you and I were brought up. Religion is the external and can too often be just that—external. Yes, I believe to a degree, but I am not sure about God."

"Sun, I have grown in belief and faith. I have seen   69

grace at work. And I share your sentiments about religion. It can easily be superficial. But what is in my heart is truth. It is the presence of God."

"Then there is your compass. You must follow it. Will you promise me you will?"

"I do promise. You are helping me see that what I have been feeling and considering in these last few months could easily be God's leading. And like those passengers you mentioned, some will not understand, will question. But I promise to follow the compass."

"Your *God* talk is not something I fully grasp," Sun offered. "I'm not sure about God's leading. We were talking about the heart; I think that if we follow the heart it is sentinel enough. God made it, made us. Why can't we just trust ourselves and move forward as we see fit?"

"Oh Sun, that is difficult to answer. But I think God is at the center of our being. We would be foolish to follow anything else."

"You mean that you think God really directs in such simple matters as life choices?"

"Without question, Sun. He cares and leads and wants the best. We can call it heart if we like, but if we are in touch with God, He is our heart. He is our compass."

"Well, perhaps. But I don't share your enthusiasm. God is real; I believe that. But He is also distant. He, I believe, expects us to have enough insight to choose the best path. I don't feel that He is much concerned with such matters as we are discussing."

"Sun, this talk alarms me. I had hoped that you would have had some revelation from God that would have helped you see how very much He does care."

"Not at all; no revelations. But I am sorry that my theology disturbs you. Forgive me. You are an important person in my life and I would do practically anything to avoid hurting you."

"I know that, and there is no need to seek forgiveness from me. I hold nothing against you, not even this approach you have toward God. I admire you."

"And I you. And let me remind you that I love you. Have since childhood. I want the best for you. I want you
70

to follow your heart—or God as you choose to view it." Sun even now spoke with gentleness.

"And I will. I will follow my heart and what God puts in there as a compass."

"Good for you Rebecca. Now, what about that *but?*"

"The *but* Sun? What do you mean?"

"You said a few minutes ago, and I quote you: 'I love you, but. . . .' I interrupted you then; now let's return to that."

"Oh yes, of course. But allow me to preface that with a question."

"If you wish. Sure, go ahead."

"What is love? I said I loved you and I do, but what is love?"

"Where is Shakespeare when you need him?" Sun sighed. They smiled. Sun put his arm around Rebecca and pulled her close, his head now resting on the high plush back of the sofa.

"Love? I suppose that does deserve some serious thought! And perhaps even some categorizing. There is, as you insist, God's love That is probably out of human capability to grasp and understand.

"Then there is love for parents, siblings. This is a unique love that stands in a category unto itself. And there is the love for friends. This probably comes in degrees, depending upon the depth of friendship, but it is definitely love. But I suspect, based upon your approach to this discussion, that you have another love in mind. I would guess that the love to which you refer is that love between a man and woman, a love that would lead to marriage and building a home. That one, I imagine, is complex and has in it some components of all the others combined.

"But I am firmly convinced that it also carries a strange and special element unto itself, and that is what some may call falling in love. Yes, a marriage can be successful without that element, but I think the best relationships begin with falling in love and nurturing that love as life moves forward—through good and bad. Does that more closely relate to your question?" Sun waited for Rebecca's reply, silence filling the room.

"It does. And I should have known you would know exactly what I was talking about when I brought it up." 71

"And does that in some way touch the matter of that *but?*"

"Touches it at the very center. We can love without falling in love—that physical and emotional step that I think necessary for a man and woman to consider marriage." Rebecca felt a warm comfort.

"So do I. And that brings us back around to your statement. Could it be that after all these years and the plans of our families that you are not in love with me - Sun Bain, your friend from childhood? And could it be that you would enter marriage with me because of expectations or some desire not to disappoint even though you are not in love with me?"

"Oh Sun, this is incredibly difficult. I would in no way disappoint or hurt you. And I don't want to disregard the wishes of my parents. They have all these hopes and expectations. How can I go against them?"

"Rebecca, you have no reason to be concerned about disappointing or hurting me. I love you; you are my dear friend. I will not be disappointed by your finding happiness. And to be perfectly honest, I feel the same way as you. My love for you will follow me to my grave, and I know we could have a grand life together. But we would be beginning it without something each of us thinks essential. We have never fallen in love. Could we make that happen? Probably. Should we force it? Probably not. The compass points elsewhere. Follow your compass; I will follow mine."

Rebecca's cheeks were wet with tears. She reached and grasped the hand that was around her shoulder and pulled closer to Sun. "My dear Sun, my friend forever."

•   •   •

"Elizabeth, I'm home." Richard Bomar stepped through the door, removed a heavy wool coat, and hung it on a hall tree.

"You are early. Everything all right?"

"Oh sure, sure. Everything is fine. I just decided to
let young Clarkson close up for me so that I could come

home and visit with you and Rebecca before dinner. I am about to come to the conclusion that I work too much anyway."

"Imagine you saying such a thing Richard Bomar. Work too much! You will always work. Always have and always will. Still, I'm glad you are home. We have company—at least Rebecca has company."

"Jackson Bain I assume."

"None other. And he is more handsome and gracious than ever. He and Rebecca are in the parlor. They have been talking for almost two hours."

"How's that going; any idea?"

"Heavens no Richard. I wouldn't think of eavesdropping. I'm sure they are catching up from the past three years."

"And making plans?"

"Perhaps. But remember that we must let them make their own plans. We must not interfere. Will you promise me that Richard?"

"Elizabeth, we have been down this path before. You know I am having a difficult time dealing with all this."

"I do, and I can appreciate what you are going through. But we must not get into the lives of these two young people." Richard poured a snifter of brandy.

"Yes I know. Still, seems as if this is the perfect couple, and Boston is right for the perfect couple. Business, society, wealth—they would have it all. Boston is waiting."

"Richard, please don't forget our recent conversation about where we need to go as a couple and where we need to put emphasis. That is not on business expansion or social stature but on sharing with others and growing spiritually. If we seek God first, all other things will be added. Keep that in mind; please don't let the old infringe upon the new."

"I won't Elizabeth. I think about it often. It's just that I have had this focus for so long it is near impossible to let it go."

"I know it is. And it will be slow. But we are making progress. Let's just allow God to work. Now you mentioned William Clarkson. He is working out well, is he not?"

73

"Extremely well. He is an ambitious young man who is sure to enjoy success. He amazes me. Hard working, kind, a spiritual fellow. I see it in the way he deals with people. Always concerned with others and honest in his transactions. He is a good man."

"Good enough for a son-in-law?" Elizabeth had a wry smile on her face with the question.

"Now Elizabeth. We are not dealing with that at this time. You know I still have hopes for our daughter and Jackson."

"Yes, I do know. But from what I see, that possibility I mentioned of William Clarkson becoming your son-in-law certainly does exist. Will you deal with that in an open-minded fashion if and when it does present itself."

"Of course I will. I am still a hard man, but I am a hard man who is in the midst of change, of rediscovering myself. And rediscovering you and Rebecca. I like what I am finding and don't intend to stop looking. You have my word. Please be patient with me."

"Always my dear. Always patient."

•   •   •

"So, what will you do Sun?" Rebecca's tears had long dried and the two were concluding their conversation warmly and with mutual respect.

"I want to go to the frontier. I know you don't particularly approve, but I must explore, discover, find what is there for me, if anything. As quickly as spring is certain, I will get a saddle horse and pack animal and leave Boston. Go down through York and Lancaster. I want one of George Shroyer's rifles, a .54. I plan to take the Great Wagon Road and head into Yadkin Valley. From there it is on toward Cumberland Gap and maybe Beautiful River. I'm not sure of the exact route, but I am sure I must go. After that, I'll just have to wait and see."

"But isn't that dangerous? That is wilderness out that way. It has to be dangerous." The dread in Rebecca's eyes was real, the concern for her friend pronounced.

"Life is dangerous Rebecca. We can't live in the absence of danger and we can't fail to live because there is

74

danger. It is how we handle danger and life's difficulties that defines us. That doesn't give license for reckless abandon, but we must take some chances and explore life. I will face danger, but so will you, so will everybody who lives fully. I will be careful, but I will go and see and experience. And you will go with me—in my heart."

"And you will stay with me in the same way. You will always stay with me." Rebecca's smile gave reassurance.

"*You smiled. The day was then made perfect.*"

"That's not Shakespeare," Rebecca noted. "Is that some writer with whom I am not familiar, someone you discovered in England?"

"No; those are words straight from the heart of Jackson Bain."

"Perfect. They are perfect—as your words have always been."

"And one more Bain verse before I go: *Cry if you need to; be angry if you must; recognize that fear is real and justified; walk into grief. But always look into the mirror and see a valuable person who is loved deeply.*"

"You are incredible Sun. How will I live without you?

"You are not going to have to live without me. I am with you. We have already concluded that."

"Yes, we have. And I cherish that fact. You will be careful and you will let me hear from you, will you not?"

"Of course. And who knows? I may be right back here in Boston before winter comes again. The frontier may be more than I asked for. But I must go."

"I know. And go in peace my dear friend. May God bless you."

"And you Rebecca. You are in my heart." The embrace that followed was long, gentle. Tears trickled into the smiles on both faces. Rebecca released Sun and looked deeply once more into his eyes. She would not see him again until he returned from the frontier.

CHAPTER 13

Early April 1774

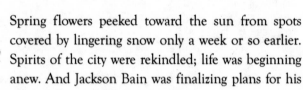

Spring flowers peeked toward the sun from spots covered by lingering snow only a week or so earlier. Spirits of the city were rekindled; life was beginning anew. And Jackson Bain was finalizing plans for his journey—first down through Lancaster and York, with a stop at George Shroyer's shop for a .54-caliber long rifle, and then down the Great Wagon Road into Yadkin Country and on to the frontier.

• • •

"But I hardly spoke to Jackson that day he was here to see Rebecca," Richard Bomar noted. "Are you sure he is leaving?"

"According to Rebecca, that is exactly what he is going to do." Elizabeth Bomar had talked with her daughter at length about her relationship with Jackson Bain and knew that he would make a journey to the frontier when spring was evident. "And Martha Bain confirms it. She tells me that Jackson is set on the frontier, even against his father's wishes. Richard, I don't think things are going well between Sun and Squire. They are at odds and need our prayers."

"I should say things are not likely going well. Bain had high hopes for that son of his. This irresponsible action by Jackson could put a chasm between them that can never be bridged. I doubt that prayer will rectify this situation."

"But that is where you are wrong, Richard. Prayer is powerful; God can touch the hearts of both these men and bring reconciliation."

"Perhaps, but I know Squire Bain to be a single-minded man. Reconciliation is not something with which he is familiar. God would have to perform a miracle to impact that man."

"And God is all about miracles. Look in His Word; it is filled with miracles. Moses and the Red Sea; David and Goliath. God worked. He is still working today."

"Have you seen any miracles lately?" There was a touch of cynicism in Richard's question.

"I haven't seen a sea parted or a giant killed, but I have seen miracles. I have seen God soften bitter hearts and bring people to salvation. I have seen God at work in this country that appears to be on the edge of being torn apart. I have seen God reshape shattered lives from within. And these miracles, the ones that happen quietly and within, just may be the most powerful of all. Yes, I have seen miracles, and you have as well if you will just admit it."

"You are correct, Elizabeth," Richard concluded. "In fact, there has been a miracle progressing in my own life. Yes, I still live for business, but God is working to show me that business is not what life is about. He has had a challenge with me, but He is working. I don't think you can deny that." Richard smiled gently as he put his arm around his wife's shoulders.

"Indeed, He has had a challenge!" Elizabeth teased, leaning close to her husband with affection. "But He has been working. I am beginning to see a new man, a man I much prefer. I thank God every day that you have been receptive to His leading. And prayer went ahead of that receptiveness."

"And I thank you for those prayers," Richard acknowledged. "I need them. Please don't stop."

"I won't. Remember, I know that God still works miracles. I will keep praying for them."

"And I suppose Jackson's leaving means that we won't see a wedding anytime soon between Rebecca and Sun."

"Now, Richard. Please don't. . . ."

"Wait, Elizabeth. I won't interfere. It is just that I, like Mr. Bain, have had hopes and plans for these two young people. Such a perfect match it seems. But that is the old Richard Bomar talking. The new one will be patient and allow God to work in all this."

"And He will, Richard. If it is God's will that Rebecca and Jackson be together, they will—if they follow Him. We can do nothing now but pray for Rebecca and Jackson, for Jackson and his father, and pray for ourselves. Pray for wisdom; pray for strength; pray for patience. We will love them and support them, regardless of the paths they choose."

"That we will my dear. That we will."

• • •

"He won't talk to me, Mother. I tried to see him twice and on both occasions he sent word from his office that I should leave. Told the messenger to tell me that he had no son." Jackson Bain was distressed, his pain obvious to Martha.

"Oh Sun, I am so very sorry. I simply do not understand your father in this matter. I have tried to reason with him, but he will have none of it. He has made up his mind that you are deserting him, are going against everything he wants for you."

"Wants for him, shouldn't you say, Mother?"

"Perhaps. Your father can be a difficult man when it comes to not getting his way. I fear that he has allowed his own desires to override all others. Please know that he is a good man in many ways, a man I love and a man who loves you. He is just blinded at the moment."

"Do you think he will ever be anything but blinded?"

"I do hope so." Martha's heart was breaking. She found herself between two men she loved deeply. "I hope and pray that he will come to accept the fact that

78

you are a man and must choose your own way. But I do not expect that to happen quickly, if at all. But know that I support you in this decision. You and your father are very much alike. He was young and ambitious and filled with a spirit of adventure once. As you are now. Those ingredients made him a successful man. And you will become a successful man, wherever you go and whatever you do. I support you."

"You can't know how much that means to me," Sun replied as he touched his mother's hand gently. "I will go with that knowledge and will do my best in every situation."

"I know that. You have never done anything less. And you will be careful, will you not?"

"Without question. You shouldn't worry."

"But that is what mothers do—worry. How can I do anything but worry?"

"I suppose you are right. Mothers do worry. And I thank you for it. But please try to put your mind at ease. I will be back. I will let you hear from me at every opportunity. I hope to get word back to you regularly, especially from the settlements. I can even get a message from the frontier. There are a great many people moving about out that way now, and staying in touch shouldn't be the chore it would have been in the past."

"And I shall treasure each word you send."

"Hug Cora, Cassie and the children for me. And tell Robert and Jonathan that we will take the fowlers to the marsh after ducks and geese when I get back." Jackson Bain handed Martha a note. "Well, go ahead and read it. It is just some little verse I wrote for you." Martha opened it with grace and gentleness: *Tears are an integral, even essential part of life. I gladly share yours.*

"Oh Sun, how eloquent." Martha choked her words through sobs. "You have always been eloquent."

"And you have always inspired the best in me, Mother. I will miss you terribly," Sun said, tears now filling his eyes as well.

"And I you, my son. Go in peace." 79

Jackson Bain was the perfect emblem of Boston society. He wore black buckle shoes, white stockings, knee breeches, a white ruffled shirt beneath a weskit and greatcoat, and his head sported a proper tricorn. His was not the garb of a long hunter. He pulled his mother close in a deep embrace and then kissed her cheek as he turned to go.

He stepped nimbly into the saddle securely strapped to a spirited, shiny sorrel gelding, behind which was tied an equally impressive pack animal. Sun tipped his tricorn and rode from the streets of Boston and out of Martha Bain's sight.

CHAPTER 14

Late April 1774 York

"I 'yest feeneeshed one like you 'vant." George Shroyer's rich German accent required Sun to listen carefully so that he could understand what was being said. "A .54, one-inch flats, 44-inch barrel, leaft-hand lock, iron 'vurniture. You should like it very, very much." Sun handled the big flintlock and admired its trim lines and exquisite inlays.

"I do like it very, very much. It is exactly what I was looking for. You do have the mold and horn to go with it?"

"Yez, ov course. A .530 double cavity. A big horn; vill hold almos' a pound of powder. It should do all you vant it to do. And I'll give you a shooting pouch to go vith it all." Shroyer was justifiably proud of his workmanship.

"Perfect." Sun Bain was more than pleased with the purchase he was about to make. The two men agreed upon a price and Sun now owned a true American rifle, a York flintlock built by one who knew his business well.

"So, vhere are you going young man?"

"First down through Yadkin Country. Thought I would then head toward Cumberland Gap and onto the frontier. Maybe on out to Kan-te-kee and along the Ohio."

81

"Dangerous country out that vay," Shroyer added as he pulled a clay pipe from his weskit pocket and lighted it. Its sweet smell permeated the air as Sun gathered the items he had just bought. "You bes' be cautious about your travels there."

"Yes sir, I will. And thank you for your concern. I've heard some tales from the frontier and understand the Shawnees can be a bit testy."

"Yez, the Shawnees and some other tribes. And the buffalo; they can hurt you. But be careful of some of the whites there as vell. Not all are hard working long hunters as they may appear. They vill sneak into your camp and take vhat they vant. They vill leave you scalped, leave you for the bears to eat. Don't too quickly trust anyone." Sun felt a sudden chill run up his spine, but he soon dismissed it as the excitement of his journey returned. Wise words, perhaps, but he would not encounter any such dangers as Shroyer outlined.

"Yes, I will watch out for all those. And thank you again Mr. Shroyer."

"Best ov luck young man. And you may vant to shed those fancy clothes bevore you get to the frontier. Folks there may think you something other than a long hunter, and I vould guess the same. You look like a wealthy merchant from east of here. Iss that right?"

"That is of no consequence to you Mr. Shroyer. I am a long hunter headed to the frontier. That is adequate information. Now again, I thank you sir. And good day to you."

"And the same to you. Hope the rifle serves you vell. And watch out for that scalp of yours."

82

CHAPTER 15

Along The Great Wagon Road
Mid May 1774

"So you the pilgrim I've been follerin' for three days." Sun startled from his gaze into the campfire and grabbed his Shroyer .54.

"Now easy with that big flinter there son. I'm friendly. Just saw your fire and thought I'd stop by and say howdy. Been on your trail for some time. Smelled you from a mile back, even 'fore I smelled your cookin'. Name's Simon Keats." The burly man, maybe in his late 50s, wore a ragged muslin shirt that hung mid thigh. His buckskin leggings were tied at the knee with a leather thong, and a woolen sash cinched his waist tightly. The sash held a small camp axe and a long-blade knife in a quilled sheath. Center-seam moccasins, obviously in a state of ill repair, showed beneath the worn edges of the leggings. The wide-brimmed hat was turned up and pinned in the back and pulled low in front.

"State your business," Sun said in an effort to thwart any potential problem.

"Just as I said. Name's Simon Keats and I was just stoppin' by to say howdy. Headed back out to the frontier   83 and thought I might share your camp for the night. Don't want no trouble."

"And there won't be any trouble unless you bring it. Come around here closer to the fire so that I can see you better. Are you alone?"

"Seems I'm always alone. Like it that way most of the time. Too many folks can make life cumbersome." Keats moved closer to the fire and let the light bounce off his weathered face. Sun was amazed to see the obvious ravages of years and a hard life that showed through a week-old growth of stubble, and he was equally amazed at the dirt and grime that coated this intruder.

"Put your rifle over there by that log and move away from it." Sun's order was clear and went unquestioned. He still held his .54 firmly, though not pointed directly at Keats. "Now come back over here and sit." Keats obliged and let out a sigh of exhaustion as he sank down by the fire.

"Been walkin' a good spell today. Ready to get to a settlement in the Yadkin. Rest up some, get a few supplies and head on out toward Kan-te-kee. Where you goin'?"

"I don't care to discuss that at the moment." Sun's words showed an ongoing concern over his current situation.

"You ain't no long hunter; I can tell that from your fancy outfit there. And that toilet water you a' wearin', I can smell it from way off yonder. You must be some big-city businessman or something."

"Don't care to discuss that either."

"Seems you don't care to discuss much of nothin'. That's fine with me. You might make a good travelin' 'panion, what with not wantin' to discuss and all. Most folks discuss too much. They just seem to talk and talk even when they ain't got no content to talk about."

"And I'm certainly not interested in having a traveling companion."

"Me neither. Remember, I told you I seem to be by myself most of the time. Don't like all that talkin' and opinionatin'."

"Well, for one who doesn't care for much talking, you surely are doing your share here tonight." Keats let out a
84   roaring laugh that bounced off the hillsides. He slapped

his leg and rocked back and forth as if thoroughly delighted with Sun's response.

"Right you are son. My 'ppologies. Guess I just got carried 'way, stumblin' up on you and such. But I didn't really stumble. I tracked and smelled and decided I'd see for myself who and what this was a ramblin' 'round out here sorta' blind. But you are on the right track if you's headed to the Yadkin. I reckon I can't fault you none there; you's keepin' to the trail purtty good."

"Well I suppose I am. After all, this road is not difficult to follow."

"That it be—easy to foller. But if you's headed on west from the Yadkin, things get a mite tedious. They's buffler traces and Indian trails and long hunter tracks runnin' in every direction. A feller gotta' know where he's a' goin' and what to look for or he'll get loster 'n a goose in a hail storm." Although Sun didn't know for certain where he was going and certainly not what he was looking for, on the trail or in life, he was more than mildly amused at Keats' comments and quaint analogy of becoming lost. Lost was not something Sun wanted. He knew the feeling well and wanted direction.

"So I'm still a' guessin' you's headed out to the long hunter grounds, out 'round Kan-te-kee."

"Suppose I am. I'm not in the mood to pass along word of my intentions, but you won't let it rest. So let's just assume that I am indeed headed to the frontier. I assume you have been there. What is your advice?"

"Oh, I've been there. Been a' ramblin' these parts for years now. Done some long huntin', some scoutin' for the gov'ment, done a little map makin'. For shore, I've been there. And you ain't even told me your name yet."

"It's Jackson. Now what is your advice regarding the frontier?"

"Got a last name you tryin' to hide or somethin'?"

"That is no business of yours at the moment. Jackson will do fine. And shall I call you Simon or Mr. Keats?"

"Simon'll do. Not much room for formality out here like they is back east. You are from back east, ain't you? I hear it in that proper talk of yours."

"East, yes. But we are not discussing me. I asked you for advice and you have yet to offer it." Keats smiled through his stubble and spat a stream of brown tobacco juice toward the fire.

"Well sir, first thing you gotta' do is keep your scalp. They's all kinda' beins' out there that'll take your scalp. Indians, no-good white folks that look like honest long hunters, bears, even bufflers."

"Buffalo?" Sun was taken aback by the inclusion of these shaggy beasts in the list of dangers.

"Shore son. They's bad iffin the situation gets a little outta' hand. Knowed a young feller once—'bout your age. We hitched up in the settlements and headed west. We split up after we made the frontier a ways and set 'bout huntin'. He shot him a young buffler bull for meat and didn't do a good job. Best I recall, his rifle was a mite too light. What's the bore on that rig you a' totin'?"

"It's .54."

"Shorely good, but you still gotta' do it right. Gotta' place that ball. Anyhow, that buffler didn't take kindly to that youngster tryin' to take his hide and tongue, and that bull trounced on him with fire a pourin' outta' his nostrils. Like one of them dragons from the old days."

"Now, now Simon. You are prone to hyperbole I believe."

"Well, maybe he didn't have no fire a' shootin' from his nose, but he shorely musta' been a triflin' upset. He pushed and shoved that feller fearus. Broke him all up and got him moren' dirty. Punched one of them horns nearly plumb through his right side. Awful scene I come up on two days later. Like ta' not got him back to the settlements 'fore he died. None of us there thought he'd make it, but somehow he did. Guess the Good Lord was a' watchin' out for him. Ain't seen that feller since he left headed east. Said he'd had moren' 'nough of the frontier. Won't ever walk right. Got banged up bad."

"And the same with bears I'd guess."

"Same. They'll get you down if you ain't careful."

"I will be careful. And I feel comfortable with a .54 should I need the extra power. And what of the Indians and those no-goods who pretend to be long hunters?"

"You ever kill a man Jackson?"

"Of course not. I have never had any cause to do harm to another human." Sun's own words put him immediately into a state of remorse regarding the situation he had left behind. He had hurt his father, maybe even his mother and sisters. Intentional or not, he had brought pain. How could he live with the choice he had made? "Why would you ask such a question as that?"

"Well, you see the frontier's a strange place. Life and death don't hold the same meanin' they do where they's more structure, more civil'zation some would say. Sometimes a man has to kill to live, and I don't mean them critters we kill to eat. I mean other folks. They will kill you iffin you don't kill them."

"Oh Simon, I'm not sure I could do that. It is not in my nature. I want to avoid any such possibility. I have no desire to fight another person. I just want to see the frontier, to explore and see what is there, and I want to do it in peace."

"Good thoughts there Jackson, but I'm afeared you a' livin' in some kinda' dream. You see, they's evil 'bout. They's folks who would think no more of takin' your life and belongins' than shootin' a big ole squirrel outta' a tree for supper. Sorry to say, but peace sometimes comes only after war. You better prepare yourself for that iffin you want to keep that scalp."

"And what about those no-goods? I understand the Indians defending their homes and families, but what is the impetus that drives those you label as no-goods?"

"Impetus! Now that's a big word I ain't heard in a long time. One of them educated words, a word not many of them long hunters know how to use. I knew you's from back east. But I know that word just the same there son, and I can tell you about them no-goods. They's the kind who can't or won't make it on their own ability. They's them men who'd ruther take it than work for it. Always a' blamein' somebody else for their misfortune ruther than gettin' out there and scrappin' for a livin' like other folks.

"And they's them that don't know nothin' 'bout the Good Lord. They dangerus. You watch out for 'em."

"I've heard that before, from Mr. Shroyer who built   87

my rifle. His warning was much the same as yours. I didn't give it much thought then, but hearing it from one who has spent some time on the frontier puts it in a different light. I will have to keep all that in mind."

"This Shroyer was a wise man. You best heed what he told you— and what I told you. A man can wake up dead out there just 'bout any day." Keats roared with that boisterous laughter again, seeming most pleased that he possessed such a clever way with words. "And when it's all said and done, ain't nothin' or nobody can save that scalp 'cept the Good Lord anyhow. You best get caught up with Him."

"You seem to talk a great deal about this *Good Lord* as you call him." There was a blatant air of sarcasm in Sun's voice as he spoke these words and gestured toward the heavens, heavens that were gloriously decorated this evening by the one to whom Sun referred with such a cavalier manner. "Are you some religious fanatic or something?"

"Ain't religious a'tall, most folks would say. Ain't been to church reg'lar since I come to the frontier. 'Course, they ain't many churches on the frontier to go to no how. Guess my church is mostly the trees and fields and rivers. Guess I'm part of the same congregation as the critters out here. But that don't mean I ain't in contact with the Al- mighty. Me and him talk reg'lar. My folks was good Christians. They raised me proper. I know right from wrong and do my best to operate in the right. And when the Good Lord is finished with me in this world, I know where I'm a goin'. Do you?"

"I never had much use for all that. I am fully acquainted with the church; my parents saw to that. And I suppose I believe in God. But this talking with God and knowing what awaits at the end of this life is something I don't think we can do. I believe God gave us intelligence and resourcefulness and expects us to use both as we live. I just can't see Him being available to talk with and such things."

"Sorry to hear that. But me, I talk to Him every day. Ain't plannin' to stop no time soon."

"And I guess you are going to tell me now that He answers you when you talk."

"Well, not so much when I talk, but when I listen He

shorely does answer. Now ain't no words I can acc'lly hear. More like this little whisper, this little tuggin' in my heart. Yup, ain't no doubt it's God alright."

"Now wait Simon. Here you are telling me of the dangers and warning me to be ready to take a life, and now you start pontificating about all your religious beliefs. I would guess that you have been in those situations in which you had to take a life somewhere there on the frontier, and if that is the case, how do you justify such action if you are so very much in contact with this God you seem to know so well?"

"A smartsome feller we got here," Simon noted as he spat another stream of tobacco juice. "And another one of them big words. But I know it son. Pontificate. Don't take me as no preacher and don't take me as pompous. I'm just a simple long hunter saved by the grace of Jesus. I told you I done my best to do right. Shorely do that. But I can't see the Good Lord a' holdin' it 'gainst me iffin I protect myself and my belongins' 'gainst evildoers. They's plenty of 'em out there. Still, it's a grev'ous thing—havin' to defend yourself and hurt somebody. Grev'ous. I hope you don't never have to, but I'll wager that you do iffin you make it to the frontier. Kinda' like some of them stories in the Old Testament. They's some good ones in there. You want to read one of 'em tonight?" Simon reached into his haversack and retrieved a tattered Bible.

"No, I don't think that will be necessary. I haven't read much in that book before, so I see no need to begin now."

"Ain't never too late to start, 'less you dead."

"Well, I suppose that would be too late. But I'm fully alive and plan to stay that way for a great many years yet. So unless you want to read it silently for your own amusement, you can put your Bible away."

"Suit yourself Jackson. But I tell you they's some good readin' in here. I think I'll do 'xactly what you said—read it myself. I'll just curl up by the fire there and read myself to sleep."

"And sleep is the primary order of business now. You are welcome to stay in my camp, but be warned that I will be up and moving early tomorrow. I need to get to Yadkin Country as quickly as possible."

"These old bones sorta' creaky and stiff, but they   89

still move me good 'nough. I'll be up and ready by the time you are. 'Course, I ain't got no fancy mount like you do or a strong pack animal, but I ain't got all them belongins' you got neither. I'll get to Yadkin just the same. You just roll up in your blanket and get some sleep. Don't pay me no never mind."

Sleep didn't come easily to Jackson Bain. He had never met a man such as Simon Keats. A man who so thoroughly knew himself and was content with life as it came. A man who had experienced difficulties and had seen the worst in humanity, yet still apparently had some first-hand knowledge of a loving God. A God who also knew him as Simon Keats, personally. Had the frontier taught him all this?

CHAPTER 16

Mid May 1774 - Boston

"Are you two about ready?" Richard Bomar called as he walked down the stairs of his opulent dwelling. "The carriage will call shortly. I understand the theater will be crowded this evening."

"What a delightful night this will be Papa." Rebecca was dressed in a most impressive Paris gown, sky blue with dainty lace decorating the neckline and cuffs. It clung to a perfect body that no longer belonged to a little girl, a fact that brought pause to Richard Bomar as he watched her descend the curving staircase in grandeur and youthful vitality. "And I just love Samuel Foote's work. This play should be the perfect way to spend an evening."

"That it will, Rebecca. Now if we can just get your mother to come along so that we won't be late."

"Oh, don't fret Papa. She is coming. She just wants to look her best for such a special event, but really she wants to look her best for you!"

"I am pleased, indeed. But she need not be terribly concerned with that on my account. Your mother always looks wonderful to me."

"Still the romantic after all these years." Rebecca smiled as she kissed his cheek and gave him a playful wink. "That is what I want—a romantic, caring husband who thinks the sun rises in my eyes. Someone who will not grow tired of and fail to appreciate me when the monotony of life begins its twists and turns. A man like you, Papa."

"I am duly impressed that you regard me so highly, but I admit that I have not always been as I now am. I have lived too much of my life for my business, thinking that I was doing it all for you and your mother. I was, but I was also doing it for myself, many times at the expense of relationships I fear. But I am a different man now. Your mother must be given credit for that."

"Perhaps to some degree, Papa. She is an amazing woman. But don't dismiss yourself. It was your decision to make a change, to see life as more than success in business. And you must recall that mother had to make similar changes. She embraced the relationship she has with you and me and turned her back on much of society's demands. No longer does she allow some misplaced social expectation to dictate who and what she is. You two are to be commended."

"Thank you. I will do my best to never again disappoint you."

"Disappoint? You have never done that. You are a knight in shining armor. Remember, I want someone just like you."

"But that won't be any time soon, will it Rebecca?" Richard Bomar's heart was pained by the thought of giving his daughter's hand to a man, one who in no way could be deserving of this grand gift of his little girl.

"I'm not so sure about that. It could be soon; it could be years away. I will just follow my heart and wait for God to direct."

"And could He be directing toward Jackson Bain?"

"Now Papa, let's not get into that again."

"Please, I meant no disrespect. I was just curious. I haven't heard many details of the last conversation you had with Mr. Bain."

"That was a special and precious time. Jackson and I talked at length and acknowledged how very much we cared for each other. He is an incredible man. He is gentle, eloquent, loving. But we both realize that we are not in love. I do love him and he loves me, but there is not that magic of being in love. So I must say at this point that Jackson is not the one I will choose for a husband. That could change, but I will just have to wait and see."

"And you are talking again of being in love. You still believe that to be a prerequisite for marriage?"

"Without a doubt. I must be fully in love with the man I marry before I marry him. Yes, I know love will change and grow and none of us can fully know a partner minus time spent together. But I will be in love from the beginning."

"I am beginning to understand. I could not have said that in days past, but I have some modicum of understanding at this point. And your mother helped me see that. I am truly in love with her, more than ever before. I want the same for you. I held out hopes for you and Jackson, but I see now much of that was of my own doing. It just all seemed perfect, proper in the eyes of society. And business. My business, as well as that of Squire Bain's, would have grown tremendously with the union of you and Jackson. But that is of far less consequence today that it was previously. I wish you the best Rebecca. I will be here for you in support of your decision."

"Thank you, Papa. You can't possibly know what that means to me. I love you."

"And I you, my dear daughter. Forever. And where is your mother?"

"I'm right here and ready to go." Elizabeth's voice, coming from the top of the stairs, was almost girlish, teasing. "Sorry to keep you waiting." Richard turned to see his wife walking down the steps. She was a portrait of elegance and grace. Richard Bomar was practically speechless as he stood with mouth open and eyes fixed upon his wife.

"Oh my, you are stunning." Richard extended his hand to greet Elizabeth.

"And you my husband will be the most handsome man at the theater tonight." Elizabeth received Richard's hand and stood beside him, a coy smile creasing her face, her eyes dancing with a touch of mischief. "You know how to treat a woman; that fact is not wasted on me. Your dividends will

93

be greater than all those received in that business of yours!" Elizabeth gently poked an elbow into Richard's ribs as she continued to look intently into his eyes.

"My goodness you two!" Rebecca chided. "This is your young daughter standing here in your presence. I should not be hearing such bawdy ramblings. Now behave yourselves. And Papa, you don't think much of being in love? I'll not believe that. Now to the carriage both of you, before things get out of hand!"

•   •   •

"It was indeed marvelous," Rebecca said as the carriage pulled away from the theater.

"That it was," Richard opined. The sweet smell of blossoms filled the air. New leaves rustled in a soft breeze. This was a grand night to be about the streets of Boston.

"Yes, quite grand," Elizabeth added. "England can't produce a better performance than that one. This is a spectacular new country. I don't know that I have ever been as happy as I am at this moment."

"That is good to know my dear, and I share your enthusiasm. Like you, I am truly happy, content. My life is full. Now if we can just get this daughter of ours properly married and from under foot!" Elizabeth jabbed Richard's shoulder with a finger and the occupants of the carriage erupted in laughter. The rhythmic clop of horse's hooves beat a peaceful and sonorous tune on cobbled streets.

"Oh look, over there on the sidewalk," Rebecca noted. "Is that Mr. Clarkson? Yes, that is William Clarkson. I wonder what he is doing out here tonight. Papa, let's pull over and talk with him, perhaps give him a ride."

"I don't know Rebecca. I'm not sure that would be proper."

"Nonsense. What could possibly be wrong with that? Driver, please pull over."

"Mr. Bomar?" The driver turned to determine Richard's intent.

94   "Yes, it is fine sir. Please pull over."

"Mr. Clarkson? William? Yes it is you." Rebecca's words were filled with excitement. William Clarkson stopped and stared in the direction of the carriage. He was dressed in his finest, but that paled in comparison with Richard Bomar's attire. Clarkson was clean and his hair pulled into the proper queue and tied with a silk band, but at best he was a workman, a hired man not able to afford clothes that spoke of wealth and prestige.

"Miss Bomar?" Clarkson approached the carriage, his steps and speech halting.

"Yes, it is me—Rebecca."

"Mr. Bomar, Mrs. Bomar." William Clarkson nodded and half bowed in greeting. "And Miss Bomar. How are you this fine evening?"

"I am just wonderful, William. And it is Rebecca, not Miss Bomar." A broad smile swept across Rebecca's face and her eyes glinted light from the street lamps.

"Yes ma'am. Rebecca it is."

"And you sir," Richard added. "How are you?"

"As your daughter, sir. I am wonderful. A grand night to be in Boston."

"Please William, will you join us?" Rebecca's words brought surprise to the gathering.

"Thank you, but I don't think that is possible. I must be getting home. My parents will be concerned, and work will come early tomorrow. But I do thank you."

"I will hear nothing of it," Rebecca countered. "We can deliver you home and you will be there long before you can walk that far. So that excuse is of no value. Please, do join us." Rebecca looked at her father for his consent.

"Yes, sure Clarkson. Do join us." Richard was reticent in his remarks, but he realized Rebecca was very much interested in adding this passenger to the carriage.

"Very well, sir. If you are sure."

"Oh, we are sure." Rebecca smiled and scooted over to make a place for William Clarkson beside her. He stepped aboard and took his seat. He was taken aback by Rebec- 95 ca's beauty, and sitting so close to her made him feel as if he were in a whirlwind of stormy emotions.

"So, where have you been on such a lovely evening as this?" Rebecca almost caught herself before she asked such a personal question, but the words had escaped her lips before she could stop them. "Excuse me. Where you have been is none of my business."

"Quite all right Miss Bomar—uh, Rebecca. I have been to the theater to see the Samuel Foote play. Superb it was."

"Well, we were there too. I am surprised that we did not see you." It was then that Rebecca recalled that the reserved boxes designated for theater goers such as her family didn't lend themselves to bumping into those who occupied the more common seats of the masses.

"Sorry that I didn't see you folks either. But I was on the bottom floor. Crowded there, it was. I am sure you were in the boxes on second level."

"We were. Papa has a box reserved there for us throughout the season."

"Yes, of course." William Clarkson spoke softly and stared nervously toward the carriage floor. "I would have expected that."

"And you are a fancier of the theater, Mr. Clarkson?" Richard Bomar quizzed.

"I am sir. I admire all the great English writers. And yes, before anyone asks, I am devoted to Shakespeare."

"Ah, Mr. Shakespeare. Quite a student of humanity." Richard's words resounded with great authority, a solid indication that he knew his literature and was inviting William into a schooled discussion of such matters.

"That he was, Mr. Bomar. I would even go so far as to say that he understood the human condition better than most. Few insights into human conduct and reasoning have surpassed those he possessed."

"Indeed. He wrote with great passion and was fully aware of the beasts that haunt us all." Richard shuffled in his seat and gazed out the carriage, a distant, reflective demeanor now growing more pronounced. "And what do you think of *Macbeth*? What was Mr. Shakespeare attempting to illustrate in that work?"

"Please Papa," Rebecca chided. "This is a weighty conversation for such a lovely evening. Perhaps Mr. Clarkson does not choose to discuss such matters."

"Not at all. And it is William!" A broad smile wrinkled across Clarkson's face as he looked again at Rebecca. For a moment he was mesmerized, seemingly detached from the immediate matter of Richard's question. "I am always happy to talk of such things. I find them stimulating."

"Interesting word, stimulating!" Rebecca's quick response caused a mild shock among the group. Its intent was not mistaken as Elizabeth daintily touched the corners of her mouth with an embroidered silk handkerchief, Richard feigned a cough, and William Clarkson blushed as he fought off a tell-tale grin.

"Yes, *Macbeth*. Perhaps my favorite." William Clarkson was glad to break an awkward silence. "It is clear that Mr. Shakespeare was highlighting the frailties of humanity in that play—the lure of greed and its often tragic ends. Also, we must not overlook weakness, when one is not strong enough to stand firm on conviction and avoid wrongdoing. And with apologies to the ladies here present, the playwright certainly dealt with the manipulative powers of women." Save a muffled chuckle that Richard Bomar attempted to contain, there was a strangling quiet.

"Surely, Mr. Clarkson, you are not saying that we women are manipulative." Elizabeth Bomar spoke for the first time since William Clarkson had joined them.

"Forgive me ma'am. No, not inherently. But male or female, we can coerce. In the case of this particular play, it appears that Lady Macbeth was the guilty party. She allowed her own greed for station in life to blind her, to permit her to prevail upon her husband to go against what he knew was right. She attacked his manhood, shamed him into committing an evil act. And we know that led to tragedy. I see it as a warning to us all."

"I think you are right." Rebecca spoke after a time   97

of contemplation on William's words. "We can all be greedy and manipulative. God created us as individuals, and for one person to wrongfully influence another is against His will. We must be careful and never allow our own desires to get in the way of what God wants for us and what we demand from others. I want to live my life in that fashion, whether as a recipient of manipulation or as one tempted to manipulate. I choose to avoid both conditions." Again, there was silence.

"My, but I would say this conversation is indeed weighty, as my daughter has already noted." Richard finally spoke after what seemed an interminable time of nothing but the sound of the clopping hooves and squeaking harness. "Perhaps the evening is too fine to spend in such depth."

"That could be," William added, "but such matters do provoke thought. And thought keeps the mind nimble. I refuse to fall into that trap of letting my mind become numb with the mundane."

"As do I," Rebecca opined. "I know nothing can be new but once, but I want to be rich and refreshed with contemplation. That permits newness, even in the everyday."

"Well said, Rebecca." William was pleased to hear her comments. "We apparently share a great deal in common." Rebecca once again wore that mischievous smile that said her interest in this young man was more than superficial.

"I must say," Richard concluded, "that I find your perception and knowledge of such things not only refreshing but also somewhat surprising. I would never have expected such."

"Never expected, sir? Why would you say that?"

"I just mean that. . . ."

"That I am common? That my parents and I don't possess great wealth and status? That I am well read, a student of literature and philosophy, yah a thinker and observer of human nature?"

"Not at all, son. I just meant. . . ."

"There is no need for explanation, sir. Now if you will all excuse me, I shall ask the driver to pull over at the next corner."

"But where do you live, William? We can drop you there." Alarm and unease were evident in Rebecca's voice.

"This is quite close enough. I do thank you for your hospitality. Now if you will excuse me. Good evening Mr. Bomar, Mrs. Bomar. And good evening to you Miss Bomar." William Clarkson stepped from the carriage and bowed.

"Please William; it is Rebecca."

"Again, good evening." William Clarkson walked away along the darkened street.

CHAPTER 17

The Frontier

"Isaac, Miss Anna; you two 'round anywhur?" Jule Chillington yelled as he approached the Walker cabin.

"Well hello Jule." Anna Walker tugged the big oak door open and allowed spring sunshine to beam through to the hearth as she greeted Jule. "We've been expecting you. Here it is approaching late May and we knew you would be headed back to the Middle Ground soon. Welcome."

"Thank ya' Miss Anna. Purt nigh runnin' late this spring. Oughta' been back out there by now. Jest stayed in the settle-ment a mite too long. Life's too easy back there a ways. Reckon I'm gittin' soft."

"Oh, that's not likely Jule. I'm sure you are still more than capable of doing your long hunting. Where are you going this time?"

"Jest out a ways. 'Hain't gonna' be long on this here trip. Wanna' be back in the settle-ment by first thing in July. Meet up with the sutlers there and git my stock for the fall. Probably jest go over through the Gap and a little ways into Kan-te-kee. 'Hain't got time to make it past the Cumberland and shorely 'hain't got time to git to Beautiful River. And 'sides, I hear things kinda' rough up that way now."

"Yes, that is what we are hearing as well. Reports are that there are Indian attacks coming regularly. The British have them stirred up over this talk of revolution. It does seem that revolution is coming, Jule."

"Don't know nothin' 'bout no revolution. Don't care nothin' 'bout no revolution. I jest need to git out there and git some buckskin, maybe a buffler hide or two and git 'em back to the settle-ment. Meet up with the sutlers, sell my wares, and lay in some fall supplies. I plan to be headed back to the Middle Ground by early September. Want to make it on up to Blue Licks this fall. But this here is a short trip. Won't be out more'n a month. Say, yore paw anywhur 'round?"

"No, I'm sorry. He is back in the settlement and won't be home for three or four more days. He went in to pick up some supplies himself. And while he was there he was going to help with work on the church house."

"Yeah, I seen all that hustle and bustle 'round there but didn't see no sign of Isaac. Shore hate I missed him."

"Well if I know Isaac, he found somebody around who needed him and he was helping them as well as working on the church. And I wouldn't be surprised if he didn't find cause to stop by the Widow Wallace's to see if she needed a fence repaired or some garden work done."

"Now go on, that sly ole fox. Don't tell me Isaac's sweet on the Widder Wallace. And here I was a thinkin' he warn't no way inner'sted in women."

"You can never be too sure. He is a healthy man and I know he misses my mother a great deal. What would be wrong with him taking a fancy to Widow Wallace and falling in love?"

"Why, nothin' would be wrong with that. Shorely would be good iffin you ask me. A man needs a good woman to keep him warm and such. No offense meant Miss Anna."

"None taken, Jule. Would you care to sit a while here on the porch?"

"Mighty kindly of ya'. I'll set a spell, git me a drink of cool water, and fill my canteen iffin that's to yore likin'."

"Well of course. Help yourself. Do you need some food while you rest?"

101

"Got a piece of fresh jerked meat? That'd fill a holler spot I got in my stomach." Anna went inside and retrieved a linen sack filled with venison jerky she and Isaac had cured and smoked the week before.

"There you go, Jule. Take all you need."

"Jest a strip or two Miss Anna. Wouldn't wanna' run you and Isaac low."

"You won't. There are plenty of deer, so we can make some more jerky. And the hens are laying eggs every day. The corn crop looks good, too. We certainly don't go hungry around here."

"Thank ya' Miss Anna."

"You are welcome at our table and in our home any time Jule. Feel free to stop by when you are near."

"A'gin, mighty kindly. Say Miss Anna, I been specalatin' over talkin' to you 'bout a matter. I can't set here a' conversin' long 'fore I git back on the trail, but I thought you might hear me out on this patic'ler matter. I done talked with Isaac 'bout it all, and me and you discussed it a mite when I's here last time. You been givin' any considerin' 'bout me courtin' you and you goin' with me to the Middle Ground come fall?"

"Oh Jule, you flatter me. I do appreciate your thinking so highly of me. But I'm not quite as certain as you that this is the right thing for me. You are a decent man; I know your intentions are honorable. But marriage is a serious matter. It is more than just sharing a warm bed on a cold night."

"That I s'pose it is, Miss Anna. But sharin' a bed ain't all bad. 'Spect it's more'n me and you ever 'magined."

"Not bad at all, I'm sure. In fact, it would be one of the grandest things God ever created—if the match is right. A man, a woman—in love and in God's plan. That would be incredible; I have no doubt about it. But just to make some hasty decision because we are at the proper age is no way to begin. For one thing, we don't even know each other very well. And we have never really talked of our dreams, our plans for the future. I just know you as a kind-hearted long hunter who is at peace about what he does. Do you plan to do that the remainder of your life?"

"'Hain't never really give it no never mind Miss Anna. 'Hain't never done nothin' but hunted and trapped. It's been a good life so far. Can't see no reason to change."

"But a wife, Jule. What would a wife do to those plans?"

"Never give that no never mind neither. A wife's s'pposed to foller her husband 'hain't she? 'Hain't that what the Good Book says? 'Course, I can't read no words writ down on paper. But that's what I hear 'bout the Good Book."

"That is somewhat correct. The man should take the responsibility of being the spiritual leader of the home, but I'm not at all sure that we are told to follow him without question, to give up our own insight and understanding and needs. I just don't think you will find that in the words of Jesus."

"Could be. Jest like I said, I can't read no words writ down on paper. Have to jest let somebody else tell me what's writ. So, you're a sayin' that you can't foller me 'round whilst I'm a tryin' to make us a livin'?"

"No, I'm not saying that at all. What I am saying is that I would have to be convinced that following you or anyone is in God's will for me. And what about children and a home? Have you ever given that any thought?"

"Oh shore. I want a bunch of little younguns' a runnin' 'round everwhur. And I could build us a cabin out there somewhur. You and the little ones could keep it up and ready for when I got back with all them buffler hides ready for market. It's as good a life as anybody could want. And I shorely can't see how it don't figger in the Almighty's plan."

"Jule, that is difficult to explain. I simply know that God is in charge of my life. He will direct me if I allow Him. As I have already said, you are a decent man and I respect your wishes and plans. I just must be sure that mine fit yours before we talk of anything more serious. I will pray about this, and I certainly want to talk with Isaac a great deal more. I have no desire to hurt you in any way, but that is all I can agree to at the moment. I hope you can understand, but that is a choice you will have to make. I can't become someone I am not just to avoid any hurt that might come as a result of my telling you I will not go with you in the fall. I suppose that is a possibility, but I don't want you to have false hopes. I feel no direction to accept your proposal right now. All I can do is pray diligently about this and think it through. I hope you can accept that and go on now with your plans for this upcoming hunt."

"Shorely not what I wanted to hear Miss Anna. 'Course, 'hain't no whole lot I can do 'bout it neither. You 'bout the purttiest girl east of the Gap, and takin' you to the Middle Ground come fall would be pleasur'ble. But iffin you 'hain't ready yet I guess you 'hain't ready yet. But I'll come back through in a month or so. Hope to find you in another disposition then. Good day Miss Anna."

"You do that. Feel free to stop by on your way back. And good day to you, Jule."

•   •   •

"I'm glad you're home, Papa." Anna's eyes sparkled as Isaac walked up to the cabin. "Did you have a good time in the settlement? What is going on back there of interest?"

"Good to be home. And yes, the settlement was fine. I enjoyed vis-iting with some of the folks there, and I even enjoyed working on the church. It should be ready by the end of summer at the latest. I also did a little work for some of the settlers around there who needed help."

"And one of those wouldn't be the pretty Widow Wallace, would it?" Anna smiled at Isaac and watched as he poked his moccasin-cov-ered toe into some soft sob near the cabin door.

"Shaah girl; none of that useless chatter. You know good and well that I have no interest in that woman."

"I don't know any such thing, Isaac Walker. To the contrary. I think you have a keen interest in her; I know she does in you. And why not? Any woman would be more than lucky to get you."

"Now stop that. Keeping this place up and trying to farm is all I can do. Women don't fit in my plans—that is except for you." Isaac's smile was gentle, revealing his love

104

for Anna. "Enough of this talk about women. I'll gather some wood so that we can cook supper. Then I'm going to the creek and wash some of this dust off. We'll sit on the porch and talk after we eat. It will be a fine evening to sit and watch the stars dance across God's heaven. His creation still amazes me, and I missed being here in the quiet while I was back in the settlement. How does that sound?"

"That sounds just fine. As quickly as you get the wood in, I'll start supper."

●　●　●

"Papa, do you ever have a longing in your heart, something that you can't quite identify but know it is there?" Anna sat on a hand-hewn pine bench in the cool night air, Isaac across from her on a short stool and blowing smoke rings from his pipe. A shooting star zipped across the sky. Anna closed her eyes and whispered a wish. Crickets chirped and owls hooted from nearby woods. "I'm just not sure what it is, but I have a longing. It is almost like summer lightning. You know that lightning when we desperately need rain. You see it brighten the sky in the distance but don't know exactly where it came from or what it will bring. Too often we are disappointed; we don't get the rain we hope for. You know that lightning, don't you Isaac?"

"I know it well, girl. You hope and wait and watch. But then the promise disappears in the heat of a summer night. It leaves you empty, afraid to hope the next time it comes. Yes, I would say I know it first hand."

"I felt that you would."

"And I know the longing you mention. It takes many forms for me: Longing for your mother, longing for success here on the frontier, and definitely a longing to see you happy and fulfilled. I fear I have failed in that last category."

"Please don't be concerned about that. I am content with what we have. I love my life here and can't imagine living it anywhere else. In no way have you ever failed me."

"But what of that longing? I'm sure it has something 105

to do with you being alone out here like this. And you are here because of me. I can't help but worry about that from time to time."

"But you shouldn't, Isaac. I tell you again, I am content. Yes, there is a longing, but until I can identify it adequately, I'll continue as I am—here and happy. And since you have mentioned worry, I worry about you. You need companionship other than that I offer. That is just natural. And please know that I understand."

"Yes, but your mother. . . ."

"My mother—your wife—is gone. That is not your fault. It simply is a fact that can't be changed. If we could talk with her now I'm sure she would tell you and tell me to live life. To celebrate every moment God gives us. She would not want either of us to waste time in worry and remorse."

"That's true. Your mother enjoyed life fully. Even on that long trip to the Yadkin and then the hardships we faced here on the frontier, she wore a smile. I recall many times watching her struggle up the hill with a bucket of water, only to stop and gaze at the colors of fall and smile her approval up to God. She would hum softly as she bent over the fire while cooking our meals, perhaps pushing a wayward strand of hair back behind her ear. If she saw me watching, she would put on the most beautiful grin anyone has ever seen and let her magic eyes dance across my face. She was splendid. What she saw in me I will never know."

"She saw a gentle man who recognized all her special attributes, a man who loved her unconditionally, a man of God. That is what she saw, Papa."

"My goodness, girl." Isaac tapped the spent tobacco from his pipe and tucked the pipe into a pocket of his ragged weskit. "You do find the good in people, don't you?"

"I always try. But with you that is not a difficult task."

"Thank you, but enough about me. Have you talked with anyone else about all this? A woman would probably have more insight than I do."

"Mrs. Jacobson and I talk often. She understands."

"I would imagine she does, and I'm glad you have her."

"So am I. But. . . ."

"But that summer lightning?"

"Yes. It has often brought disappointment. It has failed to fulfill our hopes for rain."

"Disappointment is a part of life, Anna. We will never be free from the risk of disappointment while we are here on earth. God is the exception; He never disappoints. But while we are here and dealing with humans, the potential for disappointment exists. Some disappoint us willfully; some do so out of carelessness. Either way, we are hurt. But wouldn't it be sad to live life running from hurt? Is that any way to live?"

"No, I suppose it isn't. But that doesn't take away the dread."

"No, it doesn't. There is dread, and there is real risk. When we lost your mother I thought life was not worth living. But I have come to realize that I would not trade those memories of the good to escape the pain of losing her. She was a gift from God and I would now be far less than what I am had I failed to accept that gift. Painful. But the rewards are enough to last a lifetime. Besides, look at you. You are part of the gift God gave me through your mother."

"Special words, Papa."

"Only truth, Anna. I mean everything I just said, mean it all from the depths of my heart."

"I believe you. I would never question your sincerity. And I thank you for the words, the encouragement, the understanding. I'm just somewhat confused about life at the moment."

"And life can be confusing. My only advice to working through the confusion is to be patient and wait on God. He has the answers."

"Jule Chillington stopped by two days ago. He said to tell you hello and that he would be back in a month or so, probably early July."

"He still wants to court you, I suppose."

"I think that is his plan. But he didn't seem too terribly interested in courting. He was more interested in my keeping him warm on the trail this fall. He has visions of my packing up and going with him to the Middle Ground when he heads back in August or September."

"Not a very romantic sort of fellow, is he?"

"No, at least not the kind of romance I am looking   107

for. I see deep, lasting love as more than just bundling up in a buffalo robe in some rude camp and watching the sparks fly—from the fire and from Jule's eyes!"

"Oh, I don't know. Could be just the thing you need!" Isaac winked at Anna and spread his aging but handsome face into a wide grin.

"Isaac Walker! Hush up with that kind of talk."

"Only chiding you girl. You know I agree with you. Love is more than that. It includes that, but love is much more. I fear poor Jule is not thinking that profoundly at this point. Are you considering his offer?"

"He can't even read, Papa."

"I guess you would just have to read for and to him, though I doubt reading would be the first thing on his mind."

"Come, come now Papa. I'm trying to be serious."

"Yes, I know girl. I'm sorry. Just making light of a heavy line of conversation here." Isaac reached over and patted Anna's hand.

"I can't say I haven't considered Jule's proposal. He is, as you have often said, a decent man. It's not like I have a long list of suitors coming by on a daily basis here on the frontier. I suppose I could do worse."

"And you could do better as well. Just because you could do worse is little reason to act. That lightning you mentioned could be real. Jule Chillington, even though he is a decent man, could bring to one such as you a heavy dose of disappointment. Is this what God wants for you, Anna?"

"I'm not sure, Papa. How can I be sure?"

"No easy answer there. No easy answer at all."

• • •

"Well, there's Yadkin Country, Jackson. Is it what you 'spected?"

"Beautiful land all about, Simon. Beautiful. And a bit more settled than I imagined. Not quite Boston, but there are people about."

"Boston? You from Boston son?"

"Did I say I was from Boston? Just because I mentioned that city doesn't mean that I have ties there. And where I am from or where I am going is still nothing you should be concerned about."

"Don't go gettin' all testy and 'cited there son. You shore are a strange one. Just the least little hint of me a' mentionin' your past and you get all bothered and such. I ain't meanin' no harm 'bout it all."

"Forgive me Simon, but my past is my past. It in no way is anyone's concern. We will make it better to just let that rest. Is that agreed?"

"Agreed son. Now we gotta' get you fixed up proper for long huntin'. Ain't no benefit in you a' goin' off toward the frontier dressed up like a dandy. You gonna' stop in at some of the sutlers and get some buckskin. I'll make you up some moccasins and leggins', but you best watch close. Ain't gonna' make you but one pair, and they won't last long on the trail. You a' gonna' have to make the next ones! And get you a long shirt or two. Maybe get you a frock. Ain't travelin' on the long hunter trail with some dandy from Boston."

"What? We are not traveling together. I don't want a traveling companion."

"Me neither there boy. Don't want nobody 'round me when I'm a' travelin'. I just thought you was a' goin' toward the Cumberland and I know I'm a' goin' toward the Cumberland; figgered we'd just 'panion up for the trip. The Good Lord knows you could use the 'struction I could give you in a' keepin' that purtty scalp there."

"Perhaps I could use a bit of instruction; I know very little of frontier life. But I don't think I am interested in finding a companion for the journey."

"That's just plumb good with me iffin that's the way you want it. It don't make me no never mind. I been a' trekkin' these trails for years and am finely comfortable by my lonesome. It's you I's considerin'. Just thought I'd make a offer to wise you up a speck if you's a mind to let me. Tell you what. We'll get you all fixed up for the trail and see where it all leads after that. Won't take no more 'n a day or so and we'll be ready to head to the Cumberland. You got time to reckon on all this travelin' 'panionship after that. What you say to that?"

"Oh, I suppose that will be fine. But we are just traveling on out toward the Cumberland together. I don't want any great deal of comment regarding my plans. I am simply interested in some exploring and don't want to be hampered by meeting someone else's schedule. Is that clear?"

"Shorely is clear." Keats gave that boisterous, roaring laugh again. "Yes sirree; you's a strange one. Ain't the least bit concerned with a' keepin' that scalp. But the choice is yours. I'll not be the one to stand in your way. Now let's get to a sutler and get you some fittin' clothes for this big 'venture you a' headed to."

Boston

• • •

"You are quitting Mr. Clarkson? I am sorry to hear that. Are you sure about this decision?" Richard Bomar was taken aback by William Clarkson's announcement.

"Never quite sure about such matters Mr. Bomar, but I think it is the right thing to do. I appreciate the opportunity you gave me to work and learn, but I feel it necessary to move on now."

"I can appreciate that Mr. Clarkson. A man will seldom reach his full potential working for someone else. But I had hoped you would stay with me; I had even considered the possibility that you might work into a more prominent position in my business endeavors. Similar hopes were in place regarding Jackson Bain, but my daughter tells me they will not likely marry and he will not be a part of this family, at least not any time soon."

"Yes, Mr. Bain; I have heard the name mentioned often. He comes from an influential family, the perfect match for Miss Rebecca." William Clarkson spoke the words with some distaste evident in his manner.

"I agree—the perfect match. Or at least I would have agreed in the past. But now I am beginning to see things differently. My daughter has helped me grow into this. The perfect match, according to her anyway, begins with

110

being in love, not some social standing. That was difficult for me to digest, but I genuinely think I am beginning to see it all more clearly."

"So social standing does not matter in all this?"

"I would be less than honest if I said it didn't. You have seen Boston society. Business focuses around the socially elite. My family has been fortunate to be among that group all my life. Business contacts are from that group. It just seems a natural progression of events. So I can't say with certainty that social standing doesn't matter. But I can say with great certainty that I no longer consider it the paramount ingredient for a full life, and Rebecca has been a leading figure in helping me see that—and of course my lovely wife. The two embraced the change first and I have followed, sluggishly and obstinately, but I have followed. That has made a tremendous difference in my life."

"But I am not among the elite Mr. Bomar. My parents are poor; common laborers they are. In fact, without my income to assist them, they would be in a pitiful condition. You are aware of that. And that awareness, I assume, was the impetus for your surprise at my being schooled and interested in theater. I'm sure you haven't forgotten our discussion recently after the play."

"Is that what this is all about Clarkson? My comment? You are quitting because I found it amusing that you knew Shakespeare? You are interested in business and committed to success and you are willing to walk away from a grand opportunity just because your sensitivity was bruised by a comment that you misinterpreted? Foolish son; truly foolish. You will never enjoy success until you put the past in the past and look toward the future. There will always be incidental remarks that will scar you. And besides, I was in no way referring to your upbringing or social level. I simply found it refreshing that a young man was so aware of the great writers. And now you go and determine to make some lame decision based upon what you thought you heard."

"Mr. Bomar, I. . . . I. . . ."

"No need for additional comment Mr. Clarkson. You have made your choice, a choice I fear you will regret. And my daughter will regret it as well. She is terribly fond of   111 you young man. And so am I. As I have just said, I had hopes for your future. You will be difficult to replace, but replace you I can—and will. Your salary to date will be waiting for you at closing time. Now good day Mr. Clarkson."

"But Mr. Bomar, Sir, I. . . ."

"Good day son. And God's speed."

CHAPTER 18

Late June 1774 - The Frontier

 "Ain't you never gonna' get ready to hit the trail there boy? We done laid 'round this settlement for nigh on a month now. And here you are a lookin' fine and proper for long huntin'; done put away them fancy clothes of the Boston folk. I'd say you's plumb ready for some true frontier life."

"That I am Simon. You just keep fretting and fuming and I am growing weary with it all."

"Not half so weary as I am with your lollyin' 'round. I'd like to be deep in the Cumberland by July. It'll take us that long at a steady walk to get there. And besides, I'd find it fanciful and fittin' to stop by and visit the Walkers on the way. Don't never pass up Anna and Isaac's hospitality."

"And here you are talking about my, as you say *lollyin'*. Seems you have some lollying on your mind as well. And who are the Walkers? I don't know that I care to stop and visit anybody. I am interested in the frontier, not some remnant of civilization."

"Maybe that's so, but you won't go a' regrettin' stoppin' by the Walkers. Even iffin it's just stew they serve up, 113 it'll be the best you ever had. And by the time we get there, you'll be more'n ready for some victuals."

"Mrs. Walker must be a good cook, Simon."

"'Ain't no Mrs. to it. It's miss. Miss Anna. Isaac's daughter. Courtin' age, too. But I 'spect somebody's done looked into that. Purtty girl like that gonna' draw a whole passel of suitors. You better watch your step or some of 'em'll crook that high-class Boston nose of yours over that girl."

"Oh, a real frontier beauty, is she? Well, I'll have to see for myself. I can't imagine any woman being prettier than those I left behind in Boston. And besides, the last thing I am interested in is a woman. I want to see the frontier."

"So, it is Boston after all. You's from Boston. I figgered as much."

"Now Simon. I thought we had reached an agreement. You are not to pry into my past or question my future. You are only to tag along to the Cumberland. I will have it no other way."

"Still spunky 'bout that, ain't you son? Can't see where it makes no never mind iffin you tell me where's you from. And mark my words, Miss Anna'll cross them blue Boston eyes of yours."

"And I can't see what difference it makes to you where I have come from or where I am going. All you need to know of me is that I am headed toward the Cumberland."

"Got a last name?"

"Simon Keats, you are insufferable. I have a good mind to leave you here and move on alone. You are beginning to fray my nerves more every day with your useless questions and speculations."

"Leave a lovable sort like me behind, boy? I ain't worried 'bout such as that. First, I can make it just fine on my lonesome; and second, your life would shorely be incomplete without my comp'ny. Where would you find your amusement?" Simon's big laugh echoed across the landscape. "Now I'm a' gonna' be spectin' you to be ready to get out of this settlement and head west at first light."

"Don't you fret about that. I'll be ready. You just make sure you are ready old man."

"Born ready, still ready boy. And you's the one who
114   don't need to fret."

• • •

"Well what a sight! I figured you had withered up and blown away by now Simon. Don't you know you are too old to be heading back to the frontier?" Isaac Walker gave Simon Keats a hearty handshake and a slap on the back. The eyes of both men sparkled with the recognition of a long friendship and the joy of reunion. "Good to see you old friend. Good, indeed."

"And you Isaac. Guess I am a mite more withered than the last time we met, but the years do that. Been healthful, though. I'm still on this side of dirt. The Good Lord's blessed. Still lets me marvel at His handiwork, visit old friends, and laugh at all the things that's just plumb hum'rous 'round me. Plenty of hum'rous things 'round. Lots of 'em folks. And this here's Jackson. Ain't got no last name."

"It's Johnson. Jackson Johnson. Glad to meet you Mr. Walker."

"And glad to meet you Mr. Johnson. But please, it is Isaac."

"And it is Jackson. Thank you."

"Simon, Jackson, tie up your animals there at the rail; you two come up on the porch and sit. You can stand your flinters there by the wall.

Boston

• • •

"And where did you see young Clarkson dear daughter?" Richard Bomar peered over a stack of papers piled on his desk.

"I just happened to meet him on the street. He is working odd jobs as he can about town but has nothing of any great import. He appeared disheveled and somewhat downcast." Rebecca's tone was sympathetic, her feelings for William obvious to her father.

"Sorry to hear that Rebecca. Clarkson was a good and solid employee. He has real potential for the business world. It is indeed tragic that he was unable to control those emotions that led to his rash decision."

"Agreed Papa, but perhaps we had some impact on those emotions. I know how we view him and that your comments were certainly not out of order. He is probably insecure with his station in life. If so, I can better understand his reaction."

"That is true, all of what you say. But I am not responsible for Mr. Clarkson's reaction. It is he who must gain control of who and what he is. That is the only way he will succeed in this difficult world of business."

"I'm sure you are right papa."

"Of course I'm right. A man must be in touch with himself and take control apart from what someone else thinks."

"And who better than you to help him do just that, Papa?"

"What are you saying girl? Am I to take this young man under my tutelage and assure him success?"

"Not assure him success. He must be responsible for that. But you possess the expertise that he needs in business, and you have definitely learned to focus on what is important in life. I have always admired your business savvy. But in these last few months you have more completely blended these elements into the family and become the perfect father and husband—not that you weren't close to perfect all along!" Rebecca wrinkled her nose and winked at her father in a manner that always softened his sometimes calloused business heart.

"Well daughter. You really know how to manipulate me."

"No manipulation. Just simple truth. You are my hero. And I think mother would agree."

"So I suppose you want me to locate young Clarkson and have a long talk with him? Perhaps even attempt to convince him to come back to work here, to learn this business, to welcome him into our family as it were?"

"See, you do understand; you do know me completely. That is exactly what I am suggesting. William Clarkson needs us; we need William Clarkson."

"Could it be that it is you who needs him, not us who need him?"

116

"Now Papa. I can't deny my attraction to Mr. Clarkson; you are aware of that. And I suppose I do *need* him and want to get to know him better. You are not the only man in my life!" Rebecca flashed a demure smile; her eyes twinkled with enthusiasm.

"You have again convinced me to do something I would never have considered on my own. Now off with you." Richard Bomar gestured with a swish of his hand. "I have to get back to work. And where may I find this rebellious Mr. Clarkson?"

"You just leave that to me Papa." Rebecca bounded from Richard's office and fluttered through the merchandise, exhilaration filling each step.

CHAPTER 19

"I am concerned about your father, Cora." Robert Jamison said as he sat with his wife after the evening meal. "Jonathan and I have been discussing it and we think he may not be well."

"I concur. Cassie and I have concluded the same thing. And we have talked with mother about it. We think a great deal of the problem is this thing with Sun."

"Blast Jackson. He should know better. He has everything anyone could want in life and he does this."

"Now Robert, let's not too quickly criticize Sun. He is young and filled with struggles and is doing what he feels best. Your criticism of him is ill placed."

"Perhaps it is as you say, but I can't comprehend his stubborn resolve to disobey your father's wishes. He is tearing this family apart. Can't you see that?"

"He is tearing this family apart only if this family allows that to happen. A family should be understanding, supportive. If one doesn't find these qualities in his or her own family, where will he or she find them? Your obvious disgust will do nothing but add to the fragmentation."

"Cora. Are you turning against me and choosing sides with your brother?"

"Choosing sides? We are all a family. We don't choose sides and do battle. How could you accuse me of such a thing?"

"I'm not accusing you of anything."

"But you just said that I was turning against you and choosing sides with my brother. Be assured that I will never turn against you. And as for my brother, he is after all my brother. And even if he weren't, I still think that we must allow others to find their own way. Manipulation is a tactic of selfishness."

"Cora, I am sorry. Your father is not well, the business is a tremendous responsibility, and I often feel the entire world is caving in around me. All that is at the core of my discontent."

"Discontent? You are not content with our life?"

"Content with most of it, Cora. But there are times when I want to run away screaming."

"Run from me?"

"No, not particularly. But I do admit that I sometimes want to leave everything and everybody behind. But I know life would be a miserable journey without you. I love you Cora, and I am sorry that I even mentioned that urge to flee."

"No need for apologies Robert. And I love you. If truth be told, we all likely consider running from time to time. But maturity helps us see that running is no real answer. God gives us strength and direction to not only endure but to enjoy conquest in times of trouble. I believe that. I know you believe it as well."

"That I do. And I am dedicated to that premise. There will be no running in my future."

"Robert, could it be that part of your frustration with the situation and part of your disapproval of Sun is a disapproval of and frustration with yourself? Could it be that what Sun is doing is what you wish you had done before settling into your routine?"

"Those are complex issues Cora. It is unsettling to even talk about such matters."

"Perhaps it is unsettling. But never do I want to stand in your way of discovery, or your coming fully to know yourself and love the person you are."

"But I have responsibilities."

"*We* have responsibilities. You are not in this alone. Life is a joint effort that is shared."

"Oh Cora, you are right. And thank you for reminding me. I do at times feel alone, but I know you are there. I would have it no other way. Forgive me."

"Again, no need for apologies. I understand. And I again remind you that it is *we* and not just *you*. Now, tell me more. What are your feelings, your aspirations, your desires? Where do you want your life to go?"

"My life is fine as it is. Why would you ask?"

"Because I have seen of late that your life may not be as you want it. I have seen the frustration."

"But to verbalize something gives it power. It is best left unsaid."

"There is power in talking about a matter, but in this case it is not likely best left unsaid."

"I think it is, Cora. Please, let's not deal with this. The last thing I want to do is cause pain."

"But pain is inevitable. We don't go through life without pain. We are taught in God's word that trials perfect us, help us grow. Do I need to tell you again that I love you, that I am for you and not against you?"

"No, you don't need to tell me, but I do enjoy hearing it. A man enjoys every time a beautiful woman fawns over him!" A broad smile and teasing eyes brightened Robert's face, expressions Cora had not seen in far too long. "So please, feel free to tell me on every occasion you see fit."

"My pleasure. I'll not forget to do so more often. Now, on with the disclosure of those dark secrets you have hidden away. I will gladly listen."

"As you wish. I hope I am gentle."

"You can be nothing but gentle. That is one thing I love about you."

"Your father is a good man. He is successful and pays us well. I have no complaints there."

120

"But?"

"But, he is also difficult at times."

"Temperamental?

"Well, yes. Temperamental."

"Don't forget that I have known him longer than you have. I grew up in his household. And yes, he is a good man. And he is also temperamental. Your conclusion comes as no shock."

"I should have known you were aware of that. As you say, you have known him longer than I. But I want to be careful that I don't sound too crass. That would serve no purpose other than to hurt you."

"Robert, put your mind at ease. Now please continue."

"He comes in often with not so much as a word of greeting. Jonathan and I know he cares, but he gives no indication of it. He seems to view us as buffoons that must be tolerated, not appreciated. As insignificant weasels who, under the cover of pretense, wooed his daughters into the trap of matrimony so that we two could benefit from his benevolence. Jonathan hardly ever mentions it, but I feel as though I am some evil that Squire accepts rather than a valuable member of his business team."

"I know for certain that your conclusions are not totally accurate, but I can see how his actions, or lack of actions, can impact you as they do. You can't help how you feel. But the only sure change can be accomplished in oneself; we don't have the power or the privilege to change others. The change needed to deal with this situation must come from within you."

"Yes, I think you are right. But it is too late to change anything."

"It is never too late. Life is filled with change. God is a God of second chances."

"I wish I could believe that, but the responsibilities I have. . . ."

"That *we* have Robert."

"Yes, that *we* have. How can I make wholesale change in the face of these? The cost would be too great. I am not an irresponsible man."

"Of course you are not, and I admire you for that. But don't live life in misery, limping on the crutch of false ex-   121 cuses. Consider those to whom you are responsible, as I know you do and will continue to do, and then make your decisions from there. You must not allow this or any other situation to dictate life. If it is not my father's business you want and need, then recognize and act upon that."

"But we have so much; we are accustomed to. . . ."

"Limping again on the crutch of false excuses?. Limping along and feeling sorry for yourself?"

"Yes, I suppose I am, but. . . ."

"But what? True, we are accustomed to opulence, but how much of that is really needed? Our needs are met far beyond expectation. We can do with much less. If that is the stumbling block you fear, you must set that fear aside. It is not a valid reason."

"But I must not be careless. I must remain responsible."

"That you must. You, we must choose wisely, but we must not allow ourselves to be trapped by possessions or some false sense of security. No, you, we can't put our family at risk of destitution, but I doubt that will happen. You are too cautious for that."

"But the world is a dangerous place, particularly in business endeavors. I fear. . . ."

"And who lives minus danger? And who lives without fear? Trust in God and our family is all we have that is genuinely reliable. Now, what other excuses do you have—or legitimate reasons for that matter? Where are they?"

"I suppose they don't exist. I suppose that my reticence is based on irrational fear."

"It is correct to be careful, perhaps even reticent as you say you are, and it is correct to consider all possible outcomes, but if you choose wisely with all this in mind, all will be well. God will direct if you will follow. Now, what do you want to do? Be honest."

"That I will, Cora. And I suppose my honesty must begin by being honest with myself. I think I admire Jackson rather than despise him.

He is a threat to me, not because he, as I said, is tearing this family apart, but because he has courage. He stepped out to find his own way, even in the face of unquestioned danger. I never have."

"Are you sure you haven't, Robert? You had the courage to marry and settle into a regimen of providing. You had the courage to become a father. You had the courage to carry on in the mundane. That is courage, and you have a generous supply."

"But at least Jackson had the decency to remain single and not involve a wife and children in his fanciful ramblings."

"Is that another one of those flimsy excuses I hear? Sounds as if it is. If we enter this journey together and in agreement, it is not a reason but an excuse. It is something you may later regret. Now go on; what is it you feel you must do?"

"I'm not completely sure, but I feel I need to explore, to branch out, to determine how I would do in the world with decisions that I—no, we—make apart from the dictates of your father's business. The frontier is somewhat appealing, but so is business here in Boston. I just feel that I have somehow lost or failed to find my true self, and I now need to do that—with you and the children by my side, of course."

"And that is where we will be—beside you. We will not be without the same fear that grips you as well, but we will be beside you."

"But I am just not sure what to do. I just know that I need to change the direction I am now taking, at least to some extent. I may remain where I am in your father's business, but I may opt to explore other avenues. Are you in agreement?"

"Well, it is an undertaking filled with uncertainty, but I am in agreement as long as you are convinced that you are in God's will. Let's begin praying now that He will direct us and that we will follow that direction. If we do, the journey will be one filled with satisfaction."

"Yes, let's do. We will begin praying earnestly and discuss this more thoroughly. And never forget that I love you." Cora and Robert stayed long in an embrace that spoke of newness in the midst of familiarity.

CHAPTER 20

The Frontier

"Anna, look who is here." The satisfaction of renewed friendship was obvious in Isaac's voice.

"Well Simon Keats. Good to see you. It has been far too long. How have you been?"

"Just fine Miss Anna. Ain't no complaints to be found nowhere, 'cept maybe for these old bones. God's been good."

"He always is, Simon. What brings you out this way?"

"Oh, this here is Mr. Johnson, Jackson Johnson. We's headed on out toward the Cumberland. Jackson here wants to explore, see something 'sides that fancy life in Boston that's made him soft and edge'cated."

Anna was without words when she looked into Sun's eyes, eyes that spoke of longing and desire, eyes that made her very being soar and immediately filled her with flights of fancy. Her heart raced and her breathing quickened, a condition with which she was most unfamiliar and by which she was shocked.

"Pleased to meet you Miss Walker." Sun bowed. *Simon was right—a frontier beauty. Simple, but truly beautiful.* Sun straightened from the bow and smiled, his handsome face radiating and his muscular physique rippling beneath a long hunter shirt and buckskin leggings. The sash cinched around his waist was as expertly tied as was the leather thong that held his manicured queue.

"And pleased to meet you Mr. Johnson," Anna managed to squeak out. "But please, it is Anna."

"And it is Jackson. In fact, it is just Sun, with a 'u'. My mother was responsible for that derivation when I was a child, and the designation stuck. Feel free to use it; I certainly answer to that. And I must say that I would likely answer to any name a lovely lady such as you chose to employ!" Anna blushed, cast a downward glance, and turned again to her cooking.

"Sun? Well here's the two of us been close friends for nigh on to three months and you ain't never mentioned nothin' 'bout your little name there." Simon was jovial as usual. "I'm crushed there Sun, shorely crushed. Guess Miss Anna here just brings out something in you that I failed to. Told you she was a beauty 'fore we got here, now didn't I? 'Weren't never no doubt that she would get your 'ttention. Never no doubt."

"That you did Simon, and you were right."

"Now you two hush up. You are embarrassing me. You'll make me spoil your supper."

"My sincere apologies Miss Walker. . . . uh, Anna. I can't speak for my companion here, but I never intended any embarrassment. Forgive me."

"No apologies needed Mr. . . ., uh, Sun. I have grown to expect such nonsense from Simon, but I don't know you and was caught off guard. Thank you; I am flattered."

"No flattery intended either. Just simple truth."

"Goodness. Again, thank you. Now off with both of you. Out of here and onto the porch. Supper will go lacking if you persist."

"See, I told you that gal would cross them eyes of yours boy." Simon turned to lead Sun from the cabin and onto the porch, his good-natured laughter echoing off the hillsides. "Let's go sit a spell. Might even help Isaac with the chores. Yessirree, cross them eyes of yours!"

• • •   125

"Yo, Isaac, Miss Anna. You two at home there?"

"Well for the life of me if that ain't Jule Chillington a'comin' down the path yonder." Simon smiled at the recognition of another frontier personality he knew well.

"Hello Jule," Isaac yelled from beside the house. "Come on around. Have a look see who is here with me."

"Simon Keats. You ole coot. Thought you wuz shorely dead and buried under a rock by now. Whatcha' doin' out this way? Don'tcha know you's too old for such shenanigans?"

"Now behave yourself Jule and hush your mouth up 'bout bein' old," Simon bellowed." I'm still young enough to skin the hide offin' a young upstart the likes of you. Come on over here and let's get started. I'll break you from suckin' eggs." Again that familiar roaring laugh indicative of Simon's nature erupted.

"Good to see you Simon. I's just thankin' 'bout you yesta'dee. Wonderin' how's you doin'."

"I'm doin' just fine Jule. A mite stiff on a cold mornin' but doin' fine." Simon grasped Jule Chillington and placed him in a monstrous hug that caused the younger to groan.

"Still plenty strong I see," Jule managed to say when he caught his breath. "And ugly as the last time I seen you. 'Hain't you gonna' git no purttier in old age?"

"Not likely. 'Sides, I'm purtty 'nough now that the women foller me everywhere I go. That's why I can't stay in no settlement; women follerin' me 'round and such. Makes a man a trifle tiresome."

"You 'hain't changed a bit. Still mighty high on yoreself. Women follerin' you. Shaah, they's more likely runnin' in the other direction when they see that ugly face. You can't fool Jule Chillington."

"Enough you two," Isaac chided. "Jule, welcome. And let me introduce you to Mr. Jackson Johnson. He is traveling with Simon. And Jackson, this is Jule Chillington, a long hunter and friend. He's been on the frontier for the last few weeks. Headed back to the settlement for a while Jule?"

"That's right. Gonna' go back in and resupply 'fore headin' out agin in early fall. And pleased to meet you Mr. Johnson."

"Same here Mr. Chillington. But I have determined that formalities are foreign to the frontier, so it is just Jackson."

"And just Jule with me."

"Told Miss Anna that she could call him by the pet name his mama give him, Sun. And he spells that with a 'u'. 'Course, that don't make no never mind with you Jule. You can't read writin' no way, so I don't 'spect you'd know a 'u' iffin it walked straight up to you and said howdy." Simon burst into laughter once again. "'Spect he'll let you call him that if you don't cross him."

"Yes, that will be fine. Sun is more than adequate." Sun shook Jule's hand with a firm grip.

"Then Sun it'll be. You figgerin' on doin' some long huntin' out this way? And don't tell me you made such a mistake as to hire this old man as yore guide."

"May do some hunting. Primarily want to explore the frontier, discover some things about myself and determine which direction I really want to take in life. And regarding your reference to Simon, no I didn't hire him as a guide. In fact, I have been trying to rid myself of him since way back before we reached Yadkin Valley. Just can't seem to shake him. I suppose I should have shot him that first night he stumbled into my camp."

"Rid yourself of me, this lovable feller that the women all foller and the Shawnees have chased 'round a tad over the years. Shorely you don't mean it. Why, I reckon you'd be plumb lost now without my comp'ny. A feller like me just sorta' grows on folks. They get a taste of high quality like me and they ain't never satisfied with nothin' less in days to come. Boy, you'd be 'a lookin' for me in 30 minutes after I got outta' your sight. You ain't foolin' nobody with that useless talk, and fancy talk it is, too." Simon rubbed his scruffy chin and winked in the direction of Jule and Isaac.

"He is a mite fancy talker, now 'hain't he Simon. Don't reckon I ever heard nothin' like it, 'specially not from nobody like you. You best stick close to this stranger   127 with the babyfied name. Some of that explorin' and discoverin' he wants to do could end him up with no scalp. Don't 'spect he'd be so pleasome lookin' with no scalp."

"Jule, Simon—you two stop that racket. Mr. Johnson here is our guest, new to the area. All your banter will have him running for . . . Where did you say you were from Mr. Johnson?"

"I didn't say. I don't know that that is a matter of any concern at the moment."

"He's a mite ticky over his where'bouts Isaac. You and Jule would do well to just let that be as it is. He's done straightened me out 'bout that moren' once. But iffin I had to guess, I'd guess he's from Boston."

"A big city boy, huh?" Jule's voice held a hint of contempt. "And I bet he's all edge'cated and such like. Don't reckon he's got much understandin' 'bout us common folk from out here on the frontier. What brings you outta' the city anyhow? You in trouble with the law?"

"Of course I am not in trouble with the law. I was taught to obey man's laws and I always have. Always will, if that is any of your business. And I told you I wanted to explore, to discover. Now that is as far as I intend to go with explanations. This discussion is over. If you persist gentlemen, I fear I will have to divest myself of your presence and move on at this very moment."

"Now not so hasty there boy." Simon had a sympathetic and understanding look Sun had not seen from him before. "See, I told you two he was a mite ticky. Let's not spoil everything by continuin' with this. Sun here has his own reasons for thinkin' as he does, and I know we all do the same. We don't want nobody 'a meddlin' in our business. Let's just leave it at that and enjoy Miss Anna's cookin' and some good times on the porch. 'Nough trouble like it is all 'round without us a' creatin' more."

"I agree Simon," Isaac walker opined. "Mr. Johnson, I apologize for this episode. I'm sure Jule meant nothing by it. And please know that you are welcome here."

"And my apologies Mr. Walker. I just don't want to be interrogated, to be some creature of intrigue. I am simply

128

Sun Johnson, headed to the frontier. And although I find the setting aside of decorum odd, I rather like it. So it is Sun, not Mr. Johnson."

"And it is Isaac. Again, welcome. Now let's see if Anna has the pot boiling and supper ready. Jule, wouldn't hurt if you went to the creek there and washed off some of that Cumberland dirt. I'm sure you would be far more presentable to Anna. And don't poison the catfish with your grime!"

"Poison 'em? Shaah, they's gonna' all swim lickety split upstream when they get a whiff of that one a' even comein' close to the creek." Simon reared back with laughter and pointed at Jule. "You ain't got no worries 'bout him gettin' close 'nough to poison 'em. Wouldn't have a catfish for a mile or more iffin Jule got in the creek very often. Come on Sun. Me and you'll just wash up in a bucket 'fore supper. We's gentlemen. We couldn't get as dirty in a month as Jule does in two days."

•   •   •

Boston

"Oh, I'm not sure that is a good idea Rebecca." William Clarkson was yet aloof and kept at his task of unpacking merchandise for the hardware store. "I appreciate your contacting me, but I feel your father made it clear how he feels about me. I don't care to subject myself to that again. So if you will excuse me."

"William Clarkson! You are being as stubborn as some of the old men I know around Boston, my father at times among them." Rebecca Bomar's voice had a bite to it that shocked William into an upright stance. He looked into her eyes. "You will let some innocent comment that wounded your pride interfere with an opportunity that may well shape your life? How foolish. If you are going to react by running from every remark that stings you, you will never become the man you can be. My father was making idle conversation; he meant no harm. And even if he did, why would you not want to move on and prove him wrong? Why would you sabotage yourself in a misplaced effort to get back at my father?"

129

"Rebecca, I. . . ."

"And why would you want to sabotage us?"

"Us?"

"Yes; you and me. Why would you be so blind and bullheaded as to ruin any chances that we might have for a future together?"

"A future? Together? Why Rebecca, are you saying that you, that we. . . ."

"And why do you find it difficult to believe that there could be a *we* in all this? Are you so stubborn that you dismiss any possibility that the boss's daughter could hold some interest in the hired man? You are entirely exasperating William Clarkson. Exasperating. I don't know why I even bothered coming to tell you that my father would like to see you. I don't know why he would want someone with a head as hard as yours in his employ in the first place." Rebecca stood with her hands on her hips and fire in her eyes. Yet, she had a depth of concern deep in those eyes, eyes that would not unlock William Clarkson from their magnetic grip.

"I'm just not sure I understand all this. I am flattered but confused. Never could I meet your father's expectations, particularly not when it comes to you. I am just not prepared. . . ."

"And now you are throwing away more opportunities for that preparation. I am not sure any of us can be fully prepared for life in the business world and certainly not life as a husband or wife. It is a growing process. We follow our hearts under God's guidance and move forward on the path that is set. We do the best we can with what we have and know. Nothing more can be expected from anyone; not even my father can expect more."

"But Rebecca, this is all foreign and unsettling. I just don't know."

"Nor do I. I think I know my heart and I know I am following God's will, but past that I don't know anything more. It is a step-by-step process, and I see my father's interest in you as a step in the direction you should consider. Don't let pride spoil any of this for you William. I care deeply. I want the best for you."

"But your father. . . ."

130

"Wants to see you William. He wants to discuss your

employment again in his business. Past that I can't say. But that is the next step in that journey. Please take it and see where it leads. God will guide."

"You are a persistent one. You won't let this rest, will you?"

"Only if you give me a firm no. I will otherwise pursue this until you sit down and talk with my father." Rebecca's face softened; a gentle smile touched her lips. "I have only the best of intentions—for you and for us." William was taken aback by her beauty and forcefulness. Her womanhood blossomed before him and he found her impossible to resist.

"Please, let me think about this for a day or two. I will let you know my decision."

"And will you think about me William?" Her eyes glinted with hope, intrigue, promise.

"I will think of little more. Have thought of little more since that night on the way from the theater. Seems you capture my thoughts even with my best efforts to push you from them. Now off with you. If you don't leave soon I will have no job at all." William Clarkson's face brightened with a smile, the first he recalled in days. "Yes Rebecca Bomar, you are a persistent one."

"Thank you William. And good day to you." Rebecca turned and walked away, William Clarkson's eyes following her every step, his enthusiasm for her growing with each breath he took.

•   •   •

The Frontier

"Just as good as I remembered Miss Anna. Your cookin' is as good as it gets." Simon Keats pushed himself away from the table.

"Well thank you Simon. You are always gracious when it comes to my cooking. And believe me, it wasn't anything special. Just venison stew and apple pie. All easy to make. You are just a hungry traveler, so anything would be good."

"Oh, not so." Sun was also obviously pleased with the meal. "Simple, perhaps, but absolutely superb. My sincere compliments."

"And thank you sir. I'm sure you are accustomed to more elaborate meals. But I am glad you enjoyed it."

"Enjoyed it thoroughly. A thing doesn't have to be elaborate to be a thing of beauty." Sun smiled at Anna Walker, his subtleties not lost on her.

"Again, thank you."

"And I must say that the company around this table added immensely to my enjoyment of the meal. I haven't heard anything but Simon's endless chatter for three months now. And when it comes to a treatment for the eyes, in no way can he compare with what I have seen sitting across the table from me tonight."

"Now he's right there Miss Anna. I do tend to chatter on a mite. But then, I ain't had nothin' too very pleasesome to look at myself. Just this here fair-skinned boy from the big city 'round the campfire every night, green as a new goard. Makes a man chatter to keep from goin' plumb crazy. The Good Lord's got a sense of humor a puttin' me in such comp'ny as this one. Yessm' Miss Anna, you's a pure sightful pleasure for these weary old eyes."

"Now you two stop it. You will have me flattered to the point that I will want to do nothing more than groom myself and sit on my throne. None of that on the frontier. Off with you all. Go outside and sit on the porch while I clean up from supper. I'm sure you have things to discuss among yourselves."

"That we do." Isaac had been quietly listening to the gleeful banter with an eye on Anna and this new arrival to the frontier. "I'll take these gentlemen outside and get them from underfoot."

"But please, can I help you with the kitchen chores." The other three men looked at Sun in astonishment.

"Well, I. . . ." Anna was clearly dumbfounded. Isaac did his turn at cooking and cleaning, but his primary work was outside in the fields and woods and with the small collection of livestock. "No Mr. Johnson; I wouldn't hear of it. You go on with the others. I will have this done in no time and join you all on the porch."

"Yes, please do join us. But be assured that I will be

more than happy to assist here." Sun smiled, his charm filling Anna's heart with a song.

"I am sure you would be glad to do that, but I can manage easily. So please feel free to go on outside. I would not have you miss out on all the culture you will find with Jule and Simon. Isaac? Now that is another matter. Ample culture. My father is an amazing man." Anna's admiration for Isaac was evident, and Sun was pleased to see it expressed.

"As you wish Miss." Sun bowed, took Anna's hand and kissed it, and turned in a military manner to go outside.

"'Spect I'll jest set here and have a talk with Miss Anna iffin youin's don't mind." Jule Chillington had listened to the previous conversation and observed Sun's treatment of Anna. He was visibly shaken and showed signs of mild anger.

"That will be fine Jule. I'll just take these two other guests outside and catch up on what is happening along their travels. Is that all right with you Anna?" Isaac was careful not to take his daughter's wishes for granted.

"Yes, that is acceptable Papa. You three just go on. Jule and I will talk until I finish these chores and then we will join you."

• • •

"Jule still sweet on Miss Anna I see," Simon said as he plopped heavily onto a wooden bench on the porch, his battered flintlock leaning against the wall nearby. "Still 'a wantin' to court her?"

"Yes he is," Isaac offered. "But I fear he is not having any great amount of success. Anna has a mind of her own. Jule's wooing is not producing the results he had hoped for."

"It appears that Jule is adamant about winning Anna's hand," Sun observed.

"Yes it does. He has mentioned this possibility every time he has been by here for the past year. Even talked with me directly about it a few months back."

"And your feelings on the matter?"

"Well, that is Anna's decision. I have made that clear to her and to Jule. I will stay out of the choosing. I know it is customary for the father to have more input than I am exercising, but I want Anna to be happy, to find the one she connects with and feels it God's will to marry. Jule is a descent enough fellow, a hard worker, but one with little ambition outside long hunting. That is an adequate profession, but I don't see it as long term, nor do I see that lifestyle as one Anna would prefer. Oh, she can hold her own on the frontier. Even made a hunt by herself and got us a deer when I was down from a nasty rattler bite awhile back. But Anna is intelligent, insightful, a thinker. She is far more reflective and spiritual than these surroundings may indicate. And well read, too."

"Yes, I detected as much. And Jule?"

"Well, as I said, he is a descent enough fellow. But insightful? I hardly think so. And he has no exposure to the finer things. Can't even read. His understanding of a woman is someone to cook and maintain camp and keep him warm on chilly nights. I can't even imagine his being able to sit down and have a conversation of any depth with anyone. To settle for that would put Anna into a situation of survival, not living. I just hope. . . ."

"And you are saying nothing in this?"

"No. It is Anna's decision. She will follow what she believes to be God's leading."

"I admire you for that—staying out of the decision making. But I can't help but believe that you should at least make your observations and speculations known."

"Perhaps you are right Sun. But I am hesitant to do so at this point. I want to let this develop more before I speak up—if I ever do speak up. I must trust Anna's judgment."

"Isaac, that Miss Anna—she's a smart one." Simon slid a clay pipe from his pocket and stuffed it with tobacco. "And purtty as a speckled puppy. She's gonna' choose right. Never mind that. She ain't no Jule Chillington woman and you ain't got no need to worry 'bout such."

134

"I imagine Simon is correct Isaac. It seems that Anna

is not the match for Jule—or rather Jule is not the match for Anna. I predict that she will turn him down flatly. Probably with gentleness, but firmly. I see little need for concern."

"I hope you two are right. But I also know that Anna is a woman now, a woman with natural needs and desires. I just hope she won't settle for less than she deserves."

"I can understand," Sun added. "But I am certain that is not going to happen."

"Yep, me too. I think this smooth-talkin' foreigner here is right. He don't usually say much, but when he does he has something to say. And I think he says right in this situation. Rest easy Isaac. That daughter of yours is like you; she's got a good head and even better heart. Now rest your brain. God's gonna' take care of everything."

"True. And worry is senseless; it is against God's wishes. I'm praying for patience and leadership. God is in control."

"That He is my friend. You just rest easy. Now, what are you a' hearin' from the frontier? Sun here wants to do some explorin', wants to see what's out there."

"Basically peaceful close in they say. Plenty of buffalo, deer, and elk on out toward the Cumberland. But I understand things get out of hand from time to time a bit north. The French and English got the Indians all stirred up, especially the Shawnees. I would be careful if I were you anywhere out past here. You just never know."

"'Spect that's true. And bein' careful is a good idea. Me, I've done it 'nough now to have a' extra sense 'bout it all. 'Course, since I can't run like I could when I was a youngun', its purtty smartsome to have some sense 'bout it. A time was when I could strike up and flat-foot out run a whole swarm of Shawnees. Kept this mangy scalp of mine several times a' doin' just that. But now I gotta' rely on my smartsomes."

"Smart? You, smart?" Sun wore a boyish grin and teasing eyes.

"Well shore boy. And watch that uppity Boston mouth of yours. I's smartsome as anybody, 'specially 'bout the frontier. You just stay close and watch when we get out there a' ways. I'll show you smartsome. And book smarts too. Ain't I done showed you I's smartsome when you was a' usin' them   135 big words back there when we first met. All your spoutin' off didn't hinder me none. Remember?"

"Oh Simon, I remember. And I was duly impressed. In fact, I must tell you that I am even more impressed now than then. It does seem that you have some solid insight into life. I admire that."

"Well bless my soul boy. Never thought I'd hear no words of compliment a' comin' from your edge'cated mouth. Why, I'm nigh flattered. And you gonna' be more impressed when I save your hide out yonder. Yessireeee, bless my soul." Isaac, Simon, and Sun smiled simultaneously.

"Mr. Johnson, you are in for an adventure with this one!"

●   ●   ●

"Blast that woman!" Jule Chillington slumped to the steps of the front porch with his knees spread and elbows resting on them. He jerked a pipe from his hunting pouch and began stuffing it with tobacco. "I can't git her to show no reasonin' 'atall. Hard headed, she is."

"Trouble in your courting Jule?" Sun was obviously entertained by Jule's behavior.

"I don't see my courtin' as none of yore never mind. I'll thank you to do like you told me and stop askin' into my business."

"As you wish Jule. But I'll be happy to make suggestions based on my observations of the situation."

"And I'll be happy for you to stay outta' my business. 'Sides, what 'uz a smart talkin' city fellar know 'bout my courtin' or my business out here on the frontier. Be best for you to jest keep yore mouth shut and maybe head on back to Boston or everwhur it is you's come from."

"Now you two. Settle down there." Isaac detected a possible confrontation. Sun was gloating and Jule was angry from rejection. "This should be a pleasant evening. God has given us a beautiful day and starry night. Let's enjoy the gift."

"Isaac's right. Now you two upstarts just cool off. Ain't no need to get all huffy and spoil the visit."

"Sorry Isaac, Jule, Simon. Yes, it is a grand evening. Look at that sky."

"I shorely hain't in no mood to look at no sky. Jest the same ole sky I see ever' night," Jule fumed. "Isaac, what's the matter with that girl of yorn? I done offered her all I got. Told her I had us a handy rock shelter out there toward the Cumberland. A good fire pit, a cookin' pot. Got a big buffler robe on the floor and 'nother one to cover up with. She'd never be cold; I'd see to that. And 'spect she'd keep me a mite warm too. What's the matter with her?"

"I don't see that there is anything the matter with Anna, Jule." Isaac felt his own anger rush to his face. "Anna is free to choose for herself. I don't see her choosing other than what you think best as anything being the matter. Have you looked at yourself in this situation Jule?"

"Me? Whatcha' mean by that? You a' sayin' I ain't good enough for yore daughter?"

"Not at all. I'm just saying that you have used that same approach on several occasions and Anna has rejected it every time. Take a look at yourself before you go passing blame to someone else. After all, you are asking Anna to become your wife. If you can't woo her as you are, consider some changes."

"Changes? Why, I's what I am. And that's jest gotta' be good 'nough."

"Well, apparently it is not, so in that level of thinking you may not be good enough for my daughter. But it is her decision, and you would be wise to evaluate it for what it is rather than requiring her to make concessions and me to encourage it all. I won't. I have told you it is Anna's choice."

"Well I never. 'Taint never seen nobody as stubborn and bull headed as you two Walkers."

"Now Jule, be careful with your words. I know you are disappointed, even angry, but you know we have always been accepting and treated you with respect. You can't find fault there. And we want to continue to do the same. But that now rests upon you. Don't put blame where there is no blame.   137

It will make you a bitter man. One thing a man needs to come to grips with as he grows is that he can change no one but himself. What others do and how they react is up to them. How a man deals with that is up to him."

"Well I jest don't know 'bout them fancy words there Isaac. Sounds to me like you's 'gainst me from the start."

"No, not against you Jule. I want the best for you. But the same goes for my daughter. And I know she will make her decisions wisely and under God's leading. I suggest you do the same. But if you choose to be angry and cast blame, there is nothing I can do about that."

"Perhaps a woman of Miss Anna's fabric might prefer a more genteel approach," Sun added, his eyes twinkling with delight as he seized another opportunity to goad Jule Chillington. Isaac flashed Sun a scathing glance and gestured with his hand to circumvent an almost certain and unpleasant encounter between the two.

"Now there you go a' gittin' in my business agin. I think I'll jest git up here and give you a good thrashin.' I done told you to stay outta' my courtin' and my business. Wanna' come out here in the yard and let me whup you all the way back to Boston whur you belong?"

"Oh, I suppose that meeting could be arranged, but I somehow doubt that you'll whip me back to Boston—or whip me to anywhere for that matter. This is not the gentlemanly thing to do, but if you insist on a confrontation, I shall not deny you."

"Now stop it you two hot bloods." Simon spoke with authority. "We'll have none of that here on this peaceful evenin'. You two's just like a pair of young buck deer, a chasin' 'bout and stiff leggin' and noddin' heads back and forth. Makes 'em look silly and they's just dumb animals. You's God's own and a' actin' like that. No sirreeee, we ain't havin' none of this."

"Simon is right. This is out of place. Now you two settle down. Sun, you are welcome here but not welcome to incite Jule. Jule, as always, you are welcome. But you must accept Anna's answer and deal with it as a mature man. Anything else is less than what is expected in this household. Now, do you two understand?"

"Understood." Sun had maintained his calm demeanor throughout the exchange.

"Well, I may understand in a strange sorta' way, but I don't have to like none of it. You know what my plans wuz Isaac. You a' seein' 'em vanish right here tonight. Is that suppse' to make me happy?"

"Probably not. But happiness is external. We can't always control the externals and as a result we may not always be happy. But we can have joy in our hearts, and that is the most important ingredient. Externals change. Joy is with us even in the sadness. I suggest you think on that some."

"Well, I'll try it Isaac, but I can tell you for shore that hit's gonna' take a triflin' long time 'fore I'm happy 'bout any of these shenanigans."

"Your choice Jule. I hope you won't chew on this until you get sick. A man needs to be healthy. Anger and bitterness get in the way of health. You must decide which it will be."

"And Mr. Smart Mouth there, whatcha' mean a gent'till approach?"

"Okay, careful now again. Remember what Simon and I just told you two. No more of this ill natured bantering."

"Agreed Isaac. May I answer Jule? In a helpful way I might add." Although Sun spoke gently, his words and countenance still emitted an aura of disgust and superiority.

"Yes, but let's keep this all civil."

"Without question. Civil I will be. *Genteel*" The word rolled from Sun's lips with grace, perfectly pronounced. "This has to do with elegance, things such as good taste, refinement, polite society."

"And I'm a' guessin' you's brought up jest like that—all polite and such."

"Well, in large measure. But it can be just like that choosing that has already been mentioned. You can choose to be genteel if you exercise a modicum of good judgment and exercise a willingness to learn, to adapt. Just consider those around you and select your words appropriately."

"Oh, you's a fancy talker for shore. Don't 'specially   139 like it none, but I can foller yore big words and purtty way of puttin' 'em all together. So, what's yore lesson in this gent'till you's talkin' 'bout?"

"Well, if I were relating it specifically to my relationship with women, I might consider a bit of poetry."

"Po'tree. I don't know no po'tree. 'Hain't never read none 'cause I can't read nothin' writ down and hain't never heard no po-tree, 'least not none I thought worth listen' to no how."

"Well, you might be surprised if you listened closely. Most poets have an uncanny eye for the human condition, and they put their observations and understandings of it into a beautiful art form."

"'Hain't got no never mind to do none of that. 'Sides, I don't know none of it and don't plan to learn none of it. Jest me, but that's how 'tis."

"Again, your choice. But if you don't know any from the masters, consider writing your own."

"Can't write."

"Yes, forgive me. Then make up your own in your mind. It would be most genuine then."

"I reckon it would. Whatcha' got in mind?"

"If I were compiling poetry of my own to tell a woman how I felt about her, I would focus on being away and my desire to once again be in her presence. Or maybe how the days are just not the same without her. That type thing. For example:" Sun took on a reflective posture and gazed toward the sky. "*I miss you. It is not that life without you is no good. But it is that life with you is far better.* Or try this: *There was no sunshine today, but there was the memory of you. The day was bright.* See. That's all there is to it. But it must be sincere."

"Oh how high falutin'." Jule scowled at no one in particular and recoiled at the thought of coming up with and speaking soft words such as these proffered by Sun Johnson. "Whatcha' think I am anyhow. A edge'cated fool? No sirreeee, I ain't sayin' nothin' like them words. They'd make me spit out my pipe and hang my head in shame. 'Taint no woman gonna' coax me to makin' a fool outta' myself."

140

"Is that right? What is Miss Anna doing right now? Do you think you are acting in any fashion other than foolish?" Sun was persistent in his clever but pointed prodding of Jule.

"Now watch yore mouth agin Mister. I still 'hain't decided I 'hain't gonna' jump right up and knock you into next week. You's so big on manners I think I'll teach you some straight from the frontier."

"Jule, Sun, remember what Simon and I just said. We'll have none of this. It would truly be shameful for two old fellows to have to wrestle two younger ones around in the dirt because they won't behave themselves. And win I might add." Simon smiled at Isaac's comment.

"And we'll do it iffin we have to. We still tougher 'n buffler leather and can handle you two iffin you don't straighten up. Right Isaac? Yessireeee, just like two buck deer pups. All full of salt and pepper and chargin' 'bout the countryside at each other. Be plumb disgustin' iffin it weren't so down right funny. Both of you's a little green there. Miss Anna done got in your heads. I can shorely understand. Isaac, bet'chew can too. We's young once, remember?"

"You young Simon?" Sun seemed relieved that an element of humor had again entered the conversation. "You were never young. And if you were, you are now so old that you surely can't remember. So don't give me that business about being young once." Sun smiled in good-natured fashion toward Isaac.

"Now watch out there Mr. Johnson. You are my guest, but Simon and I won't be insulted by you." Isaac returned Sun's smile while speaking. "Yes, we were young once and recall it quite well. And yes, we will roll you and Jule around here in the dirt till you spit peddles if we have to. Just doesn't seem the appropriate thing on such a beautiful night."

"Isaac's right. We's still rough and ready. And did I mention we's still handsome as a yeller bug? And smartsome too. Years ain't dulled our edges none. So iffin you two wants some learnin' in matters of romance, you's lookin' at two who can shorely teach you something."

"Oh, we have already heard that the women follow   141

you around Simon." Sun was jovial. "You have told us that several times."

"True too. And I just bet same's true with Isaac. Bet he has to run from the Widder Wallace every time he sees her."

"Simon Keats; you old rascal. What's this about Widow Wallace?"

"Isaac, I done heard. You's got your eyes on the handsome widder. And she's shorely got her eyes on you. 'Course, can't say I blame you none. Shorely can't blame her none. A good catch, the Widder Wallace. And you's a good catch."

"I'm not interested in making a catch and am surely not interested in being caught. Now just put this out of your mind. We were discussing these two youngsters. No need to discuss the two of us."

"But we's the most interestin' ones to discuss, Isaac. Smartsome, handsome like, all learnt' up on the ways of life. Purtty interestin' iffin you ask me."

"I fail to recall anyone asking you Simon, but since you brought it up it could be rich material for some in-depth musings." Sun glanced at Simon with dancing eyes and that captivating smile. "Tell us. What about your life of love?"

"Well, I shorely got one. Had me the purttiest girl you ever see'd when I was younger. Guess the frontier life got in the way. I fell in love with a' ramblin'. Shorely cost me a bunch. Maybe I shoulda' stayed with that purtty girl 'stead of chasin' 'round out here and a' runnin' into the likes of you and Jule. Yessrieeee, think now I mighta' made some mistake in my thinkin'."

"You still have time Simon. Is that pretty girl still back in a settlement somewhere?" Sun asked.

"She is. And a widder now, too. Guess I might just go back and call on her one day soon."

"What is stopping you? Time is wasting. Go back and get reacquainted," Sun suggested.

"I might just do that, but first I gotta' see that you come from your first trip to the frontier with all that purtty scalp o' yours. Be a cryin' shame to abandon a tender youngun' 'fore he got some learnin' tucked 'neath his sash. And 'sides, I'd miss gettin' to visit with Isaac and Miss Anna and good folks like them iffin I tore off toward some settlement a' lookin' for a woman. And keep a' rememberin', they's women a' chasin' me everywhere I go anyhow. Ain't got much need to go a' lookin' for 'em."

"So you say Simon. So you say." Sun chuckled under his breath.

"True too. But iffin you's a' wantin' to hear some real romancin' and womenfolk talk, let Isaac do the tellin' He's the one what really knows 'bout them things."

"Now Simon, you hush up. I don't want to talk about any of that. You leave these young ones be and let them work out their own emotions—unless of course that working out involves verbal assaults and fist fights. We have already established the fact that there will be none of that here."

"And there won't on my part Isaac," Sun noted. Jule Chillington sat quietly, sullen and puffing his pipe, seemingly detached from his surroundings. "But please," Sun continued, "tell us about those matters of the heart Simon thinks you know so well."

"I'm not sure I know any of that so well, but I do know that I have had one great true love. Patience was my life. And then Anna just added to it. I struggled getting free from my indenture, and heading west was even more struggle. But the love of Patience and God's leading made it possible. I love Patience now as much as I did when I had her here with me. I grieve her loss daily, but the grief pales when compared to the love we shared, to the daughter we produced. God has been good in it all. I am a happy man.

"And I found that poetry you mentioned earlier most interesting. I am certainly not a poet, but Patience inspired any poetic spirit I might have. I told her things like you said. I told her every day of my love for her and the empty spot in my chest when I was away from her. Even a man with a weary back and calloused hands can be gentle, yes, poetic. She brought that out in me, and I have no shame in saying so. Patience and Anna are the best parts of my life. Absolutely, no regrets."

"Well said, Isaac. I admire you. In fact, I envy you.   143

Not the pain and grief, but surely the exhilaration that you have had. A true love. I'm not at all certain that I know what that is. Yes, there is some envy."

"But you will know that true love when you find it. I never doubted it with Patience. It was deep and pure and everlasting. You will know it."

"Perhaps, but for now I want only to know the frontier. To experience life and the unknown and the thrill of freedom."

"Iffin you can keep your scalp there boy," Simon chided.

"That is all good; I have no quarrel with any of it. I guess I had a touch of wanderlust when I was your age. But Patience changed my thinking. I had no need to ramble and explore. I had found my place. We came to the frontier to establish a home, to have a place of our own. I came in an attempt to make life better for my family."

"And I'm sure you did just that."

"Sometimes I wonder. If we had been in a settlement or back east in a city, perhaps Patience would not have died. There is no way to know for sure, but I can't help but wonder. Even blame myself at times."

"Is that fair—blaming yourself? I don't think so. Life is life. We take what comes and make the best of it."

"Sun's right there Isaac. You can't never know what's gonna' happen. You's just gotta' trust God and keep a' livin'. And I know you trust God."

"That I do Simon. And you and Sun are right. There is no blame. We do the best we can under God's guiding and make decisions based on the knowledge we have at the time. And we trust God for the rest. I do. I have. I will continue to do so. And thanks Sun for your favorable acceptance that I am, or was at least, a poet. Patience deserved nothing less."

"Well, that jest may be all good and proper for you soft gent'men, but I 'haint innerested in bein' no poet. 'Haint gonna' spout no po-tree to nobody. Not Jule Chillington. He's gonna' stay a man. He's 'hain't gonna' let no woman spoil his man-hood. What he's gonna' do right now is gather up his blanket and wander off yonder by the creek and git some shut eye away from you's tender gent'men. He's gonna' git up 'fore sunrise and head out to the country that needs real menfolk." Jule turned to Simon and Sun. "And iffin you two run up on him out there on the frontier, he's gonna' be a' showin' you both what a real man is 'bout." Jule grabbed his flintlock and stormed from the porch, throwing his blanket and shooting pouch over his shoulder as he left.

"A mite sore ain't he?" Simon opined.

"I'd say. Jule could be trouble. I have no spat with him and I hope he doesn't create one. But I will surmise that he will find a way to blame me, or at least blame someone, for Miss Anna's refusal. A sad thing, but he is the one who must choose how he reacts. That is outside my power."

"Poor Jule." Isaac Walker was sympathetic. "I was afraid of this. I wish Jule well, but I do see a potential problem. Had such an outburst occurred earlier, I'm sure I would have had my say to Anna. I'm glad it didn't come to that. But it is clear now that Jule Chillington is not the man for my daughter. Now I only hope this is over for good. An interesting evening. And if you *soft gent'men* will excuse me, I think I'll go to bed. Daylight will come early and I have plenty of work waiting for me. You two are welcome to throw out your blankets there by the hearth."

"Thank you Isaac. 'Spect I'll do just that 'bout right now. These here old bones done got a mite tired."

"Yes, thank you Isaac. I'll sit here awhile longer and enjoy the stars. Don't see this much in Boston."

"Yessireeee; it's Boston after all. You can't keep no secret from a wise one like Simon Keats. This here brain is just full of knowin', and it is all wrapped up in a purtty head and face."

"Well by all means Simon. Go get your beauty rest. I'll do my best not to disturb you when I come in. Surely wouldn't want to cause any sort of distress that would impede your good looks! Good night old man"

"Boy, you's still just a' itchin' for a scuffle. Too plumb wore out to do it now, but I'll take care of you soon in the mornin' iffin you like. Show you who's old. Now   145 hush up. I'm gonna' go roll up in my blanket and mind you that you don't bother me none when you decide to close them baby blues of yours. And who knows, Miss Anna may just come out and sit with you a spell. Iffin she does, you be shore to serenade her with them purtty words. But I'll beat Isaac to a' skinin' your head iffin you even a' considerin' troublin' her in any way. Yessireeee; skin your head. Now let this old man go get some sleep. And you best be on your good behavior and ready to roll out quick come day. You hear me?"

"Oh, I hear you well. Put your old brain at ease. Now off with you."

CHAPTER 21

"Enjoying your evening Mr. Johnson?" Sun turned somewhat startled to see Anna Walker standing in the door of the cabin. Gone was the apron she wore while in the kitchen. Gone was the worn house dress, this replaced by Anna's simple but best Sunday attire. Gone was that bundle of hair that circled her head while at work. Instead, it hung below her shoulders and encircled a pleasant face and beguiling eyes. Her skin glowed in the night's dim light, her lips full and curved into a soft smile. Jackson Bain found himself staring and felt his breaths come in short bursts.

"Why yes. A most beautiful evening. And may I say Miss Walker, you look radiant."

"Thank you kind sir, but it is just Anna."

"Forgive me. I forget that formalities are left behind here on the frontier."

"Oh, not all of them. And they are most welcome. Makes one feel respected, of importance. Still, we are more casual. First names, if indeed the individual indicates that permissible or preferred. I like that just fine, so Anna will suffice. And I shall call you Sun."

"Yes, please. I am just not yet accustomed to such manners, but then I don't find them offensive in any way."

"I'm glad to hear that. I am far more comfortable with these frontier manners than I am with Bostonian etiquette. 147

Though that too is well received. So if you find yourself vacillating between the two, that is no matter for concern. I fully understand. Please, do what is comfortable." Anna's smile burned into Sun's awareness.

"Thank you; I shall. And you as well. But please, allow me to ask a rather personal question."

"Personal?"

"Not inappropriate I hope, but it is personal."

"You have my permission."

"Why do you call your father by his given name, Isaac? That is certainly not the norm back home. I trust you don't mind my asking."

"Not at all. I know it must sound strange. First, let me assure you that Isaac is my father, a treasured parent. I would never disrespect him. But you have already discovered that the frontier ways are different. Such breaches in protocol as my using my father's name are more common here. I can remember my mother telling me that when I first began trying to pronounce his name I said *Idj-jek*. She said he would laugh and tell me that was the sweetest sound he had ever heard. He even insisted I continue, so Isaac it is. No disrespect."

"No, of course not. I appreciate your sharing that. And I now understand. I was just a bit mystified by it all."

"I'm sure you were. But that is the reason. I see no purpose in changing that."

"And neither do I. Thank you again."

"So, have you enjoyed yourself so far this evening?"

"Yes, of course. It has been delightful to this point, and with your joining me here it holds even more promise. I am rarely in the company of one filled with mystique."

"Mystique? Me? You have it all wrong Mr. . . .uh, Sun. I am anything but filled with mystique. To the contrary. I am a simple woman of the frontier. Nothing mysterious about me."

"Not so. I find you fully mysterious. Please don't misunderstand, but I would expect to find individuals such as Jule Chillington out here. But you are quite the anomaly. Simple to the degree this life demands, but also intriguing."

"And there you go with another word that in no way

describes me—intriguing. Please sir; you flatter me." Anna gazed away into the distance.

"No flattery. The full truth. I mean, in the midst of crudeness I come across you—and Isaac of course. Your speech, your manners, your apparent insight—these are not what I expected to find out here so far from civilization."

"Certainly you are not saying we are uncivilized." Anna's voice was gently jovial but held a keen edge of honest inquiry that cut into Sun's very being.

"Oh, absolutely not. Please forgive me. In risk of digging myself deeper into a hole of misunderstanding, allow me to attempt an explanation. I simply mean that this, these surroundings," Sun gestured out toward the creek and beyond, "haven't yet been touched by the culture that I have come to conclude as depicting civilization. Back there, in the East, there are cities and theaters and commerce. There are civic and social gatherings. There are institutions of learning. But out here there are none of those entities. There is only openness. And beauty. This country is indeed beautiful. And I must say that you add to its decorative allure." Sun smiled and Anna blushed.

"Now there you go again with flattering words. I'll have none of that. I know who and what I am, and your descriptions are filled with hyperbole. But I have to say that you simply soared from that hole of misunderstanding you had excavated!" Anna's eyes sparkled with delight. She whisked away a strand of hair that fell across her cheek and fumbled with an unimposing broach that hung from her neck. She raised her face to gaze directly into Sun's eyes and temporarily lost herself in some form of imagining she had never experienced. She and Sun were both silent, caught up in a brief spell of wonderment.

"*The milk of human kindness,*" Sun sighed.

"What?" Anna snapped from her trance and back to the porch of the Walker cabin.

"Kindness," Sun responded. "You let me off too easily. You are kind."

"I hope so; it is my intent to be kind. But be advised that I know you have those words well out of context. 149

And you are the wrong sex. That was Lady Macbeth who spoke that phrase."

"So you know Shakespeare, do you?"

"Quite well, thank you. And Milton and Donne. Learning is not confined to those institutions you just mentioned. Isaac—and my mother while she was with us—took care to see that I was exposed to such things. Nothing formal. No institutions. And never any wealth to acquire materials. But they were thinkers. Isaac still is. They encouraged me and helped in any way they could. So yes, I know my Shakespeare."

"Why am I not surprised? I should have expected as much. And I am quickly beginning to appreciate this civilization far more than that I left behind. Intriguing and mysterious. Totally captivating."

"Is that why you came—to find intrigue, mystery? To be captivated?"

"Perhaps. But I confess I was expecting those elements in another form. The country does indeed provide these in abundance, but you accentuate them, embody each."

"Oh, you do have the gift of making one feel important. I admit I find it most pleasant, but I also know myself and am careful regarding what I allow into my heart. Still, I thank you. Your words are flattering."

"As I've said; no flattery. Just the truth as I see it. Now what do you mean by that statement *allow into my heart*?

"Oh, not now. That is a far too complex subject to address on such a beautiful evening. On to more pleasant things before I must say good night."

"As you wish. I didn't mean to. . . ."

"Of course you didn't. Do you have a dog?"

"A dog? That is a strange question at such a time."

"Yes, a dog. Do you have one?"

"No."

"Have you ever had one?"

"No. My life has never been conducive to such an acquisition. I can't imagine why I would want nor need a
dog."

"I think everybody needs a dog."

"Now why would you reach such a conclusion as that?"

"Many reasons. For one thing, they are good teachers. We may think we are teaching them, but it is they who are teaching us."

"Teaching us what?"

"Unconditional love for one thing. They are dedicated, loyal. Even when we are in a dour mood and scold them, they love us. They remain a trustworthy companion. We are more often in the wrong than they are, and yet they love us right along, always ready to lick a dirty, tired hand and snuggle up around cold feet. They don't ask a great deal, just an occasional show of kindness. We can learn from that."

"I suppose we can. Don't know that I have ever thought of such matters, but then I have never had a dog! And you? Have you ever had dog? I conclude from your observations that you have."

"Definitely. Several around here from time to time, but my dog was Snowball. A little fuzzy female pup that someone gave me when we left to come out here; I was just a child. Snowball was the teacher."

"And I guess she was white?"

"Soot black!" Anna smiled as she again twirled a strand of errant hair along her cheek.

"I recall one day when I was outside and a rattlesnake was coiled near a stack of firewood. Snowball knew the snake was there and that I was in danger. She bounced around and barked and kept herself between the snake and me until I heard him buzzing and ran inside. She prevented me from becoming a sick little girl; she may have even saved my life.

"And she maintained that air of *that was just the thing to do*. She expected no commendation. A pat on the head was adequate. She wagged her tail with glee, and later as we would all talk about that situation, Snowball seemed to know exactly what we were saying. She would perk her ears and turn her head from side to side. It seemed a smile was on her face. Isaac let her sleep inside that night, right there by my bed. She curled onto a deer-skin rug and sighed, asleep in seconds. Content, loving, fully satisfied."

151

"It is difficult, if not impossible, to find that type love."

"Not impossible. I've seen it; I've experienced it. And not just with Snowball. My parents were an example. And so are some of the neighbor families. Not all, but some. But I agree that it is difficult."

"And what about Snowball? Is she still here"

"No, and that was another lesson. I watched age work its ravages. It was then I who took care of her rather than she who took care of me. I lost Snowball over two years ago. I still miss her, but I also still smile when I remember her. The hurt of loss is less than the joy of that companionship."

"You speak with uncanny wisdom, but now it is you who have entered that realm of deep thought and pondering. Complex subjects for such a beautiful evening, I believe you said."

"I did. And they are. Let's talk about the sky."

"It is grand. I've seen it in other parts of the world. Looks different in different settings. Always spectacular, except when shrouded by the fog of London.

"London?"

"Yes, I have been there, but that is of no consequence to this evening or the frontier. London is a memory. The evening, the frontier, the sky—these are here and real. And they are certainly a more worthy topic of conversation than is London."

"I obviously have never been to London. I probably never will go and am not sure that I want to go. Still, it is interesting that you have."

"You have no interest in travel, Anna?"

"I have given it little thought. Such a prospect seems too remote even for consideration. The frontier is my home. I am content. Just like Snowball."

"Contentment is good. I have had very little of that. But there is a big world outside these hills and woods that you might want to explore."

Sun gazed again at the night sky.

"I enjoy going into the settlement occasionally. That is where Isaac and I attend church—on those not-too-frequent visits. Even with a good team and wagon, it is a

152

long ride, almost a full day. We go in to visit, buy a few supplies and stay over with friends for a church service. A new preacher is coming we understand. A young man; I believe he is from Philadelphia."

"And what church do you two attend back there in the settlement?"

"I guess you would call it a mixture of believers. This is just a group of people who believe Jesus is God's Son who came to save us from sin and give us hope here and eternal life afterward. A gracious, loving collection of Christians."

"That's quaint. And simplistic as I see it. The church that I know, and I don't hold church in very high regard, is a rigid structure of do's and don't's, with the latter prevailing. It is more likely to drain life from the parishioner than it is to actually assist that one in finding hope. It is a conglomeration of the elite, a place of social structure and business. I fail to see its relevance."

"I'm sorry. And from what you have just told me, there is little relevance. But the church I know—or more accurately the Jesus I know—is fully relevant. He shapes the core of my life. And simplistic as you see it to be, He is real; He is the one constant in this life of uncertainty."

"Well, could be. I would like to believe that. And I suppose I do believe to an extent. My mother taught me to believe. But I have just never fully trusted the entire concept. I prefer to trust myself, to follow my own lead. It is I who is responsible for my life, and I am more than hesitant to give that over to someone or something else. I do, however, see that it is important to you." Anna looked at Sun and the night sky. Sadness creased an otherwise pleasant countenance.

"But here we go again with those complex subjects you mentioned earlier," Sun added in a flippant manner. "I fear it is too late in the evening to delve into such matters. Simon tells me I must be up and ready by first light tomorrow. We will move on toward the Cumberland for a month-long trek and I am more excited about that than I have ever been about anything. So if you will please excuse me Miss Walker, I will roll out my blanket and try to sleep. Thank you for the stimulating conversation and your most decorative presence. Good night."

153

"And good night to you Mr. Johnson.

Anna stood and walked quietly into the cabin, a burden weighing heavily on graceful shoulders. She changed into her nightgown and crawled beneath a Dutch blanket in the tiny, secluded sleeping quarters Isaac had fashioned for her in one corner of the cabin. Tears streaked her cheeks and dampened her pillow as she prayed silently:

Lord, I thank You; I love You. You are my strength, my hope. Please help me in my confusion and questioning. Who is this man, this Jackson Johnson? How can I help him see You? How can I see You more completely? Follow You fully? Grant me wisdom. Help me be Your light. Thank You for Isaac. Bless him; protect him. And thank You for life, for your grace, your mercy. I pray in the name of Your Son Jesus. Amen.

Anna curled tightly against the chill, wiped tears onto her sleeve, and sighed in a soft whisper: *Snowball, I need you.* Subsequent sleep was fitful

• • •

"Well Isaac, you take care of them old bones o' yours till I get back to see to you. Can't never tell what a old critter as you are will slip up and do to himself iffin he ain't got nobody smartsome like me to keep a eye out for him. Shore be a plumb trag'dy for me to come a' walkin' back up to this here cabin in a month and not find you spry and skippin' 'bout the premises. And tell Miss Anna I said thanks for the hospitality and good victuals. Shorely gonna' miss such whilst I'm out there a' showin' this youngster 'round and helpin' him keep that purtty hair of his." Simon Keats' sonorous voice reverberated about the early-morning woods and his laughter echoed off the hillsides as he and Sun left the Walker cabin at daylight. Jackson took one last look before the trail bent and the cabin disappeared. Anna Walker was not in sight.

154

CHAPTER 22

Late July 1774 - Boston

"Cora, I did it. I talked with your father and told him I would be leaving the business soon." Robert Jamison spoke with a sense of purpose Cora had seldom heard from her husband. "I, as we have discussed, plan to seek my own way, *our* own way. I can no longer do what I have been doing; I trust that I have made the right decision."

"That is exciting; a bit frightening, but truly exciting. I am proud of you and delighted that you are willing to search for yourself, find your purpose and place. I will be right beside you." Cora's words came as no surprise to Robert, but he felt a strange and welcome calmness from her speaking them. "All will be well. And how did my father react?"

"You would think another Tea Party had just taken place. He was most vocal, annoyed. He questioned my *foolish* thinking. Asked how I planned to provide for my family—'My daughter and grandchildren,' he said. 'I'll not have them living in deprivation and falling from their social status in Boston.' I assured him my family would not be deprived, but I fear I prodded a sore spot when I made reference to the fact that social status was of little concern to us. That is something he can't grasp."

"I'm sure you are right about the sore spot, and I'm sure he can't grasp that concept of turning away from the social status," Cora noted. "He will never let go of his meager upbringing and his struggle into business and financial success. These colored his life forever. And while he shouldn't forget his past and struggles—none of us should forget—he remains a slave to maintaining his posture of power and prestige. What others think of him is an unbalanced part of his life. But know that I admire him through all that and will forever love and cherish him. He is my father."

"Of course he is; and he is my father-in-law. I appreciate him. I particularly appreciate the fact that he and your mother produced a wonderful daughter like you. And I might add, the most beautiful woman in all Boston."

"Stop it." Cora Jamison gave him a gentle shove and coy smile. "This latest decision has gone to your head, made you a man with clouded perspectives. But I think I like that! And you were saying!"

"Oh, just that you are beautiful. That I love you. That we will make this new direction one of our choosing. That we will be who and what we should be, always careful to honor God in it all.

"And what of this venture? What have you determined to do?" Cora ran through her mind the many avenues she and Robert had discussed since first entertaining the idea of leaving Squire Bain's employ.

"I think freight is the most logical and practical for immediate income. We have the funds to purchase wagons and teams, and generating business should be easy enough. There is a big demand for shipment south and west. I'm considering providing service all the way to Big Lick, maybe all the way to Yadkin Country. There is rapid expansion down that way.

"I may even look into construction or road building. The Great Wagon Road, as I understand it, could use some improvements. That could be a viable opportunity to branch out from the freighting business. There are endless possibilities. What do you think?"

"I think this all a grand idea. We may even find ourselves living on the edge of the frontier." Cora's words unnerved her, but she also found the potential exhilarating. "No Boston society to contend with there."

"Now hold up. I'm not about to uproot you and the children from what you know and consider the norm. That is too much to ask."

"Oh, don't start fretting over such matters right here at the outset. We will work this out together."

"And you would be willing to go if the business and our dreams required it?" Robert's voice was filled with trepidation but also a near giddiness he had never known.

"Remember, we agreed to *we* and not *you* when we first began talking about this matter. That has not changed. This is a family effort."

"Did I tell you that you are beautiful and that I love you?"

"I believe you did. And you are always free to do so at any time." Cora pulled Robert close and held him. "Rest easy. Think and plan and pray, but always rest easy. We are here with you. God is here with you."

"Yes, but I am concerned just the same. There is talk of war, both from the frontier and with the Mother Country. There is general unrest. Mr. Boone lost his son just this past year in what many would say was a foolish journey to explore Kan-te-kee. Such things are not essential and often bring grief. I want to avoid that and not put my family at risk."

"And you won't. We will be careful and choose wisely. The potential of war is ever present in humanity. We can do nothing to stop that. We simply must make the best decisions we can." Cora was reassuring.

"I suppose you are right, but life is just so uncertain right now."

"Life is always uncertain. Can we live without uncertainties? We can't. We just do our best and trust God. Think of the successful stories rather than those that ended in some form of tragedy: Martin's Station, the establishment of settlements. And there are new forts planned for the frontier; Lord Dunmore is seeing to that. If this move is something you feel strongly about, follow your heart in the matter. As I have already said, I am by your side and God is ever present."   157

"You are right Cora. We will do our best, and we will trust God in all things." Robert Jamison felt an indescribable calmness sweep over him.

• • •

"I am concerned about you Squire." Martha Bain recognized her husband's demeanor as quickly as he came through the door. She took his greatcoat and hung it on the hall tree without his even offering a nod of recognition. The big, influential man walked resolutely to his ever-close brandy snifter and poured it half full, emptying it in one gruff, noisy slurp before slamming it back onto the table. "I fear you are not well."

"Well as any man who is being abandoned piecemeal." Squire's response was familiarly curt.

"Please dear; you are not being abandoned. Your business, your acquaintances, your family. You are anything but abandoned."

"That is where you are wrong Martha. First Jackson; then Cora and Robert. Seems I can no longer control even my own employees. I suppose you will be next." Martha was crestfallen. Tears filled her eyes.

"Squire, please. Must we have this discussion again? I will never abandon you. I love you. And I remind you that you are not being abandoned by anyone." A powerful fist met the table top, causing Martha Bain to gasp.

"Curses woman. Why do you lecture me? Why do you always counter me? You rise to the defense of everyone but your husband, the one to whom you should be most dedicated. Is this some sinister conspiracy to destroy me, to fragment my life? I am the victim here, the target of injustice. I will not allow it. I will crush those who choose to treat me this way. Hear me; I will crush them all."

• • •

158

"I don't think he is well," Robert Jamison responded to Cora's question as they sat in the parlor and talked about the day's events. "It is partly his health, but if you ask me it is his emotional state that is impacting his physical wellbeing. His age is showing, but more than that his anger is becoming the driving force behind everything he does. His decisions and actions reveal some attempt to get even or cause harm, and his every word is filled with something approaching hatred. Please, Cora; I hesitate to bring this up. I fear he is a sick man." Robert's voice carried the distinct flavor of regret at having delivered such a message.

"I fear the same." Cora let the thought slip from her lips in a soft, long whisper. "Father is ill and perhaps of his own doing. God help us."

• • •

"Welcome back Mr. Clarkson." Rebecca Bomar flitted through Bomar's Mercantile on the way to her father's office. "I am pleased to see that you and my father worked out your differences. You are a good fit for this business."

"Hello Miss Bomar." Young Clarkson's expression revealed the slight edge of embarrassment. "It is good to be back; I feel at home. Uh, I didn't intend to sound presumptuous. I simply meant that I know this place well and know what to do and. . . ."

"Shame on you William. Your face is red. Did I catch you off guard? Remember, it is still just me, Rebecca. Forget that Miss and boss's daughter approach. Now back to work. I have work to do myself. I must woo and sway my father in his dedicated efforts to pamper me!"

"I see William Clarkson is hard at work downstairs." Rebecca Bomar glided into her father's office and rushed to his side. Richard hardly acknowledged her presence. His brow was wrinkled as he shuffled papers from one hand to the other. "Hey papa; sorry to interrupt."

"Oh, I'm sorry daughter. Just deep in thought. Concerned about this war talk and how it will impact all of us."

"War talk?"

"Yes. I think there will be war. The colonies seem set for a serious revolt."

"And you papa; how do you feel about it? Do you think we should break from the Mother Country?"

"Haven't thought about it a great deal. It is not something that interests me much. But then I don't like this taxation the King is putting on us. We are not represented in the matter, so I guess that element troubles me and gets me ruffled. I am a loyal subject, but breaking away could be best. Still, it will be tragic. I thought that Tea Party incident would bring some sense to the Crown, but it appears it only exacerbated an already volatile situation. I am afraid."

"You, afraid? I have never thought of you as one who has the slightest hint of fear."

"Rebecca, you have no idea. Only a man who is not honest with himself will claim no fear. How he handles that fear is the measure of the man."

"I suppose it is. And I'm sure fear can do strange things to a person."

"It can. As can grief or anger or disappointment or failure or a host of other conditions. I have seen people strengthened by any of these, and I have seen people transformed into monsters by the same. Such difficulties test character. If character is weak, the outcome is often less than positive."

"Why is that?"

"Oh, I don't know that I can give you a solid answer. It is just that all through history individuals have responded to the same stimuli in various ways. Growth is one way; self destruction and/or the destruction of others is another way. Go back to Bible days: Cain, David, Job. You will find all types of difficulties and all types of responses. If there is war, you will see the same. That is frightening."

"It is, but I hope we won't have war."

"So do I daughter, but I think it is inevitable. And what were you saying about Mr. Clarkson?"

"I just said that I see he is back at work."

"Yes. And I'm glad he is. He is a good employee and will make a fine businessman. I'll not be surprised to

have him walk in here one day and resign—not in anger

and hurt as before but with a burning desire to move into his own endeavors. I fully expect to see Clarkson Mercantile or Clarkson Land Company or some other business carrying his name all the way to Fincastle. He has the makings for success."

"And he is handsome!"

"Now, now. I see those stars in your eyes. You young folk! Don't think I am ready to give you up to one such as William Clarkson—or to a Prince for that matter. None are good enough for you."

"That's my papa. And I'm glad you feel that way. You will surely screen my suitors adequately."

"I haven't dragged it out in some time, but you do recall that old fowler I keep propped in the hallway, do you not? It is there for a reason! Now don't you forget that."

"Never."

"Good. Now off with you. I have work to do."

"And please don't worry about war papa."

"I'll try. And the same to you. Let me do the worrying if there is worrying to be done about anything in this family. And check on Mr. Clarkson on your way out. I want to be sure he is earning his pay."

"Gladly."

•   •   •

Squire Bain hadn't slept soundly in more than a week. Neither had Martha. She could hear him coughing and mumbling and pacing the wooden floors downstairs during the night. She prayed and cried but found little peace. Squire certainly found no peace. His gradual slide into the abyss had grown more pronounced daily. He was now a bitter, spiteful man intent on revenge for some perceived wrong that had come his way. Martha recognized his illness.

God, help me help my husband. Help me be the strength he needs at this difficult time. Give him insight. And I pray that he will come to know You in a personal way, will find You in his searching. Heal him. Martha Bain closed her eyes but sleep would not come.

161

CHAPTER 23

The Frontier

"I figured it was about time for you wanderers to head back in this direction." Isaac Walker's voice was pleasant and possessed an authentic welcome.

"Shorely is good to see you Isaac. It ain't been easy a' keepin' this youngster in line and a' helpin' him hold on to that purtty head of hair. Tiresome chore it was. But I reckon I saved his hide and taught him some valuable lessons out there. And how you and Miss Anna been a' doin'?" Simon Keats removed his haversack, propped his big flintlock against the steps and sank onto the porch.

"Oh, we are fine. What's it been—a month now since you and Mr. Johnson left us?"

"Something like that. Time just loses its meanin' out there. Makes a man forget he's a' getting' on up in years. Me and you oughta' spend all fall and winter over yonder toward the Gap since we's the ones lettin' them years creep up on us. But that don't make no never mind; we's still the smartsomeest and best lookin' gentlemen 'round these parts." Simon's laughter once again echoed about the Walker place. Isaac felt its warmth.

"And you Mr. Johnson—how did you like the frontier?"

"Thank you Isaac. It was grand. Nothing like I have ever seen. And don't you for one minute think that it was Simon here who was tending me. It was I who had to look after him. This old man would still be out there trying to find his way back if it had not been for me."

"Hush up there boy. You ain't foolin' Isaac here. He knows I am more 'n capable of takin' care of myself—and you for that matter. You just a wastein' your breath with such nonsense talk."

"I see you two are still at it." Isaac wore a wide grin that revealed his pleasure at having his old friend close once again. "The frontier didn't change that. And what about Jule? Is he not with you?"

"Didn't see much of Jule. He stayed ahead of us most of the time. We did bump into him once or twice. Said he was a' lookin' for new ground to hunt and trap when he got back out come fall. Said he didn't like keepin' comp'ny with the likes of Mr. Johnson here and since I was gonna' be friendly with Mr. Johnson didn't much like keepin' comp'ny with me neither. Said he didn't want nobody a' intrudin' on his country out there and said he was a' headin' back to the settlement to get supplies. Planned to be back out 'round the Gap by early September. He didn't stop by and say howdy to you folks when he was a' headin' in?"

"No, we haven't seen him." Isaac's voice portrayed a touch of sadness. "I hope he won't become a stranger because of that episode with Anna awhile back."

"Can't never tell. Jule's sore as a old settin' hen robbed of her eggs. Guess his pride's a touch wounded. But if I know Jule, he'll sull up for a spell and then get on back to doin' what he always does. And part of that is comin' by here for a hot meal. I wouldn't worry none 'bout Jule."

"You are probably right Simon. Still, I hope he doesn't let this ruin a friendship—with you or with Anna and me."

"Iffin he knows what's good for him he won't. Where's he gonna' find smartsome and handsome friends like me and you?" Simon again exploded with his roaring laugh.   163

"'Spect he may be a touch shy 'round Miss Anna from now on, but he can't help but purely treasure the likes of me and you. We shorely are treasurable."

"No Simon, you are insufferable. I fail to see the treasure." Sun smiled in fondness for Simon. "But you are talking too much and I am tired of hearing you. Do you mind if I have a word in this conversation."

"Not a'tall boy. I reckon you got some real spoutin' off to do after you done spent time in the comp'ny of great men and enjoyed yourself in God's wonderland. Have your say."

"I was just wondering about Miss Anna. Is she here Isaac?"

"No. Just the same as when you two first came. She has taken a berry pie to the Jacobsons. And I'm sure she will sit and admire that little one for a while. She said that baby would be half grown if she didn't get back over there soon. She'll be back before sundown."

"That's good. I would like to see her."

"I'm sure she would like to see you as well."

"'Spect both of 'em would like to see the other. Don't you reckon Isaac? You remember how it was, don't you?"

"I do remember, and I imagine you are right. So when Anna gets back you be sure to give them some time and stay out of the way." Isaac once again smiled at his long-time friend.

"Me get in the way? Why Isaac Walker. Miss Anna and Sun here could use some instructin' and spectifyin' by the likes of me. And the likes of you, too. We's the ones who knows what life's 'bout. These younguns ain't got no clue. They's just got romancing' eyes and romancing' dreams."

"As it should be Simon. Just as we were at their age. Now you mind your manners and leave them alone in this."

"Iffin you insist Isaac. But they's a' missing a jewel a' sittin' right here in their midst." Simon slapped his leg and tucked into a bundle of pure merriment. "I'll shorely behave myself. Now let's me and you wander off down by the creek. Might even wash some of this dust off 'fore Miss Anna gets home. Mr. Johnson, you might consider doin' the same. I know you think of yourself as plumbly handsome, but you got some soiled spots here and there that could use a little 'ttention. 'Spect Miss Anna would find it favorsome iffin you's a bit tidied up when she gets here."

"I'll do that Simon. Not because you think I need it but because I am a gracious sort who is willing to humor an old man such as you. Isaac, do you need me to haul in some wood or something for you?"

"That's kind, but I have supper wood split and stacked by the hearth. And we won't need the fireplace tonight. So you just make yourself at home and do as you wish. Let's go Simon. You can tell me about the goings on out near the Gap. Trouble brewing out there as it is in Boston and Philadelphia?"

• • •

Squire Bain paced the floor and scowled: *I am a victim. I will not be victimized.*

• • •

The dust gone from his face and hair and a clean long hunter's shirt beneath his weskit, Sun sat on the porch. He looked into the distance toward Cumberland Gap and wondered about his future. Anna's moccasins made only the faintest shuffle as she walked up to the cabin.

"Well Mr. Johnson. Imagine seeing you here."

"Hello Miss Walker."

"How was your first visit to the frontier?"

"Oh, fine. And thank you for asking. It was much different than I imagined it would be. Not at all what I expected. I was just telling Isaac that I had never seen anything quite like it."

"Not even in London?"

"Especially not in London. London is crowded and always busy. It is dirty in places as well. Out toward the Gap, there is none of that. It is clean and unspoiled and inviting."

165

"Any trouble out there?"

"Not anything to cause great concern. Word is that there is Indian trouble in spots, and we did see sign of that. Also, word is that revolution is coming. There seems a general unrest, even out there in the wilderness."

"Does that alarm you?"

"Well, it is certainly not comforting. But I would prefer to stay detached from it all if possible."

"And do you think that is possible?"

"I would hope so, but probably not. I fear the colonists will have to take a stand one way or the other. Revolution was even discussed when I was in London. Cedric, my friend while I was there, avoided the matter at all costs. We knew it would likely divide us."

"So you would be in favor of revolution?"

"Not in the actual act, the probable war. War is not something I would want. But to be free from outside forces would be best for the colonies I believe. These people deserve the right to govern themselves, not be subjected to rule from abroad. And what are your feelings on this Miss Walker?"

"Freedom is always preferred. Isaac brought us here so that we could build a life of freedom. Yes, I think separating from England could be beneficial."

"And costly."

"Yes, I suspect you are right."

"No question. The King will never agree to the type freedom now being discussed, so war will be the only way to gain it. And war will be costly—in every avenue of life. It will be tragic. I have always wondered why humanity has had to resort to war. Seems terribly foolish."

"Wars and rumors of wars. We read that in the Bible. Man rose up against man at the very beginning. And yes, it is foolish. I fear it will continue until Jesus returns."

"And I suppose He is going to return? Is that what you believe?"

"Fully. I have no question about that. He will return. Don't you believe that?"

"Apparently not with the same measure of conviction that you do. I have been told that, but I am not completely convinced. I would like to believe it; I would like to feel that I know God and that He is in control, is with me daily. But I find it difficult to grasp. After all, He gave us the ability to reason and work things out, so why would He have any interest in exploring the frontier with me?"

"Exploring the frontier and visiting London and traveling with Simon Keats. God is with you. He not only has an interest in it all but knows you personally. Knows the number of hairs on your head we are told in Scripture."

"And Simon intends to see to it that God won't have to do any updating regarding that number. The man is constantly worried about my scalp." Anna smiled at Sun's words. "Enough of this talk. Tell me how you have been."

"Fine, Mr. Johnson. Thank you. I have been fine."

"Please. No more of this mister or miss. It is not the way of the frontier, or so you told me."

"That I did. But the last time we talked you. . . ."

"Left you wondering? Perhaps even bruised your spirit with words that were less than kind?"

"Yes; in fact you did. You cut the conversation short and hurried me along. I was a bit wounded. But more than that, I was concerned. I was grieved that you found spiritual matters of so little consequence."

"Not inconsequential. Just not something to which I have given great thought. Please try to understand that I am on an adventure, a man filled with dreams. And please forgive my harshness the night before Simon and I left."

"I forgave you that night, and I prayed for you. Prayed that you would have a safe journey and that God would open your eyes to His love and goodness."

"Seems your prayers were answered, at least in that safe journey part. And while I don't fully understand what you mean when you say you asked God to open my eyes to His love and goodness, I do know that my eyes are

167

open to an extraordinary individual in Anna Walker." Anna smiled softly and looked away.

"Now there you go again, just like that night before you left. You paint all these beautiful portraits with your words, portraits that don't in any way resemble me."

"I see things differently. My words are accurate."

"No, no. Not at all."

"As you wish, but we must disagree on this matter."

"And as you wish as well,"

"You prayed for me. I can't say I did the same for you; I don't do much praying. But I did think of you; I thought of you often. At night while I lay there under the stars trying to sleep, I thought of you. Of course, Simon's obnoxious snoring kept interrupting." Anna and Sun both laughed aloud. "That man can rattle the tree tops!

"And when I finally dozed, sleep was often fitful. There was distant thunder rolling through my dreams, pleasant but haunting. That thunder was the recall of you, Anna Walker."

"Distant thunder? That is an interesting analogy. I think I understand the idea of distant thunder."

"Yes, I'm sure you do. It is something that is far removed but simply won't go away, won't let you rest."

"And did this distant thunder cause you distress Sun?"

"Oh, I suppose it did. It was something unfamiliar. Made me feel vulnerable, perhaps a bit out of control of my own destiny. Just like a huge storm that comes through and changes all the elements of a journey. It controls the traveler, not the other way around."

"It does. And I do know it well. My parents and I left what we knew and moved to the frontier. That required an adjustment we had never known. And then my mother's death. That was surely a storm. But storms pass."

"Some do. This one? I'm not convinced. It just keeps rumbling."

"Now you are the one who is wading into deep matters."

"Yes, this is all too complex. Too much so for such a lovely setting with a lovely woman."

"Your perfect words again."

· · ·

"Yep Isaac, I do think trouble is a' brewin' out there. And must be just 'bout everywhere. Talk I'm a' hearin' ain't good. Looks like we's headed for revolution. The Indians upset out there too. Kinda' a dangerous situation iffin you ask me."

"And what I hear from back east is bleak. Talk of revolution. And here on the frontier there are Indian uprisings. Seems somebody is always stirring up unrest. I thought the problems were solved around the Middle Ground, but things are a touch uneasy again."

"Me, I'm too old for revoltin'. Just want to stay sorta' outta' the whole matter. Shorely wish this world could live in peace. But I guess that ain't happenin' till the Good Lord comes down here and straightens everybody out good and proper."

"You are right about that Simon. It is disturbing. War and unrest. Seems an ongoing part of the human condition. And it does cause me concern for the younger people. Consider Anna and Sun."

"And wonder how them two's a doin' back up there at the cabin?"

"I'm sure they are fine, and you remember to mind your manners and leave them alone in this." Isaac again smiled gently at his friend.

"Oh, I'm shorely gonna' do just that. Leave them alone and let them work out their own doin's. 'Course, that boy could use a little advisin'. He ain't got the sense God give a frog when it comes to womenfolk like Miss Anna. He's just foolish enough to let her get right on by him, whilst he's out there a' lookin' for adventure and such."

"Well you are the one to talk about such things Simon Keats. Didn't you do a similar thing when you were about his age?"

"Reckon I did. And that's why I's the one to do the advisin'. Shorely ain't regretted my travelin' 'round, but shorely think I missed out on a good life. And I just may go back and find that fine lady one day soon now. Quit all this ramblin' and a' raisin' youngsters with stars in their eyes. Gettin' too old for such shenanigans."

"No time like the present."

"Now don't go a' rushin' on me Isaac. I still got work   169 to do with that one up yonder at the cabin with Miss Anna. A good heart in that boy. And he's smartsome. Just ain't got no sense yet. Smartsome and sense don't always live under the same roof."

"I suspect you are right. And what else do you think about Jackson?"

"I'm 'specalatin' that he's a rich youngster from Boston. Maybe from a powerful family. And I've already said he's smartsome. All full of books and school and stuff. But he's a' hidin' somethin', a' scared of somethin'. Maybe his daddy. Maybe scared of findin' out his true self. But every man's gotta' do that—find his true self. A scary thing it is, findin' yourself."

"That it is. Truly frightening at times."

"Yissireee. Makes a man wear his own responsibility. Makes him decide iffin he's gonna' be happy or unhappy. Won't let him blame somebody else for his life. Findin' himself can scare a man a touch. But it's gotta' be done and I'm here to help that youngster do it iffin he needs me."

"I'm sure he needs you Simon. Not sure he wants you and not sure he realizes he needs you, but he does. He'll come to see that at some point."

"'Spect so. I'll just have to wait awhile 'bout goin' back to find a woman. 'Course, ain't gonna' take no lookin'. I know where the only woman I'd tolerate is. And she's a' waitin' for this handsome face to round the bend." Simon's laughter could be heard all the way back to the Walker cabin.

"Don't you mean the only woman who would tolerate you Simon?"

"Oh, truth be known, I 'spect you's right Isaac. But let's me and you just keep such matters 'tween ourselves. And a fine woman she is. Shorely 'spect I missed out on a good life with her. Ain't too late, though. I got plenty of livin' left in me. I'll still put her head in a spin."

"Hush up you old rascal."

"All true Isaac. And you too. You's got plenty of years left for a' spinin' the Widder Wallace's head."

"As I said, hush up. Now let's head back to the cabin.

I need to get a fire going in the hearth. I imagine you will be complaining about near starvation within the hour. Can't let you go hungry."

•   •   •

"I would conclude that our conversation is for the most part over Anna. If I am not mistaken, that is Simon Keats and Isaac coming up the trail. When Simon is around, there is little conversation other than his." Sun smiled.

"Seems you are fond of Simon. But I'm not surprised. He is an interesting character."

"Interesting, to be sure. How could I not be fond of him? I find him a study in contradictions."

"Contradictions?"

"Well, yes. I at first thought him a wanderer looking for a handout, perhaps even a misguided soul who didn't fit in with society. That was back along the Great Wagon Road when he first came into my camp. I didn't trust him. But now I find him anything but that. In fact, I find him extremely insightful. Curiously educated in a non-formal sort of way."

"Insightful and intelligent. I have heard Simon and Isaac in conversation that would rival any scholar. Don't misjudge Simon Keats. Or Isaac Walker for that matter. They are resourceful, spiritual men who care deeply for people. I admire both."

"And I am coming to do the same. You are right; I am fond of Simon. Still don't want him in my business, but I am fond of him. He makes travel more enjoyable. And I admit that he taught me a great deal out there. I'll try to hold on to him until I go back out in September."

"So you are staying to do some long hunting?"

"'Course he's stayin'. Couldn't leave no gracious and smartsome man like me behind and wander on back toward Boston. And 'course, he couldn't leave no purtty woman like you neither."

"Simon, I told you to leave these two young people alone."

"That you did Isaac. And that's just what I'm a doin';   171

I'm a' leavin' them alone. I'm a goin' right in there and start the supper fire. Can't nobody say I don't earn my keep."

"Nor can they say you can stay quiet for more than 30 seconds. Unless you are asleep. And even then you are at the center of the most ungodly din the human ear has ever heard. And probably that has ever been heard on the frontier. I am surprised that we got those two deer for our food while we were there. They must surely have heard that rattling all the way to Beautiful River. See Anna, I told you our conversation would be cut short!" Sun touched Anna's shoulder as he nodded toward Simon.

"Now there you go again. Hadn't a' been for me, you'd a' gone plumb hungry out there. It was you a stumblin' and knockin' 'round that put the critters on edge. A plumb wonder I's able to shoot a thing for victuals."

"You shoot? Don't you recall that it was my York that got that velvet-horned buck?"

"Another plumb wonder. And it was shorely my old flinter that got the next 'un. You still got a lot of learnin' to do 'fore you's ready for long huntin'."

"You two would go on all night if I allowed it." Isaac stepped onto the porch. "Simon, do as you said you were and go start that fire. Anna and I will have supper ready before you know it. Sun, you are welcome to come inside or sit out here and watch the day come to a close. It has been a good one. We owe God the thanks."

• • •

"Excellent as always." Jackson Bain pushed back from the table.

"Thank you. And as always, you are most kind." Anna was pleased that the men seemed to enjoy their supper.

"I agree daughter. Your cooking is superb."

"Shorely is. Don't never get nothin' but the very best at the Walker cabin. Thank you Miss Anna. 'Course it can't live up to them trail suppers Mr. Johnson here put together out there while we was a' trekkin' 'bout." Simon burst into laughter. "That boy'd a' starved plumb to skin and bones hadn't been for ole Simon a' lookin' out for him."

"Need I remind you that it was I who was looking out for you?"

"Just ain't so. You didn't even know how to skin that buck you shot. No sirree; it's me doin' the lookin' out."

"Let's just all agree that it was each looking out for the other. And all you go outside while I get the supper dishes cleaned and put away." Anna's smile brightened the entire cabin.

"I insist; I will help this time," Jackson added. "I won't have you doing this without assistance."

"Well, I will take that offer. And see if you can get my father and Simon from under foot. That will make everything easier, and it will certainly remove much of the clutter!"

"Isaac, Simon—you heard the lady. Off with you. She and I will have this chore completed quickly and join you. Now go."

"Reckon we'd best do as we've been told Isaac. Let's creep on outta' the way. Maybe we can get these old bones to take us as far as the porch."

"That we can. And maybe our old fingers are up to filling a pipe. It is a fine evening for sitting and smelling that sweet smoke rise in the night sky." The big oak door of the cabin closed behind Isaac and Simon as Sun handed Anna four bowls from the table.

"I need to get a message back to my family," Sun said as Anna poured hot water from the hearth pot over the bowls. "Is that a reasonable possibility from out here?"

"Not from here, but when you get back to the settlement there is some service. Slow and unreliable, but a letter will probably get delivered in due time."

"That will be fine. Simon and I are going in tomorrow. We need to supply for our September hunt out toward the Middle Ground."

"Dangerous out that way I hear."

"Perhaps. There is some unrest among the Indians. Seems this talk of revolution and the rumblings between the British and French is touching just about everybody."

"I would imagine. Would it not be best to let this settle some before going out?"

"I suppose it would be safer, but we can't always put our lives on hold for safety's sake."

"Nor should we rush foolishly into something. Impatience can be the undoing of anyone."

"I concur. But life without danger is an impossibility. Potential hurt is around every bend. Avoiding all risk is a recipe for missing out on what life has to offer."

"I suppose you are right, but we should always be careful that our decisions are wise. We choose not only for ourselves. We must choose with the wellbeing of others in mind as well."

"And whose wellbeing is my responsibility? Who must I consider before making a decision?"

"Well, your family is a good place to start. There is someone back somewhere who cares deeply for you."

"Perhaps a few. But I fear my decisions have already fractured that relationship."

"Not likely. Oh, there may be some disapproval, but family is the most forgiving and supportive group we will ever find. Consider them as well as yourself."

"I'm afraid it is too late for that. You simply don't understand."

"Maybe I don't. I don't even know for sure where you are from or who makes up your family. But I would still guess that at least some of them care and understand."

"Certainly not my father. But Anna, please, I don't want to deal with that at this time. I will say that I am from Boston, but past that I have nothing else to say."

"I will honor that. But there are others who care for you as well."

"Oh?"

"Sure. Simon for instance. He is fond of you. He sees something in you that is rare. Otherwise, he would not be so ready to help."

"Agreed. And while I don't want Simon to hear me say it, he is a work of art. Not sure I have ever met anyone like him. Or like you and Isaac for that matter."

"See. There are others who care. Isaac. He cares. You are not obligated to him in your decision making, but he can be added to the list of those who care about you."

"I recognize that. Isaac is the type man I will never be. I admire him."

"You should be who you are, but he is a worthy model for you or any young man to follow. As I said; he cares for you. Cares for all God's creation. And. . . ."

"And?"

"And I care."

"You?"

"Yes."

"Even though I have already been gruff and bruised your spirit?"

"Even after that. Remember forgiveness?"

"Yes, but I have neither received nor given much forgiveness so far in life."

"I'm sorry to hear that. Forgiveness is essential—both the giving and receiving. That is one primary element of God's love—forgiveness."

"Oh Anna, I don't know. I just can't envision a loving God. I may come to do so, but for now I find little need for some far-away God ready to strike me down with vengeance."

"And neither do I. The God I know and serve is not far away. Nor is He all vengeful. He is near by and He is loving. Forgiving. I wish you could come to recognize that."

"And perhaps I will, but not now Anna. I am just not ready for such thinking at this time."

"I will pray for you Sun. I will accept and pray. Never condemn."

"And you are among those who care for me?"

"Of course I care. I see in you something that is not often seen. Not just those beautiful words that you so easily speak, but something more. Now don't misunderstand; I appreciate those words. They make me feel special."

"And you are."

"Thank you, but past the words is a kind man, a man   175

with potential, a man who can do great things, but a man struggling to find himself. And I think much of that struggling will end with finding a personal relationship with God."

"Could be, but I'm just not prepared to find this God you so freely talk about."

"I understand. And I will never coerce."

"I appreciate that. And you have my respect. Now, let's go check on Isaac and Simon."

"Come join us," Isaac said as Anna and Sun stepped from the cabin. Smoke from two pipes filled the night air with a pleasant aroma.

"You get them supper dishes all cleaned up there did you boy?" Simon offered Sun a sly smile.

"Cleaned up and put away for future use. And what are you old folks talking about."

"Shorely talkin' 'bout more smartsome stuff than you could 'magine. We just full of spectifyin'. Important stuff like God's goodness and His creatin' abilities. Stuff like how it would be to soar 'round up there like them birds'll do come daylight. Stuff like how them wild geese can come a' glidin' down this way in the fall. They'll be here soon."

"That is intriguing material Simon. Does it have your old brain aching yet?"

"No sirree. You a' lookin' at two who's got young brains just full of learnin'. They ain't gettin' one bit tiresome."

"That's true Sun. Simon here always amazes me with the things he can discover to, as he says, *specify* about. Keeps our brains active. Keeps us in touch with God and the more significant things of life."

"You both amaze me," Anna added with a gentle smile. "I love to hear you two talk. In fact, much of what I ponder is the same as you. Guess I've maybe heard too much of your ramblings."

"Can't get too much of wise 'uns like me and Isaac there girl. "Course, I 'spect Mr. Johnson's words are a mite more pleasin' to you at times."

"They surely can be pleasing. Makes a woman feel important."

176

"Now don't go gettin' a' carried 'way there Miss Anna. Mr. Johnson is a smooth talker; that he is." Anna looked toward the heavens and admired the starry spectacle above.

"And an honest man when it comes to my words directed toward Miss Anna. She brings out the poetry."

"You two are embarrassing me."

"Sorry," Sun said. "No embarrassment intended. Just the truth."

"Thank you, but let's change the direction of this conversation. I hardly want to be the center of attention here."

"Agreed Anna. Yes, let's change; that is if these philosophers will allow."

"Fine with me. I have heard about all of Simon I care to hear for one evening. It is good to have you two out here with us to bring new life to us old men." Isaac removed the pipe from his teeth and smiled at Simon Keats. "Please carry on Sun."

"I admit that I have found this country most refreshing. It is more than I had imagined when I left Boston. A bit more settled than I thought it would be, and there seems a steady stream of new arrivals every day. Things are changing."

"And I shorely hope for the better. Too many folks can foul things up a mite. Shorely like the quiet out here. Hope that don't change no time soon."

"And it probably won't be soon. But the fact is that there are people moving west. There is not enough available land back east to accommodate new families and homesteads. This place will eventually be settled thoroughly."

"And I imagine you are right. Just since Anna and I have been here, there are a great many new homesteads. And the settlement is growing daily. Things will change."

"That they will. Don't 'spect they'll be no bufflers left in these parts much longer. And long huntin' will go away. Kinda' a trag'dy for the Shawnees and such folk too."

"You are all right. But then I must consider that Isaac and I also advanced this change. We would have to fault ourselves if we begin to grieve the change com-   177 ing to the frontier. We wanted a new life; so do the others who are coming."

"No fault there Miss Anna. Just the way things are, all this changin' and the like. Can't fault nobody for doin' what they think's best for they families."

"That's right Simon. Anna, Patience and I came to find freedom and create a life out here. Harm was not our intent. Nor do I expect it is the intent of the majority of those who have or will come. What is your opinion on this Mr. Johnson?"

"I agree. Just look at history. People have moved and created change since time has been in existence. Most were just looking for something better. Yes, they may have brought disruptions, but that is the essence of change. Disruptions. All we can do is consider those we are impacting and do our best to respect them."

"Well, that is an interesting comment." Anna turned toward Sun. "Seems we were just discussing such a matter back there in the cabin."

"That we were. And I want to give it more thought. Thank you for reminding me."

"So that means that you will reconsider going to the Middle Ground in September?" Anna hoped for an affirmative.

"This youngster not go the Middle Ground? Ain't gonna' happen. He's set on a' losin' that scalp of his I reckon."

"Not so Simon. I plan to keep my scalp. And you will no doubt be there to see that I do."

"Shorely will. Iffin you insist on a' goin' back out there, I'll be right beside that tender hide of yours to make shore you get back here for some of Miss Anna's good cookin'."

"I appreciate that. But it would be more pleasant and quiet without your constant chatter. I might just choose to leave you behind after all."

"You know bettern' that. We done talked this through. You just 'bout can't do without this handsome face and smartsome brain a' keepin' you in line. Now hush up 'bout leavin' me behind. I'm a' stickin' close."

"I imagine you will. And I admit that I would miss you in a strange way. Something like missing a sore thumb after it heals. I simply couldn't do without Simon Keats."

"Now there's a smartsome youngster. Done recognized greatness in his presence."

"So what are your plans Mr. Johnson? Or perhaps I should say your and Simon's plans."

"My plan's just to keep this boy all healthful like. Can't say what he plans. 'Course I 'spect them romancin' eyes figger into them plans some."

"Enough Simon. Allow me to address Isaac's question."

"Gladly boy. Simon Keats ain't never stuck his good lookin' nose in nobody else's business!"

"So you say. But regarding my plans, I definitely want to go out toward the Middle Ground and do some exploring and hunting. I would like to stay out all of September and perhaps into October. Then I would like to come in and try to get back to Boston before Christmas. It would be good to see my family if I can make the trip. And I do want to write and send a letter home before we head back out in September."

"Service will be slow, but I can help you get a letter into the right hands in the settlement."

"Thank you Isaac. I would appreciate anything you could do to assist."

"Gladly. In fact, Anna and I plan to hitch the team and go in Saturday. We will stay over with friends and attend church Sunday. It has been too long since we have done that. When do you two plan to go that way?"

"What's today—Monday? 'Spect me and the boy here will head on out tomorrow, Wednesday at the latest."

"And you'll be there when Anna and I arrive?"

"'Spect so. We gotta' get supplies and such. And these old weary bones could use some settlement pamperin'. 'Course we'll prob'ly sleep on the edge of the settlement rolled up in our blankets. Be 'bout the same as stayin' out there 'round the Gap."

"You may plan to do that, but I will find more suitable lodging. Even if it is in the block house. There is a block house, is there not?"

"Shore; shore. Got a block house. 'Coure, aint' much purpose for it back there. No trouble in the settlement for some time now."

"Oh, there will be lodging. If nothing else, someone will take you in for a few nights. Simon knows everyone there and can handle that."

"And they's all kinda' pleasesome toward Simon Keats. He ain't never been put out in the night air by nobody. Folks know quality when they see it." Simon offered his laughter to the wilds of the frontier.

"Naturally." Sun rolled his eyes and looked toward Anna.

"Simon, Sun—what about you two meeting Anna and me for church on Sunday? We will all be there, and as I understand it, a new preacher will be in town. A young fellow from Philadelphia. And of course there will be a dinner on the ground after service."

"You can count on me Isaac. Simon Keats ain't never been one to miss out on some good churchin' and the like. What about you boy?"

"Not too much in favor of church."

"In favor of dinner on the ground, ain't you?"

"Don't recall ever going to a, as you say, dinner on the ground. I can't make a judgment on that."

"Well boy, you shorely done missed out on the finer things in life. I'd a' 'spected you to be all 'cquainted with such goins' on as dinner on the ground. You see, ain't nothin' like it in this whole world. Them womenfolk, they put together all sorts of victuals and spread 'em out under a shade tree. A plumb social event. You can't miss that boy."

"And what of this new minister? What do you suppose he will have to say in his first sermon?"

"We don't know," Anna noted. "But the ones before have been gentle, spiritual men. They all spoke of God's love and grace. I would imagine this one will be no different. I do hope you will join us."

"At your request, I will be there. Certainly don't want to miss this grand gathering. And I can tell those back in Boston about dinner on the ground." Anna smiled at Sun's acceptance, but her heart sank at the mention of his return to Boston.

"And tell me more of the plans you have past this fall's hunt."

"Not a great deal more to say. My plans are somewhat short term at the moment. But I have been considering business prospects, these primarily focused on the westward movement I have seen."

"So you's a businessman there are you boy?"

"Not really Simon. I am acquainted with business; I grew up in it. But I have never had a keen interest in that pursuit. But it seems some real opportunities await out this way. Freight, supplies, even a trading post and draft stock. The needs are here already and are sure to grow in the future."

"Unless war stops it all." Anna's voice was filled with trepidation.

"That is possible. But even if war comes, it will not last forever. More people will move westward and will create a market that can only grow stronger with time."

"You are likely correct in that thinking. Anna and I, in fact all the people on the frontier, have to wait a long time to get supplies brought from back east. And even then there are a great many things we need and can't get. The service could certainly be improved and expanded." Isaac concluded.

"Exactly. And that is why I may give some consideration to this idea. It could be the right thing to do at this time."

"Iffin you get back from the Middle Ground with your scalp. Kinda' hopin' you gonna' change your mind 'bout that little journey 'fore late August."

"Not much chance of that Simon. I want to go back out. And you will, as you so often tell me, see to it that I return with my scalp—and all other parts of my body for that matter. Besides, the trip on out into the frontier will help me better evaluate the prospects of business in the area."

"'Spect business gonna' be a mite slow with the Shawnees all stirred up and such. Nobody wantin' or needin' nothin' more'n stayin' alive and a' keepin' what they already got."

"True, but that too will change with time. There won't always be the same level of unrest and danger as there is now. This will all end, and it is the wise businessman who is ready to provide services when it does."

181

"And that means you would be in this area to supervise your business Sun?" Anna could scarcely avoid her question.

"Possibly. I would have to have someone here to see that everything went smoothly. But then someone would also have to be back east. That is where the goods would come from, so procurement and shipment would require tremendous attention. It is just too early in this to make such determinations. For now, I am simply interested in a September trip to the Middle Ground—and in dinner on the ground this upcoming Sunday!" Anna smiled at Sun's agreement to meet for the church gathering.

"It's shorely gonna' be a get-together like you ain't never seen, promise you that. You'll want to stay right there forever after you go once. Now iffin you all will excuse me, I believe I'll roll out my blanket. My feet's kinda' tiresome and old back kinda' hurtsome. Warm enough I think I'll just sleep down there by the creek under God's sky. You gonna' join me boy?"

"In short order. And by the creek sounds good. I'm getting accustomed to being in the open."

"I think I'll go inside and get in the bed myself." Isaac tapped his pipe against the porch floor. "Lots of chores tomorrow. Good night to you all."

"Same to you Isaac. Hope Sun here don't disturb me when he comes a' knockin' and scramblin' on down to the creek. That boy can make some horrible noise when he's a' walkin' 'bout. Horriblest I ever heard. Ain't no deer or buffler this side of the Gap can't hear him."

"I know the truth about all that noise you mention since I have tried to sleep with your snoring these past few weeks. Now that is *the horriblest* noise I have ever heard. You are one to talk about noise." Simon waved his hand in dismissal and walked toward the creek. Isaac stood to go inside.

"Good night papa. I'll see you in the morning"

"Will you stay here and visit with me awhile Anna?"

"Only a short time. Morning chores come early."

"And you have more than your share."

"Not so much. Chores are just a part of the frontier. I

182   would have it no other way."

"So, a life in the cities back east wouldn't interest you?"

"I've never given it much thought. But I am most attracted to the frontier. I don't know that I would adapt to the cities very well."

"So a city socialite you would not be?"

"Hardly. I am common. I am more suited for the frontier."

"Suited for the frontier, perhaps. But common? Not at all. Most uncommon I would say."

"Your words again."

"And again I remind you that I speak only the truth."

"I would like to think that, but I admit to some concern."

"Concern?"

"Yes. You are free with those absolutely perfect words but not free in other ways."

"And how is that?"

"For one thing, you have not provided much information regarding your past. That remains a mystery. And you remain a mystery. You are guarded."

"I have told you that I have been to London, that I am from Boston, that I might have an interest in business out this way."

"Yes, but something is missing in all this. You are, as I have just said, guarded. Why is that?"

"It pays to be guarded. Divulging too much information can hinder a great many things."

"Does that guard cover your emotions as well?"

"To a degree. There is hurt in every direction. A little guarding is wise."

"But it was you who told me that life is not without risk. Seems you may not take your own advice."

"Perhaps you are right. But I am just not ready to go beyond where I am at the moment—with emotions or giving out information until I better know myself."

"And then—after you know yourself?"

"I can't answer that. I will just have to make the discoveries and see where everything leads."

"And I trust you will do that. Perhaps the Middle Ground will help. Now if you will excuse me, I must go inside. Have a pleasant evening. And if you and Simon are gone before I see you tomorrow, I will look forward to Sunday. Good night"

"And to you Anna. Yes, Sunday."

CHAPTER 24

Boston

 "Cora, have you seen your father?" Martha Bain's voice was strained. "He was gone when I got up this morning and I have been unable to find him."

"No, I'm sorry. I haven't seen him. What is going on with father?"

"Oh Cora, this is tragic. Your father is becoming someone I hardly know. He is sullen, withdrawn. I am afraid."

"You know he is not the most personable man alive at his best."

"Yes, I do know that, but this is something different. I fear he is not well."

"I agree. And I believe this illness is more than health. Do you think so?"

"I do. He is angry at the world it seems. He thinks everyone has turned against him. This condition can only worsen if something is not done."

"And what do you propose? This can be solved only by father. We can do little for him until he determines to do something for himself that will point him toward recovery."

185

"You are right, but I just want to reassure him that I am by his side. He won't even listen. He thinks I am among the conspirators set out to destroy him in some sinister fashion."

"You said you were afraid mother. Do you see him as some threat to you?"

"Of course not. He would never do anything to harm me—or anyone if I know him as I think I do."

"Perhaps that is true of the man we both have known and loved, but he is now different. He is not that same man. Your fears may be legitimate."

"Yes, that could be. But I just can't believe. . . ."

"Can't believe what?"

"Oh Cora. He said recently that he would crush those forces that are against him. Could it be. . . . ?"

"Be what mother?"

"That he would actually seek to do harm to someone?"

"I can't believe he would, but he is ill. He may be capable of doing something that none of us would consider possible."

"What are we to do Cora? How can we help Squire? I love him; I am devoted to him. And I know he loves us. He has simply lost control of himself and has begun to blame that loss on others. Robert, Jackson, perhaps even you and me. What are we to do? When will Robert be home from Philadelphia? We need him."

"He should be back now within a week. And yes, we do need him. Now I too am frightened. What shall we do mother? What shall we do?"

• • •

Frontier Settlement

"Liam Sullivan, sir. Good to have you with us today."

"Yes, Reverend Sullivan. Pleased to meet you. I am Isaac Walker. This is my friend Simon Keats."

"Mighty fine message there Reverend. Shorely am pleased to meet you and have you in these here parts."

"Pleased to meet you Mr. Keats. And thank you for your kindness. I just try to proclaim God's goodness."

"And you did so well. Have you met my daughter Anna and her friend Mr. Johnson?"

"Not that I know of. But this is my first day and getting names sorted will take some time."

"Well, maybe it will with some folks like me and Isaac, but Miss Anna—you won't have no chore a'tall a' keepin' her in mind once you see her. Just about the purttiest thing this side of the Gap. And here she comes now. Miss Anna, Mr. Johnson, this here is the Reverend Liam Sullivan. Shorely shucked the corn for us this mornin'."

"Miss Walker, Mr. Johnson, most pleased to meet you."

"And pleased to meet you Reverend." Sun extended his hand to Reverend Sullivan and offered a firm grip.

"Yes, a pleasure. My father and I have been looking forward to your arrival."

"Why, thank you ma'am. I have been excited ever since I received the call to come out this way. It is nothing like Philadelphia though."

"Philadelphia? That is a big city. I am newly arrived here from Boston."

"Well, that is good to know. Glad to discover that I am not the only one new to the frontier."

"I can shorely tell you one thing. Iffin you's a' wantin' help 'round the frontier, Mr. Johnson ain't the man for you. Hadn't been for me, he'd still be out there a' tryin' to find his way back."

"Reverend Sullivan, please excuse these two." Anna's voice was light and filled with good-natured humor. "They have yet to determine which of the two is the more skilled on the frontier."

"Ain't no determin' 'bout it all. I's the one with the smartsome skills."

"Again you remind us Simon. But perhaps the Reverend would like to talk uninterrupted to Anna and Isaac." Sun looked at Anna and smiled, the corners of his mouth wrinkling a handsome face that seemed to delight in Anna's presence. That smile brightened her heart.

"That is a good idea Sun," Isaac added. "And perhaps the first thing we should do is advise him of frontier ways when it comes to names—at least to our names. We don't hold with formality here Reverend."

"I can appreciate a lack of the formality to which I was accustomed back east. Philadelphia society is often stiff."

"Shorely ain't in these parts. You gonna' like the way we conduct business out here."

"I'm sure I will. Please, Mr. Walker explain what you mean about the formalities."

"Well for this group of four, you need not bother with Mr. or Miss. It is Anna, Jackson—he prefers Sun—Simon and Isaac. That will do just fine. And welcome to the frontier and this church family."

"Kind of you all. I am most pleased to be here. My prayer is that great things will happen in this congregation."

"God's moren' capable of seein' to it that great things happen. He's a great God."

"That He is. And I hope you all will attend services regularly."

"Shorely will when I am here. I gotta' give this youngster here some more learnin' on the frontier for a month or two, but I'll be back in the settlement for a spell after that I 'spect."

"And we will attend at every opportunity," Isaac noted. "Anna and I live out farther west, so we are not often in the settlement. We really miss the fellowship of church when we are away, but we simply can't be here every week."

"I can understand that. But know that you are welcome any time."

"Thank you Reverend Sullivan. Isaac and I are in church as much as we can be. Not as much as we would like, but that is the way of the frontier." A dove fluttering into a tree top caught Anna's attention and she turned to watch. The sun outlined her face, a face that beamed with life and vitality.

"I am already beginning to see that. As I said, this is definitely not Philadelphia. Perhaps I could come visit you two out there."

188

"That would be fine Reverend," Isaac concluded. "But it is quite a trip. If you have a good mount or buggy horse, you can make it there and back in a day. It will be a daylight-till-dark run. If you have to walk, best plan to spend the night."

"I will have a horse soon. And please, I would never want to intrude."

"No intrusion Reverend. Isaac and I would welcome you any time."

"That we would. I'll give you directions before we leave today, and feel free to come at your leisure."

"I fear there will be little leisure for a few weeks at least. I have to get settled and find my way around first. But visiting church folks is high on my list of things to do."

"Certainly. Anna and I understand. The frontier demands some understanding from all of us."

"And you shorely won't regret none a visit to the Walker cabin. Miss Anna will fix up the best victuals you ever had. Ain't nothin' in Philadelfee can compare. And what 'bout your wife? Is she somewhere visitin' 'round with the other women folk?"

"I'm not married Simon. I have been busy with studies all my life it seems. Just haven't had the time yet for family. And I haven't found that perfect match anyway. That is something I will consider now that I am finished with my preparation for ministry." A sting rushed through Anna Walker as she heard the Reverend's words: *That perfect match.*

"So tell me about your family back in Philadelphia." Sun felt compelled to redirect the conversation.

"I am the youngest of six—two brothers and three sisters. They are all married. The sisters and one brother are in Philadelphia. One brother is a minister in New York; the one in Philadelphia works with my father. They are carpenters."

"I would imagine carpentry is a good profession there in the city. It is growing quickly." Sun thought briefly of his father and the chasm that had progressively grown between them.

189

"Yes, they are busy most of the time, winter excluded. Heavy snow can slow building."

"That it can. We get the same in Boston."

"Shorely don't have to worry much 'bout that out this way. Least not like it is up there. 'Course, we get snow here and the winters are a mite chilly, but usually ain't nothin' like back east. A long hunter'd be hard put back there. He'd need a whole passel of buffler robes to sleep under the stars outside Philadelfee'."

"So you are all long hunters?" Reverend Sullivan's voice was filled with intrigue.

"Not Anna and me." Isaac was quick with his answer as he held his hands up, palms out. "We are settled farmers. We do some hunting for food, but we certainly don't trek far out onto the frontier for a livelihood."

"And this here boy ain't one neither." Simon nodded toward Sun, who had fallen suddenly quiet and introspective. "He wants to be one, but I reckon he's got a whole lot of learnin' to do 'fore he can be considered a long hunter. 'Cept for me, he'd be lostern' a stray dog. Ain't that right there Sun?"

"Excuse me Simon. I'm afraid I wasn't listening. Had something running through my mind other than your useless chatter."

"I's just a' tellin' the Reverend here that you fancy yourself a long hunter but you's a' dependin' on me to keep you all straightened out yonder in the wilderness."

"Uh . . . suppose you are right Simon." Sun was detached, a strained look furrowing his brow. "I want to do some exploring before I head back to Boston Reverend. I may consider some business opportunities after I see what I have come to see."

"Yes, yes. That is wise. And what type business are you considering?"

"Nothing firm at the moment. Perhaps freight. Shipping hardware. Maybe even household goods at some point."

"My father and brother, the carpenters, also build fine, sturdy furniture. Perhaps I could put you in touch with them."

"Perhaps. Furniture might be good at some point in the future. Most of what I see out here is roughly built. It is strong and serviceable but crude to a degree. No disrespect Anna and Isaac."

"None taken Sun. And you are right. Anna and I use only what I have put together from timbers available out around the cabin. It is crude, but it is all we need."

"Agreed. But as the area becomes more settled with people from back east, there will likely be a demand for additional goods, furniture included. So thank you Reverend. Perhaps I can and will contact your father and brother in the future."

"And when do you plan to return to Boston?"

"I can't be sure, but I would like to head back that way by late October. Guess I'll miss your sermons for a while." Anna looked away with rejection painting her countenance. Sun's talk of going back to Boston caused an unidentified alarm to sound in her heart.

"I wish you well. Now if you fine folks will excuse me, I must get around to everyone and visit. Please, enjoy your meal, and again I tell you that you are welcome here any time. And Isaac, please give me directions to the Walker cabin before you leave today."

"That I will."

•   •   •

"So this was dinner on the ground?" Sun smiled as he spoke and looked into Anna's eyes. Those eyes were not as bright as they had been.

"That it was. And now you have something else to tell those people back in Boston."

"Shorely was a sumptuous affair there boy. What do you think of our frontier ways now?"

"I'm very pleased with them Simon. You told me I would enjoy it."

"Ain't never wrong neither. Simon Keats knows what's good and what ain't."

"Well, at least I agree with you on this particular   191

event. It was good. I'll miss such gatherings when I get home."
Anna turned and walked away, her shoulders slumped.

"Isaac, Simon, excuse me. I need to talk with Anna."

"That you do boy. Best get over there and see what's a troublin'
that girl. Can't say I've ever seen her so downsome and such."

"Simon!"

"Sorry Isaac. I did say I'd stay outta' these young folks' business
didn't I. 'Spect me and you oughta' ease over there and see who we can
find to talk to. Is that the Widder Wallace over yonder a ways?"

"That it is, but I'll thank you to mind your own business in that
matter as well."

"Shorely will. Wouldn't think of interferein' in no way with your
courtin' of the Widder Wallace."

"I'm not courting the Widow Wallace you old snoop."

"Well you shorely oughta' be. I'm a' thinkin' you ain't got no sense
a'tall when it comes to women. You let the Widder Wallce slip by and
you gonna' regret it till your dyin' day."

"Hush up Simon. Now let's go visit the church folks."

"And iffin you just kinda' stumble over toward the Widder Wallace, I'll sorta' stay outta' the way and let that handsome face of yours
work its spell. I bet the Widder'll be brightern' sunshine when you
come a' strollin' by."

"Simon, Simon." Isaac Walker shook his head in feigned disgust. Ar-
guing with Simon, Isaac had learned, was an exercise in futility. Jackson
had already walked to Anna's side and placed his hand on her shoulder.

"Anna, what is troubling you." Sun's voice was gentle, filled with
concern that he hardly recognized. Anna removed his hand with a
shrug.

"Nothing is troubling me."

"I can't believe that. I have not seen you like this. Something is
troubling you."

"Well, if you must know, it is all this."

"All this?"

"Yes. The families. The fellowship. The children. All
of it is troubling."

192

"In what way? I thought you enjoyed the church gatherings."

"I do. But I can't help being disturbed."

"Why?"

"Perhaps it is because I see in them all something I want."

"Oh?"

"Yes. Families. Husbands and wives. That is all appealing."

"It can be. And I am sure you will have all that in due time."

"Due time? When is due time?" Anna's tone was injured and sarcastic.

"I can't answer that. I wish I could, but I can't."

"I'm not so sure about that."

"And what do you mean?"

"I don't care to discuss it."

"As you wish, but I am sorry to see you so apparently tortured by all this."

"And it is torture, at least at times. I try to be strong and keep hope alive, but that is more than difficult."

"I think I understand that to a degree. If hope fails, we lose our focus. Yes, I can understand that." Sun was yet gentle, his concern growing. Still, he was not in complete touch with the enormity that Anna felt over her situation.

"Oh, I'm not sure you do. I don't think you understand fully. I don't think you know. . . ."

"Know what?"

"Nothing. It is nothing. Let's not talk about it now."

"When, then should we talk about it?"

"I just don't care to discuss it."

"Don't care to discuss this, this *vague something* that is troubling you?" Sun waved his hands toward the surroundings and its inhabitants as he spoke. The gesture only enhanced Anna's already distraught condition.

"See. I knew you didn't understand. Men seldom do."

"Is that right? Well, you might just give me a chance here."

"No need for that. You are going to the frontier and then to Boston."

"So my leaving is troubling you?"

"Don't flatter yourself Jackson Johnson. Why should I care what you do?"

"I don't know. Why should you?"

"It's just that. . . ."

"Just that what?"

"You are impossible Mr. Johnson."

"So it is Mr. Johnson now, is it?"

"It is. Now I don't care to discuss this any more. Please leave me alone and go about your business." Anna's words were sharp, filled with something akin to panic.

"That I will do. I will leave you to wallow in whatever level of self pity you choose. I want to draft a letter to my family, and I will take this opportunity to do just that. Good day Miss Walker." Sun moved away in haste, his jaw clinched tightly and his face crimson.

"Good day Mr. Johnson. *And good riddance.*" Anna whispered her last response so that Sun couldn't hear. Tears came, regardless of how hard she tried to hold them back. "*And even where hope is absent, faith remains.*" Anna let the thought materialize into a breathy pronouncement. "*God, You are there. I know You are there. Forgive me, but I now doubt if my faith is enough. Help me.*

•   •   •

"Simon, you know Marybeth Wallace don't you?" Isaac's eyes danced as he spoke.

"Shorely do. And how you on this fine day Marybeth?"

"Well Simon Keats, you old rambling ruffian. I haven't seen you in months. Figured you were stuffed under the sod somewhere by now."

"Shorely ain't Marybeth. Still as handsome and smartsome as ever. Ain't in no hurry to be in that sod; 'course I'm ready when the Good Lord is. And what do you mean *ruffian?* Ain't no lawless bone in this nearly 'bout perfect body."

"Oh, of course not Simon. You are a gentleman. And

rubbing shoulders with Isaac here can only help improve that. Good to see you. Did you two enjoy the service and dinner on the ground?"

"We plumb did. That Reverend Sullivan told about the Good Lord just right this mornin'. And the victuals spread by you womenfolk—why, they's what a man dreams 'bout. 'Spect I could get usen' to such."

"Well as I understand it Simon, there is someone over near the Yadkin who would be glad to settle you down and see that you had all the *victuals* you could want. Have you seen Nora Jean of late?"

"Ain't seen her. To tell the truth, I ain't been a' lookin' for her. But iffin I can get this new boy that's a' courtin' Miss Anna out and back from the frontier with his scalp in place, 'spect I just might go speak to Nora Jean."

"That would be good Simon. A fine woman, Nora Jean. And she has been widowed long enough for everything to be respectable. And so have I for that matter!" Marybeth looked coyly toward Isaac. Simon slapped his leg and let out a burst of uproarious laughter.

"'Spect that's right. You hear that Isaac?"

"Simon!" Isaac Walker proffered a frown to Simon, this to no avail. "And had Simon not so rudely dominated the conversation, I would have said we did indeed enjoy the service and the meal. It is good to be in the settlement and in the company of fine folk such as you. A day or so with Simon will make a man seek refuge in beauty and culture."

"Ain't so. A man can't want no more culture than he'll find in me. And handsome like too. 'Course beauty is something else all together different. Can't fault Isaac none for a' seekin' that out. And I have to say Marybeth, he shorely done found it in you."

"You haven't changed one bit Simon. And I thank you. A woman is fond of hearing such things. Do you talk to Nora Jean like that?"

"Ain't in some time now. 'Course that's just 'cause I ain't seen her of late. 'Spect that'll change come fall."

"Fall?"

"Yeah. I gotta' get this youngster business took care of 'fore I start a' lookin' up womenfolk or a' makin' fancy plans and all. The Good Lord done put me in charge of that boy."

"And who is this young man who is courting your daughter Isaac?" Marybeth smiled, her face aglow as she spoke.

"His name is Jackson Johnson. He met Simon somewhere along the Great Wagon Road and found his way on out to our place. And I hardly think he is courting Anna. They are simply acquainted, thanks to Simon."

"Ain't so. He's a' courtin' her all right. Boy'd be plumb foolish iffin he wasn't."

"Well, we will just have to wait and let them work that all out. Seems I can't get Simon to mind his own business in that matter. Marybeth, have you seen that daughter of mine? We need to head on back home soon."

"I did see her briefly. She spoke, but only with a nod. It appeared she had been crying."

"See, I told you that them two's a' courtin'. Makes folks cry a bunch when they first get in love and all flustered and such."

"Disregard him Marybeth. Where did you see her?"

"She was over by the church. I believe Reverend Sullivan left some of the other church members to go talk with her. He's not married you know. And a handsome young man he is. That Mr. Johnson best get busy if he wants to keep the Reverend away from your daughter."

"You may be right Marybeth, but I have determined to stay out of Anna's decisions regarding her courting. And I have warned Simon to do the same. You know how difficult it is for him to keep his nose out of anything that arises."

"Ain't so. Ain't so a'tall." Marybeth and Isaac took pleasure in Simon's denial. The three of them laughed with abandon.

Boston

• • •

"Mother is worried about you father." Cassie Spencer drew near Squire Bain and put her hand on his shoulder. He looked up with eyes that spoke of little sleep and too much brandy.

196

"There is nothing for that woman to worry about." Squire's voice was gruff and minus affection.

"And I am worried as well. Something is wrong father."

"Must you trouble me too?"

"Trouble you? Father, I am not here to trouble you. I am here because I love you. Jonathan, the children—we all love you and want you in our lives."

"Perhaps daughter. But that puts you in a small group who wants Squire Bain in their lives."

"That is not true. A great many people love you deeply, want the best for you and need you."

"If that is the case, they have a strange way of showing it. And after all I have done for them."

"But father. . . ."

"No Cassie. There is no *but*. I am being abandoned without thought of what I have done, what I have created for those who should care for and support me."

"Support you?"

"Yes. I am the head of this household and deserve respect. I demand respect."

"But who has treated you with disrespect father?"

"Who? You ask who? Look around; it won't be difficult to see. First Jackson, then Cora and Robert, and now your mother. I suppose you and Jonathan will be next?"

"Father, no. You see this all wrong. There is no disrespect."

"Enough daughter. It is you who sees this all wrong."

"But we are not against you, not abandoning you."

"That you are. At least most of you. Why, I had the business set up so that Jackson could step in and take over. And what does he do? He leaves to become a dirty, worthless long hunter and ramble about the frontier. He has no gratitude, no respect. He is no longer my son. And Cora and Robert are little different."

"Surely you don't mean that."

"I mean it, and I would thank you not to counter everything I say."

197

"I'm not. I am simply trying to reason with you and help you see this differently."

"Reason with me? Do you think I am a man without reason?"

"Of course not."

"Well then you have no cause to *reason with me*." Squire Bain spat the words with disgust and anger. He reached for the brandy and filled a snifter.

"Father, please. Please don't drink any more today and please allow me to speak without your becoming so angry."

"I will drink when I want and as much as I want. As for my allowing you to speak, I feel that you have had quite enough to say already. Did your mother put you up to this."

"I will have you know that she did not. How can you be so cruel to even insinuate such a thing?"

"Cruel? I am the one who is cruel? What about the cruelties that have come my way? Explain those to me. Cruelties heaped upon one who doesn't deserve such treatment."

"No one deserves such treatment. And no one has intentionally *heaped* cruelties upon you." Cassie's voice was forceful. Squire's tone and words had prompted a protective and defensive posture in his daughter. "Now, you can wallow in some misguided pity and harbor anger if you wish, but you are wrong about all this. It is your choice father; I can do nothing more. None of us can. But be assured that you will destroy all you are and have if you elect to live in this condition. It is up to you." Cassie turned and walked away in haste. She slammed the door before she heard Squire Bain's words.

"I will crush everything that stands in the way of Squire Bain." He gulped the snifter dry and crashed it onto the table. "Crush everything and everyone."

CHAPTER 25

Early August 1774 - The Frontier

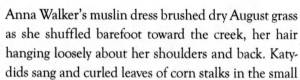 Anna Walker's muslin dress brushed dry August grass as she shuffled barefoot toward the creek, her hair hanging loosely about her shoulders and back. Katydids sang and curled leaves of corn stalks in the small field rustled. Anna searched the sweet gums and hickories for promise of autumn, but it was yet distant. No color spectacle or cooling breezes for another month. The entire countryside seemed to sigh from summer's burden, cry for relief from the heaviness, pray for the cessation of sameness. Anna did likewise. A covey of quail flushed from the path ahead but she scarcely noticed.

Lord, where are You? Forgive me. Where is my faith? Is it adequate? And who is this man Jackson Johnson? Have you put him in my life? Who, God? And why? Help me I pray. Let me see You in this struggle.

The rattle of a wagon crept into Anna's awareness. *Isaac is back.* Isaac had gone into the settlement the day before for supplies and was eager to get back home to Anna.

"Are you here girl?" Isaac's voice was always kind and welcomed. He was the man Anna most admired.

"Down here papa. I've been to the creek."

"That's good girl. I just wondered where you were. Is all well?"

"Fine Isaac. Nothing out of the ordinary here. And the settlement? All well there?"

"All well. Busy around there. Lots of new folks. I saw a few long hunters preparing to head out to the Middle Ground. I even saw Simon and Sun. They are making ready as well. In fact, they will probably be through here day after tomorrow. Here; this is a letter Sun sent you." Isaac handed Anna a folded piece of paper and smiled. "And I didn't read it."

"Never expected you would."

"I'll unload the supplies and unhitch the team. You just go on with your doings. I'd guess reading that letter is high on the list!" Isaac looked at his daughter with kindness and understanding. Anna walked inside.

> *Anna, this is not really a letter. Just some short verses I wrote for you. I hope you enjoy them. Sun.*
>> *I look forward to all days with great anticipation—some days because I will surely see you, others because the potential of seeing you exists.*
>> *A smile, an acknowledgment from you and life is suddenly filled with wonderment, beauty, mystique.*
>> *I saw you Sunday. Today is only Wednesday and already I miss you.*

You are your beautiful words, Anna thought. She held the note to her breast and cried. She then tossed it into the fireplace where it would become ashes along with the supper wood. "I will not," she said, her fists clinched tightly and her body trembling.

Boston

• • •

"I am sorry mother, but we argued." Cassie Spencer was distraught. "I tried to reason with father, but he would not listen. He just accused and scowled. I could not tolerate his conduct and I became angry—with my own father. My heart is broken."

200

"As is mine Cassie. And please, don't fault yourself. Cora and I have been unable to get through to Squire. In fact, he has virtually disowned Cora and Robert, particularly Robert. Squire is a sick man I fear."

"Your fears are justified. He is sick. And he will only become worse unless he decides to do differently. But that decision will be up to him. We can do no more than what we have done."

"Yes. All I know is to keep praying for Squire. He is no longer the man I have known these many years. And while I do love him, he is not the man I fell in love with when we were young. Heartbreaking."

"And I am profoundly sorry mother. I want to go see Cora. Do you care to join me?"

"Yes. I think it is time we three discussed this. And how I wish Jackson was here."

"So do I. It seems father blames him most. That is tragic. Jackson will find himself and do what is right. I only wish father could realize that and allow him the freedom he needs at this time."

"And I the same. But it may be too late already. Squire is sinking deeply and quickly."

"He is. What must we do mother?"

•   •   •

The Frontier

"There you two are; I expected to see you today. Headed back out?" Isaac Walker extended his hand to Simon and Sun. "Beautiful day for traveling. Still hot though. Fall can't come soon enough to suit me."

"Shorely right on that Isaac. Sweatin' and swelterin'. A little autumn breeze would be welcome." Simon Keats was clean shaven and wearing a new set of leggings and moccasins. And thanks to Sun's generosity, Simon rode a handsome bay that pranced about proudly.

"Hello Isaac. Good to see you again. And yes, we are heading to the Middle Ground—if I can keep this old man here moving. This new mount I bought should help his creaky bones stay on the trail."

"Just looky at what I have to contend with Isaac. Shorely makes a man tiresome a' listenin' to such disrespect all the time. Shorely does."

"No disrespect intended Simon. I'm just trying to properly care for my elders."

"It'll be me a' carein' for the likes of you when we get on out there in the wilderness. Just you wait and see. But I'll get you there and back in one piece."

"I am sure you will Simon. Never any doubt about that."

"Will you two dismount and sit awhile?" Isaac pointed to the porch. "You can't be in such a rush as to miss some good company."

"I ain't never in no rush, but this youngster here musta' been born a' rushin'. He's plumb dead set on bein' out yonder a ways 'fore dark. But I reckon we can sit a spell. Maybe smoke a bowl in our pipes."

"But nothing more." Sun looked first at Simon and then at Isaac. "I do appreciate the offer, but my goal is to roll out my blanket closer to the Cumberland tonight. There are four hours of daylight yet. Simon, see if you can get your stiff back and legs off that mount and fill your pipe. I'll talk with Anna while you two visit if that is okay."

"That would be fine Sun, but Anna is not here." Isaac detected the disappointment that rushed across Sun's face. "She went to the Jacobson's. A sudden decision it seemed to me. Just started early this morning, baked a pie, and said she would be back by dark. I'm sorry, but I guess you will miss her today."

"So am I Isaac. Sorry. And would you please tell Anna that for me?"

"Be glad to. I know she will also be sorry that she missed you."

"I am not so sure of that."

"Why?"

"Well, I fear Anna and I were not on the best of terms when we parted at the church gathering three weeks back. She did get my note didn't she?"

"I gave it to her day before yesterday when I got home. I'm sure she read it." Sun's shoulders slumped and he looked off into the distance, as if he were hoping to see Anna walking down the trail from the Jacobson cabin.

"I see. Thank you Isaac."

"You are welcome, and I wouldn't worry if I were you."

"What'd I tell you and Marybeth back there that day at the dinner on the ground Isaac? See. Just young folks in love and such. A terrible condition, it is. Plumb terrible. Ain't got no reasonin' when they's in such a condition."

"Oh, hush up Simon and fill your pipe. Let's visit a little before you move on. You two care for some cool water, maybe even some coffee? I brought some in from the settlement." Sun continued to stare off down the trail.

"Sun—water, coffee?" Isaac recognized that Sun was deep in thought.

"Uh, sorry Isaac. Nothing for me. Thank you."

• • •

Late August 1774 - Boston

"A letter for you Mrs. Bain." The courier was a polite young man wearing a bright smile.

"Thank you." Martha Bain took the envelope. It was worn and stained from poor treatment in transit, but was yet expertly folded and sealed with wax. As quickly as the courier turned to go, Martha began breaking the seal to get at the contents beneath. "Sun! Dear, dear Sun." Martha's heart danced as her eyes flooded with tears. The letter was dated a month and two days before its delivery.

Dear Mother,

I hope all you back in Boston are well. I am writing this from the last settlement east of the Cumberland. I have just been to a frontier church service and dinner on the ground. A gala event! I will explain it all when I get home.

I am well. This country is intriguing, beautiful. It is a bit more settled than I thought it would be. And there are good people here. I have met several and am well received. Three in particular have become quite close. They are Simon Keats—he is traveling with me - and Isaac and Anna Walker—a father/daughter team who are true frontier folk. Rather well versed they are. Not just plain country folk as one might expect to find out here. They are most gracious.

Simon and I will be leaving this settlement within a week I think. We plan to be on the frontier by late August and hope to get to the Middle Ground for some hunting and exploring in September. If all goes well there, we plan to stay until early October and then come back to the settlement. I do hope to be able to get back to Boston before Christmas. I will do my best, for I want to see you all.

I am excited about some business opportunities I have been considering. This area is growing; new people are coming in almost every day. There is a great need for better shipment of supplies, and I am giving thought to establishing some freight service, perhaps even a trading center out near the frontier. I hope father will be interested to know that I share his enthusiasm for business and am considering all these potential projects. In fact, he could be of tremendous benefit in this. Perhaps even partner with me. The name Bain could become a familiar one on the frontier as it is in Boston, known for providing goods and services.

Mother, I miss you. I want to get back soon and see you. Please give Cassie and Cora my love and hug the children for me. Know that I care deeply and wish no ill that some feel is evidenced by my decision to come here. I will do my best to be back there at year's end. With love and respect.

Sun

Martha Bain clutched the letter close to her heart and sobbed.

On the same day Sun's letter arrived, Squire Bain sat blurry eyed and red faced across his desk from a riotous man with a thick accent. Sullen and unkempt, he was a new arrival in Boston and said he was going to New York or Philadelphia or wherever he could to stay one step ahead of the law who didn't appreciate his conduct.

204   "It is Jamison Freight. And make sure this happens on

the Wagon Road. Now take your money and get out of my sight. Don't ever contact me again. And I don't want to know your name. Now get out of here, and see to it that this is done." Squire frowned and cursed and slammed his fist onto the desk. *I will not be betrayed.*

*   *   *

The Frontier

"I guess they are out toward the Middle Ground by now, Simon and Sun I mean." Anna Walker was pensive.

"Oh, they could be. May be taking their time and exploring around the Gap. Sorry you missed them when they came through."

"I don't know that I'm sorry."

"Why? What happened between you and Sun?"

"Papa, I've been foolish. I let those pretty words of his go to my head and thought that maybe. . . ."

"That maybe he was the one?"

"Yes, I fear that possibility crossed my mind. But I was horribly wrong. Nothing could ever work out for us. I'll probably never even see him again. He will come through and go back to Boston before he finds some new adventure to occupy his time. No, there is no possibility with that one, and I'm sorry I even let it enter my mind."

"Now, now girl. Don't do that to yourself. First, your response to Sun was only natural. A handsome, intelligent young man from back east. Powerful words. Why would you not be attracted to him?"

"Maybe so."

"And second, you shouldn't reach any hasty conclusions. You can't know what God has in store—maybe even for you and Sun."

"That's not likely. God has his hands full with that one before I would agree to any serious relationship."

"And God is more than capable. He never has His hands full. Patience girl; patience."

"That has worn thin Isaac. I'm sorry, but it has worn thin. I'm tired of being patient."

"I know; we all get that way from time to time. But things will work out for you. God is still in control. What say you and I hitch up the team and go into the settlement tomorrow. Maybe stay a day or so. Nothing is pushing here. We could go to church Sunday, see the new Reverend and other folks."

"And Widow Wallace?" Anna offered that familiar smile that warmed the hearts of all who saw it.

"Well, yes. And the Widow Wallace. I enjoyed talking with Marybeth the last time we were there. She is a fine woman."

"And you are a fine man. Yes, let's go. I think it would be good for both of us."

"Then we leave tomorrow morning early."

•   •   •

"Well there it is Sun—the cane of Kan-te-kee. Finest huntin' in this world. More deer and bufflers out this way than anywhere. What do you say boy?"

"It is grand Simon. I have heard about this country and look forward to exploring it. And Beautiful River?"

"North of here and west of here. A mite long ways either direction. Don't 'spect we'll make it close iffin you a' plannin' to get outta' here by October. 'Sides, plenty of game to chase 'round in these parts."

"I would imagine that is true Simon. Grand country, this. I am pleased to be here."

"And don't go a' gettin' so carried 'way that you forget that scalp of yours. Ain't gonna' be so pleasome to Miss Anna without no scalp."

"I don't imagine Miss Anna figures into my plans from this point forward. And I'm not really sure she wants to see me, scalp or not."

"Now watch it there boy. That's where you's wrong. That Miss Anna, she shorely got a shine for you. Ain't you smartsome 'nough to see that?"

"Well, maybe. But it is like flint and steel with us. One is always trying to chip away at the other."

"Makes a good union—flint and steel. You see them sparks it makes in your frizzen. Gotta' have them sparks to set the main charge off. And it goes off with a big boom. You don't want to miss that boom in life boy." To Sun's surprise Simon didn't howl with laugher as he usually did. He was far more reflective.

"Perhaps you are right Simon. Perhaps you are right. But for now let's just explore this country and allow me to soak it all in. I will have to deal with more serious matters soon enough."

"Not a bad idea boy. This here is some mighty fine country. Deserves a look see. And just watch that scalp of yours."

"Agreed. Now, let's see what is out there."

• • •

"Isaac, Anna, so very good to see you."

"And you Reverend Sullivan." Anna nodded as Isaac spoke. "It is good to be here."

"Anna, I saw Isaac a few weeks back but didn't see you."

"No, I didn't come to the settlement that last trip. He just came in for supplies."

"I understand. You two here through Sunday?"

"We are Reverend. Anna and I will attend church services before we head back home."

"That is good. I look forward to seeing you. And may I come out and visit you folks at some point next week? I have a good horse and can make the ride there and back in a day."

"If you rush you can. And yes, we will be glad to have you visit. We will be there. I'm trying to get the corn gathered and stored. Anna, is that acceptable with you—for the Reverend to visit?"

"Yes, of course. Please Reverend. At your convenience. We will be glad to have you."

"Kind of you both. I will try to come Thursday."

"And Anna will have a good dinner for you." 207

"Not necessary, but I would appreciate it. Miss Anna, if you don't mind I would like a word with you before Sunday, or at least before you head back after service."

"A word?"

"Yes, but it can wait for now. Just something I would like to mention to you."

"I suppose that would be fine."

"Thank you. We will find a time before you get away from the settlement."

• • •

Boston

"How would you and the children like an adventure Cora?" Robert Jamison's voice sparked with more enthusiasm than his wife had ever heard from him.

"An adventure?"

"Yes. The first shipment will leave Philadelphia in three weeks bound for the frontier. Axes, plows, gun powder. And there is flour of course. Even some coffee. That is hard to find on the frontier."

"But what adventure?" Cora was amused at her husband's obvious delight in the entire matter.

"I can arrange passage for us all from Boston to Philadelphia and we can watch the first load of Jamison Freight move westward. Better than that, we can take a wagon and go with the shipment part of the way, maybe on out to Fincastle or Big Lick. Roll up in blankets at night and sleep in the wagon."

"Well, I admit that would be an adventure. Surely would be closer to the frontier than any of us have been."

"It would. And just think what it would mean to the children. To see part of the frontier, to visit Philadelphia. And the weather is still pleasant enough. We would make it just fine."

"Robert, I don't know. The children, the lack of amenities. How would we. . . . ?"

"We would be fine. We would do as hundreds of others have done and are doing every day. What do you think Cora?"

"I think you are a bit crazed by all this and I think I am more than pleased to see you so excited and I think I love you."

"So that means we can all go?"

"I told you when you first began thinking about this that I supported you fully. Yes, we can go. You will have to make the arrangements, but we will go." Robert Jamison could hardly contain himself. He was more alive than he had been since the first day he entered the employment of his father-in-law, Squire Bain.

"And Cora, I hesitate to bring this up, but maybe we can look for property and housing around Philadelphia if we have time. I don't want to alarm you, but our moving there is a real possibility with this new business. After all, that is where the freight will leave from; that is the beginning of the route to the frontier."

• • •

Frontier Settlement

"Miss Anna, forgive me for being so forward, but I would like your permission to come visit you and Isaac with something in mind other than just calling on families from the church and getting a meal." Reverend Liam Sullivan spoke in a gentle manner but with marked conviction in his voice.

"Reverend Sullivan, I hesitate to ask, but are you saying what I think you are saying?" Anna had a cautious and curious look on her face, her speech somewhat halting.

"I think I am, and I think you understand. With your permission of course, I would like to get to know you better. I would like to discuss your thoughts for the future—again, with your permission, and with the permission of Isaac. Do you think that is something that would interest you?"

"Well to be honest Reverend, I am taken aback. You are giving me little notice."

"Forgive me. I am doing that. But no disrespect is intended. I just find you an interesting young woman. Everyone here in the settlement speaks highly of you and your father."

"Thank you Reverend. We have some dear friends here, and the church means more to us than you can imagine. I would expect those with whom you spoke are a bit prejudiced in our favor." Anna smiled and her eyes sparkled, though she could hardly imagine that the sparkle was as radiant as it had been upon her first meeting Jackson Johnson.

"Oh, I hardly think prejudiced is the correct word. They just see something genuine in you two. I perceive the same. You and Isaac are rare finds. The world would be better if more like the Walkers made up its inhabitants."

"Kind of you Reverned. And I concur where Isaac is concerned. He is an incredible man. The kind that any family needs as husband and father. I am fortunate." Anna's voice carried the sincerity it always did when she spoke of her father.

"And don't discount yourself. People here speak as highly of you as they do of Isaac."

"Again Reverend—kind of you. And kind of them. I hope they are not misguided."

"I am sure they are not. You exhibit those same traits of high character shown by you father. That is something to be admired. And while I don't know either of you well, I have grown to admire you both from what I have already seen and heard. Now what about that visit I mentioned? Do you agree that it would be acceptable?"

"I do. And you would do well to talk with Isaac about this. Have you done that already?"

"Not specifically. Only that mention that I would try to come out and visit Thursday. But I will go discuss it with him right now. If he agrees, I will be there by late morning. Good day Miss Anna." Reverend Sullivan bowed slightly and went to locate Isaac Walker.

"And good day to you Reverend." Anna felt flushed and lighthearted, the pain surrounding Jackson somewhat abated.

210

• • •

Boston

"He says he is fine and the frontier holds many opportunities." Martha Bain was hopeful that her husband would find Sun's letter of value. "He even says that he has some business ideas in mind that he would like to discuss with you."

"Business ideas? He had a business here and abandoned it. I don't think I care to discuss business with him. And I suppose he would want me to finance it all." Squire Bain refused to entertain any thought of his son. Eyes blurry and face scowling, he reached for a bottle of brandy.

"Please Squire; don't drink that. Let's talk and allow me to tell you more of what Sun wrote." Martha's pleas were dismissed.

"No more talk; it is too late for talk. I have no son. Now off with you woman. Leave me. I care not to hear anything you have to say."

"Squire, you don't mean. . . ."

"I mean all I have said. Now, out of my sight. You have nothing to say that will interest me. Leave me alone woman." Martha's sobs accompanied her from her husband's presence.

CHAPTER 26

Early Septermber 1774 - The Frontier

"Some bufflers a' comin' down the trail yonder toward the lick there boy. Pick us a young bull." Simon spoke softly, a practiced response from his many years in the presence of game. "Now easy boy. Just wait 'em out."

Jackson sat against a tree and pulled his knees up to support the York rifle. He aimed carefully and following the *clack* of flint and *whoosh* of powder in the pan, a monstrous *boom* and putrid blue/gray cloud of smoke erupted from the rifle's muzzle. The bison crashed into the canes and lay still.

"Well I reckon you do know how to shoot that big flinter after all there boy." Simon was more animated now than he was with his earlier whisper, and he wore a wide grin of genuine admiration for Sun's skilled performance. "Let's get down there and take care of that bull.

A fine robe for the market on that one. And the best meat you can find anywhere. 'Spect there'll be 'nough to jerk and take back to Isaac and Miss Anna iffin you don't eat it all and iffin you don't decide to just keep a' wanderin' 'round out here and neglectin' that woman who's back there at the Walker cabin a' waitin' for you."

"Now Simon, you know I am not interested in the Walker cabin or who may or may not be waiting for me there. I am interested in the frontier. And here you are after only a few weeks out talking of going back. Perhaps it is you who has someone waiting. Back along the Yadkin I hear."

"Shore might be right on that boy. And a wondersome woman she is. I'm just guessin' that when I get you outta' here all healthful and such that I's gonna' be the one headed east in a hurry. But that don't take nothin' away from the fact that somebody's a' waitin' for you too. 'Spect you oughta' give some considerin' to that."

"I'm not ready for, as you say *considerin'* regarding such matters Simon. I'm only ready to explore the frontier and think about business opportunities and going back to Boston to make some plans for that business. And I'm ready to care for that bull down there in the canes, so let's get on with that."

"Whatever you say boy, but young folks like you can be a mitesome foolish in the important things of life. A mitesome foolish." Simon drew a long-bladed hunting knife from his sash. "You do the holdin' and I'll do the skinnin'. Gonna' show you once and only how it's done." Autumn leaves were beginning to decorate the hickories.

• • •

"I can't help but wonder whether or not the Reverend Sullivan visits the other church members as much as he does the Walkers!" Isaac removed the pipe from his teeth and smiled at Anna. "Seems he's out this way twice a week of late. He'll soon wear that handsome mount of his to a frazzle. I just can't see what interests him so much out this way." Anna looked away and smiled, partially embarrassed by Isaac's comments.

"Now Papa."

"Shaa girl; I'm just toying with you. I know exactly   213

what the Reverend sees. And I don't blame him. And what are your feelings about all this?"

"I like the Reverend Sullivan. He is an excellent preacher and seems to care a great deal for his entire flock. He is a deep man of God."

"And handsome?"

"And handsome. He is gentle and kind and knows what he is all about. I am coming to think highly of him."

"So there is potential for a future."

"Perhaps. Yes, there is potential. I'm praying about this, seeking God's guidance. I am definitely fond of Liam."

"So it's Liam now?"

"Yes, but only when he is here with us. Reverend Sullivan at all other times."

"I'm glad for you and always proud of you Anna. You deserve the best. And if Reverend Sullivan is the best for you, I give you my blessing. But be assured that this decision is yours and yours alone. I will not interfere. But tell me Anna, do you think about Sun often?"

"Please Isaac. Let's not talk about Mr. Johnson. There is pain related to that. I choose to focus on other things."

"As you wish. I am still just a little concerned about you and Jackson. It seemed to me that. . . ."

"And to me as well. But that is not the focus now. Let's deal with the present and not the past."

"That we will. I love you Anna."

"And I you Isaac. I am blessed to have you as a father. There could be no better."

"Kind of you girl. Kind."

• • •

"So what do you think Cora?" Robert Jamison's eyes gleamed with life. His spirit showed renewal.

"It is spectacular Robert. Simply spectacular. Of course, this wagon seat is not as comfortable as the carriages back in Boston!" The countryside drifted slowly by as the wagons, loaded with freight and Robert Jamison's family, jostled along the Great Wagon Road, leather harnesses squeaking a mournful song in the autumn air. The two Jamison children were wide eyed and captivated.

"Thank you Cora, and thank you children. You are helping me realize my dream. Thank you again and again." Robert Jamison was obviously excited and pleased with his new business venture.

"And thank you Robert. Thank you for being courageous and for caring for us. All will be well; you have made the right choice. How far is it to Big Lick?" Cora Jamison smiled softly at her husband.

•   •   •

Two Weeks Later

The fire was sudden. First one wagon, then another. Canvas and wood virtually exploded into roaring flames. Livestock tugged at their tethers and stamped about in panic. The night air glowed an eerie orange from the blaze as Robert Jamison agonized over the screams of his children and wife. His dream floated skyward on a wicked, soot-black smoke. "Oh God," he cried.

CHAPTER 27

Late September 1774

"Well for the life of me iffin that ain't Jule chillington." Simon Keats stared toward a creek in the Middle Ground. "Never 'spected to see the likes of him out this a' way."

"So it is. Can't say that I am glad to see him." Jackson shrugged nonchalantly and wrinkled his brow in mild disgust.

"Ho Jule. Jule Chillington. That you? What's your scraggly old self doin' in these here parts." Simon waved a hearty greeting to Jule. Jule looked toward the two.

"Simon? Simon Keats? That is you. See you's still as ugly as a skinny pup and still ain't got no judg'ment 'bout who you's runnin' with." Spite still rode Jule's words and tone. His anger toward Jackson was yet keen.

"Just you pay no never mind to who's I'm a' runnin' with. Get yourself over this a' way and let some of my smartsomeness rub off on you. Iffin I know Jule Chillington, he shorely could use some smartsomes." Jule and Simon closed the distance until they were face to face. Simon slapped Jule on the back and extended his hand. Jule received Simon's welcome and offered the same.

 "Good to see you Simon. And shorely good to see

you's still healthful and all. 'Course, can't say nothin' much pleasin' 'bout that smooth talker yonder you's still electin' to be a friend." Jule nodded toward Jackson, disdain filling his dirt-streaked, half-bearded face. His leggings were covered with trail grime, his shirt and moccasins ragged.

"Now don't go a' gettin' all riled up 'bout Mr. Johnson there Jule. He's a alright sorta' young feller. Green as them there canes yonder, but a alright feller. Just 'cause you and him got off to a bad start ain't no cause for your belly to be in such a uproar. Just relax a mite and enjoy the comp'ny."

"Maybe yore's Simon, but shorely not hisin'." Jule remained adamant about distancing himself from Jackson. "I 'hain't gonna' have nothin' to do with that Boston smartsome feller."

"Have it your way Jule, but you can at least share a camp for the night and catch us up on all your doins'. 'Spect a little human talk won't hurt you none."

"That it won't, but I don't care to listen to nothin' that one has to say. Let's jest me and you do the talkin'. What'cha say to that Simon?"

"That'll be just fine and dandy. 'Spect we's got a lot to talk 'bout. And Mr. Johnson there can just listen. He might get some frontier learnin' from the two of us. 'Course, he done purtty good on a buffler 'while back. Made that big York he totes speak the truth. I was sorta' wonderin' iffin he knew what to do with that old .54. Turns out he does. Got us some fine buffler meat in the doin', he did. You care to share some of that jerk with us for supper?"

"That I do Simon. 'Course I 'hain't short on meat none myself. You's lookin' at Jule Chillington here—the best frontiersman to ever set foot west of the Gap. I 'hain't never goed hungry out this a' way. 'Spect yore 'panion yonder could learn a thing or two from the likes of me."

'Spect the same, but he's a' doin' toler'ble. Now you just come on and let's go over there and gather up Mr. Johnson. 'Bout time to build a half face and get firewood for the night. And mind that you behave yourself 'round   217

Mr. Johnson. I 'magine he'll be sorta' quiet 'round the fire tonight so's me and you can specalate' on frontier goin's on." Simon gestured as he and Jule walked toward Sun.

"Jule," Jackson said as they approached.

"Mr. Johnson," Jule returned. The conversation between them was terminated with that curt greeting.

• • •

"Reverend Sullivan talked with me today Anna." Isaac spoke softly to his daughter as they sat on the porch enjoying the brisk autumn evening.

"I expected as much. He told me he intended to talk with you." Anna's face was bright but showed the signs of a heavy burden. She pulled a blanket around her shoulders.

"He is interested in courting you properly and wanted my permission."

"And?"

"And I gave it. Is that to your liking?"

"Yes, that is fine. Liam is an intelligent and gentle man of God."

"That he is, but we have gone over this many times before."

"We have."

"I think he will want to move his courting along at a pretty hefty pace. If you ask me, I believe he thinks he has found his future wife."

"You are probably right. He indicates to me that he is now ready for a wife and children."

"And you?"

"Me Isaac?"

"Yes, you. What are your feelings?"

"I am praying about it."

"As you should daughter. As you should. God is the ultimate director of decision making. Let Him guide."

"That I will do."

"But Anna, what about Mr. . . . ?"

218   "Please. Let's not discuss that subject."

"My apologies Anna, but I think you must come to terms with Sun before you make any sort of decision involving Reverend Sullivan."

"And I will. In fact, I believe I have. I don't see Mr. Johnson as God's will for me."

"Perhaps you are right. I will leave that entirely up to you. I will pray with you, but the final decision is yours—and God's. But I see something in you when you are with Sun that is important to life. It is a spark, a glow. Is that present with Reverend Sullivan?"

"What Isaac? Am I to go through life glowing?" Anna smiled, grateful for the temporary relief of light humor. The two of them laughed briefly but this without conviction.

"Glowing is good," Isaac added. "I don't see that God is against glowing." Isaac's smile was then sincere. Anna joined in his obvious amusement.

"And what about you Isaac? Does the Widow Wallace make you glow?"

"That she does Anna. There, I have admitted it. And what do you think about Marybeth and. . . . ?"

"I think I want you to glow at every opportunity. I am perfectly at peace with you exploring a relationship with Marybeth Wallace."

"But I am a happy man as it is Anna."

"And I am a happy woman. I would just like a few other elements added to that happiness if it is in God's will."

"And it is. God's will is for you to have the best He has to offer. Who that is and what that is, I can't tell you. But God can—and will."

"Yes, of course. It is just that anything surrounding Jackson Johnson seems destined for disappointment, pain. That can't be God's will."

"Maybe not. But disappointment and pain go along with life. God sees us through them all if we let Him. It seems to me that part of Jackson's problem is his failure to allow God to direct. Perhaps you are the one who can help point him on the right path."

"That may be. But it will be a chore bigger than the one faced by Jeremiah. I don't know that I want to attempt that."

"I understand. And you are probably right. It will be a chore. But I know you are open to God's leading and in touch with Him. I offer no advice in that regard past what you already know and do. I will be praying for you."

"And I for you—as well as myself. Now I think I'll go inside and read my Bible. Bedtime is close. Good night Iassc."

"Good night to you Anna."

• • •

Boston

"And what do you want woman?" Martha Bain entered her husband's office, hot tears tracking her cheeks, cheeks that had aged disproportionately in the past several months.

"Oh Squire, the news is not good. Tragic. Oh Squire, what are we to do?" Martha was near panic.

"What is it woman? Why are you here troubling me with some nonsense?"

"Squire, it is Cora and the children. They have been delivered to Philadelphia. There was an accident on the Great Wagon Road. They are badly burned and near death. Oh Dear God, help us." Squire sat staring, his mouth open and eyes fixed on the opulence that surrounded him, opulence that for the first time seemed minus any value.

"Cora? The children? Martha, what are you saying?"

"There was an accident. A fire. Oh squire, we may lose them. Dear God." Squire Bain fell silent. His breath came in short bursts. He attempted to stand, but his entire right side went numb and his face contorted into a drawn, grotesque facsimile of himself. He slumped backward into his chair and then fell to the floor.

"Squire," Martha sobbed. "Squire, speak to me." There was no response past glaring eyes and an open mouth pulled downward in the right corner. "Oh God, what else can I endure?"

220

• • •

The Frontier

"Things quiet out that way Jule?" Simon Keats asked about the Middle Ground. Jackson had been sullen, quiet, his gaze focused on the dancing of the campfire since supper.

"Sorta' troublesome in spots. Shawnees stirrin' 'round 'bout everywhur. Got scalpin' on they mind iffin you ask me. A man's gotta' be moren' particler ramblin' 'round the Middle Ground. All this war talk got ever'body plumb rambunctious. You two been on past here yet?"

"Just stayin' purtty close. Touchin' on the Middle Ground some but ain't made it much past right here. The boy there, he wants to go deeper, but I'm a' tryin' to talk him out of it. 'Course he keeps a' insistin'. He don't know what he's a' talkin' 'bout though. 'Spect I'll try to keep him under control and not go deeper. He's a' wantin' to head back toward Boston 'fore middle of October, and iffin he plans to do that, he ain't got time to keep on the trail north or west. 'Spect we'll head back in a week or two. Hope so anyhow. And you?"

"Gonna' stay out 'while. Got me two good pack animals plus my mount. Wouldn't mind a' loadin' 'em down good with hides. That oughta' fetch a handsome sum back in the settle'ment."

"That they will. But you be careful out there. We don't want to lose *the best frontiersman to ever set foot west of the Gap!*" Simon offered his customary slap on the leg and monstrous laugh that made the hills practically vibrate. "'Spect I'll ease on in the half face and get some sleep." Jackson, still silent, rolled into his blanket and lay back, his moccasin-covered feet toward the fire.

"Me too Simon. Guess I'll crawl in myself." Jule stood and walked from the fire's glow into a calm, glorious autumn evening.

• • •

"Yes, he told me you talked with him Liam." Anna wore her Sunday dress as she and Reverend Sullivan sat on the porch of the Walker cabin, her hair hanging loosely about her shoulders.

"And he told me I had his permission to court you. Is that your understanding?"

"It is. Isaac said we had his blessing."

"That is good; I appreciate Isaac. And what about you Anna? Do I have your blessing, your permission?"

"Yes, of course. But. . . ."

"But what?"

"I fear. . . ."

"There is no cause for fear Anna."

"If you will allow me to finish, I simply want to say that you appear to be a step ahead of me in all this."

"My apologies, but what do you mean by a step ahead?"

"You seem already convinced that we are preparing for marriage. That we are the perfect match."

"And we are. We are both dedicated to God and His work, and we both have an affinity for the frontier, its people, its growth. What could be a better match?"

"Agreed on those points, but a match? I am not yet sure."

"And what is missing in that match?" Reverend Sullivan was perplexed.

"A glow." Anna looked into the afternoon sky.

"A glow? What on God's good earth do you mean by a glow?"

"Oh, just something Isaac said. He wants to be sure I have a glow."

"I'm not sure I understand."

"Probably not Liam."

"Anna, let's not rush this. Let's not reach conclusions before conclusions are necessary. Allow me to court you properly and give it all time. We will pray about this and see where God leads."

"Yes, we will pray—and we will see where God leads. Thank you Liam."

"And you are most welcome Anna. I look forward to our next visit."

"As do I." Anna stood and walked inside as Isaac returned from the creek with a bucket of water.

222

• • •

Jule Chillington's screech broke the calm. It was a forceful cry, filled with horror and pain. Sun rolled from his blanket and peered into the shadows even before Simon was fully awake. Jule was scrambling on the ground, blood staining his shirt along the right arm, with a Shawnee warrior, knife drawn, attempting to bury the blade deep in Jule's chest. Sun's reaction was immediate.

Without thought he ran at the attacker and pulled his own patch knife from a rawhide sheath dangling by a leather thong around his neck. Sun's shoulder contacted the intruder in the ribs, and the Shawnee fell, only to quickly regain his footing and rush toward Sun. With a move foreign to Sun, he sidestepped the attack, grabbed the warrior's hair and pulled downward, exposing the neck. He felt a sickening tingle in his left hand as the small patch knife easily created a deadly gash. The Shawnee shuddered and sank slowly.

Sun stood petrified, his breath coming in short, shallow spurts, his mind whirling in disbelief at what had just happened. He had killed a man, but before this reality had time to work its sinister scheme, Sun heard the faint hiss of a cane shaft and felt its agonizing sting burn into his upper back right of center and below the collar bone. He was remotely aware of a flint arrowhead protruding out the front of his shirt.

Sun stumbled forward, grabbed his rifle from beside his blanket and heard that familiar, metallic click of the hammer coming to full cock. As another warrior burst from the brush that initially housed the other as well, the *clack, whoosh, boom* of the big flintlock split an otherwise placid evening. The second Shawnee lurched backward at the impact of the round ball, and once again all was quiet—except Sun's emotions, which were roiling in tormented agitation. He let the rifle slip from his hands and he dropped to his knees.

"Watch it boys; watch it. There may be more. You two all right?" Simon stumbled out of the half face, his eyes still swollen from deep sleep. "Jule, Sun? You two hurt?" The essence of the attack and the carnage left behind

223

soon began to work into the befuddled minds of all three. They stayed as they were—mute statues unable to do anything other than gasp air and stare wide eyed into the woods and canes.

Jule Chillington stood, his balance less than solid, his left hand grappling at his right arm that revealed a long cut that ran almost from shoulder to elbow. He looked first at Simon and then at Jackson. "I'm cut," he managed to say. "Bleedin' bad." Simon moved quickly, his rifle steady in practiced hands.

"Come on over to the firelight Jule. Let me have a looksee. Jackson, you too. Let me check the both of you." Simon glanced toward Sun and realized that something was dreadfully wrong. "Sun? Boy, you alright?" There was no response save a glazed stare that burned into what had moments before been a spectacular autumn evening on the frontier.

"Jule, take that good hand of yours and help me with Mr. Johnson. Let's get him close to the fire so's I can see just what's a' goin' on." But even without the fire's illumination, Simon saw six inches of cane shaft and a flint head, both stained with Sun's blood, poking through the front of his shirt, a ghoulish reminder of the recent violence. The fletched portion, perhaps more than a foot in length, mirrored in back what was evident in front. "Easy Jule; easy. Don't go a' jostlin' that shoulder of Mr. Johnson's 'round much. Easy."

"He's hit bad Simon." Jule was shocked at the sight. "Reckon he's a' gonna' make it?" Sun had yet to respond, his face an ashen display of fear.

"No time to talk like that Jule. What about your arm?"

"Cut. Cut bad. Hurts like blazes." Simon pulled the dirty sleeve of Jule's shirt back and saw the wound. "You got anything I can put on this?"

"'Bout a cup of rum left over there in my haversack." Jule nodded toward his half face.

"I'll fetch it. But we gotta' save some to use on Sun." Simon walked over and retrieved Jule's haversack and found the small flask. "'Spect we's gonna' have to stitch this up Jule, but that'll have to wait till mornin' so's I can see better. What I'm a' gonna' do is wash this off for you and pour a little rum on it. I'll tie it up right tight so's me and you can see to Sun." Jule nodded in agreement as Simon set about tending the cut.

"Now Jule, get ready to grit your teeth and say your Sunday lessons." Simon put the flask near Jule's shoulder and let the firey liquid trickle downward. Jule howled and tensed, a terrific sting following the path of the rum. "Now I'll bandage this so's you can set 'bout the business of a' helpin' me." Within minutes Jule Chillington wore tightly bound strips of linen on his upper right arm, blood still oozing from the cut. "Let's get to work on our friend there." Simon stood and walked to Sun.

With Sun lying on his left side by the fire, Simon studied the situation. "Can you talk boy?" Sun barely whispered in the affirmative. "You a' doin' alright, are you?"

"I'm alive Simon." Still just a whisper.

"I'm afeared we gotta' get this here arrow outta' you boy. Ain't gonna' be purtty and shorely gonna' hurt mitesome. But shorely gotta' be done just the same. You up for it?"

"I'm in no condition to argue."

"That you ain't. But don't you worry none. Me and Jule a' gonna' have you good as new 'fore you know it. You just try to lay there and don't start up no ruckous. Me and Jule'll be doin' our best. But iffin you don't mind, first I'm a' gonna' stoke that big York of yours. Mine's loaded, and Jule you go get your flinter. 'Spect some more Shawnees might be showin' up here 'fore long." Simon hoped he was wrong about that assumption. Daylight would prove that he was.

"Now you two listen close. Here's what we a' gonna' do." Simon outlined his plan. He would cut the shaft behind the sinew and pine pitch that held the head. He would then split a section of the arrow along one of the cane shaft's joints and pour in a tiny stream of gun powder. "And Jule, when I tell you to, you poke one of them twigs from the fire in that powder. As quick as it flashes, I'm a' gonna' pull this here arrow back through. Sun, you ain't gotta' do nothin' but hold on."

With Sun's shirt cut away from the wound and his head covered with a weskit to protect it from the powder's   225 flame, Simon prepared for his last step in removing the arrow. Doubt was evidenced on his aging face, every smudged and sun-burned wrinkle filled with concern that went far deeper than the crevasses themselves. Even his proclivity for humor was not enough to brighten the moment.

"You two ready?" Simon grasped the shaft. Jule's hand, trembling at what he was about to do, neared the powder and a yellow flash erupted skyward. Simon made one smooth jerk and the arrow slid free. Sun began a bellow of anguish, but it was cut short as he went limp. "He's out Jule. That's good. He needs to stay out awhile. Maybe that flame purged the blood and dirt and other such filth that was in there. Hope so anyhow. You okay Jule?" He nodded.

"'Hain't never see'd nothin' like that 'fore in my life Simon." Jule was still shaking.

"'Bout all I know to do Jule. 'Coure, we's a' gonna' pour the rest of your rum in them holes there. Ain't nothin' but the Good Lord can do more for Mr. Johnson now. I'm a' gonna' be prayin' for him myself. 'Spect you might consider the same."

"Don't never pray much myself."

"Well, 'spect you oughta' get started Jule. Won't hurt you none. And you don't have to worry none 'bout fancy words like Mr. Johnson there. The Good Lord understands Jule Chillington words just the same. And don't forget that arm of yours. We a' gonna' get it all stitched up and clean come daylight. 'Spect you a' gonna' want to pray 'bout that a mite 'fore then."

"'Spect I might at that Simon. Hope the Good Lord 'hain't a' holdin' out for none of that Boston talk. Hope He plumb understands the simple words of Jule Chillington."

"That He does Jule. Rest easy. That he does. Now let's cover Sun up and me and you's a' gonna' stand watch kinda' quiet like. Don't want no more arrows a' skippin' through camp 'fore mornin'."

Daylight seemed slow coming. Simon nodded at the base of a tree while Jule sat beside a rock nearby. Jackson had begun to writhe and moan before the first rays of an

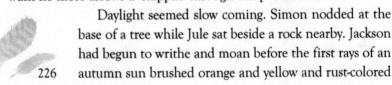

226 autumn sun brushed orange and yellow and rust-colored

leaves and tiptoed across the countryside in the morning mist. Simon stood and stretched.

"We made it through the night boys." He moved over close to Jackson. "You still with us I see."

"Still with you." Sun was feverish and faint. "Hope to stay with you."

"Oh, I'm a' plannin' for you to do just that. Don't you plan on rushin' off no time soon. Jule, you alright over there? You two want some victuals. 'Spect we all best try to eat a little something." Jule nodded in agreement.

"Just something to drink for me," Sun added.

"Maybe, but you a' gonna' need something else to get you a' goin'. Maybe some cornmeal and salt pork fat. Maybe a piece of jerk. Reckon you could get that down your throat?"

"I'll try. I just need rest." Sun lay still beneath the blanket.

"Jule, we gotta' make some plans to get you and Mr. Johnson there back toward the settlement. May take us a week or more what with the hurts you two got and all."

"You prob'ly right Simon. 'Spect I can make it purtty good, but the smooth talker yonder, he 'hain't in much shape to be a' travelin'. Reckon we oughta' try that trip?"

"Soon as we can. This ain't no place to be when you's all cut up and such. Thinkin' maybe we could rig a slide with some poles and hitch it to one of the pack animals for Sun there. Be a mitesome bouncy, but I 'spect he can make it iffin we take it sorta' slow.

"'Spect he can. But shorely do hate to leave the Middle Ground what with two more good months of huntin' ahead of me 'fore winter."

"'Magine you do Jule. But you ain't in no shape to be a tuggin' 'bout on bullfer hides and such. That arm ain't even started a' healin' yet. And you could get some troublesome stuff in that cut. Might lose a good arm there iffin you ain't careful. Shorely could. And while we a' mentionin' that arm, me and you's gotta' get it all stitched up 'fore we do anything else. Let me get my moccasin kit out and get to the sewin'."

227

"It can wait Simon. 'Spect it'll be jest finern' trail dust iffin we jest leave it 'lone."

"Ain't so. That arm there's gotta' be stitched up 'fore it's a' gonna' heal. Just gappin' open there, it is. Now sit down here and hush up."

"I'd ruther jest wait."

"Well Jule Chillington. Are you scared of something? Can't believe a strong frontier feller such as you is scared."

"I 'hain't skeert of nothin' you ole goat. Shorely 'hain't. What I got to be skeert of anyhow?"

"Maybe this here needle and thread. Maybe you scared of that."

"Hain't so. 'Hain't skeert of no needle and thread. 'Course, I 'hain't so shore you know what you's a' doin' with them there tools you a' flashin' 'round."

"Shorely do know Jule. Had to do it to my own leg once when I was a' skinnin' a fat buck. Kinda' let the knife slip a touch. Opened my leg right up. I just set in the shade a' whistlin' and a' stitchin' 'way. Ain't nothin' much moren' stitchin' up a old hound dog that's done run in on a bayed bear. 'Course that old hound dog shorely smells a mite more pleasantsome than Jule Chillington." Simon's humor had returned with the morning sun. "Now take off one of them ragged center seams you a' wearin' and start gnawin' on it. This ain't a' gonna' hurt much."

Before afternoon shadows had streaked the hills and cast fingers of solemnity across the woods, Simon and Jule had fashioned a litter of poles and buckskin for Sun. They would head east at sunrise the following day.

· · ·

Boston

"Mother Bain, it grieves me to tell you, but little Alice is gone to be with the Lord." Robert Jamison, in Boston from Philadelphia to deliver this shocking news, yet wore bandages on his burned hands. He began to weep. "She's gone," he struggled to say. "I'm so very sorry Mother Bain." Mar-

228

tha gasped and slumped onto a chair, sobs causing her entire body to tremble. "We tried Mother Bain. We tried."

"Cora; Mary Martha?"

"Mary Martha has burns on her feet and lower legs but she is doing well. Cora. Oh dear Cora, Mother Bain. My beautiful wife. Her face and neck will be scarred for life. Oh how we tried Mother. God help us."

•   •   •

The Frontier

"Good to see you again Anna."

"And you Liam. Is all well in the settlement and with the church folks?"

"All well. Two new babies born back there this week. That is always exciting. And sorry you and Isaac couldn't make it back in to service the past two Sundays."

"So are we. We really miss not being able to get to church every Sunday. But the autumn chores have had us busy. We will be there soon, maybe even this Sunday. We have the corn stored, and Isaac has finished hunting and putting up winter meat."

"Oh certainly; I understand. I was not implying. . . ."

"Of course you weren't. I just apologize for not being more regular in church attendance."

"No apologies needed. I am getting a more thorough grasp on frontier life. No explanations required. And I admit, I rather like this frontier and its ways. Think I'll stay on and grow old here." Reverend Sullivan smiled and patted Anna's hand.

"I hope you do Liam—if that is what you want. I know I will stay here, that is if it is God's will. Can't imagine living anywhere else. This is home." Anna looked away, pensive. She understood Reverend Sullivan's words and intent. But she was yet unsure of her own heart.

"And how do you feel about our situation at this point? Are you finding me to your liking?"

"Oh, I like you just fine Liam. That is not the issue."

"And what is the issue?"

"I think you should understand that by now."

"Not thoroughly. Would you care to explain it in detail—again?" Sarcasm crept into the edges of Liam's voice.

"The glow Liam."

"The glow?"

"Yes, the glow. We have discussed this before."

"Anna, I'm sure all that will come in time. Love will surely grow as the days and years progress."

"I don't doubt that. But there is not yet a glow."

"And heaven forbid that you live without a glow." Impatience was evident in Reverend Sullivan's voice. Anna crinkled her brow and resisted the urge to strike back, fighting tears that threatened her composure.

"Liam, please." Anna presented a calm demeanor. "I have agreed to see you, to allow you to court me. I will not end that soon. That is unless you insist on pushing me to a decision. A relationship must be built on many things, and understanding is one of those things, an important one. I don't feel you understand me in this. At least you are not permitting me to express my feelings without some reservation. I will be honest or I will be nothing."

"Now Anna, I understand."

"Do you?"

"I think I do. And I will try to understand even better."

"That is positive. I appreciate that."

"But let's be careful that we are not foolish and miss a gift from God."

"Foolish I don't want to be. And I certainly don't intend to miss a gift from God. His gifts are always for our good. But I will also be certain that the *gift* is from God."

"Agreed Anna. And I do want to see you again."

"And I you Liam."

"Reverend Sullivan. Good to see you." Isaac walked

230 from the fields and up to the cabin.

"And you Isaac. I see you are working hard today."

"I am. But that is common out here. We are finished with the big autumn chores. Hope to see you at church more often in the coming weeks."

"Yes, Anna has apprised me of the situation. I hope you can do that. But I understand how it is out here."

"Thank you. We do what we can and must. And how are things in the settlement?"

"Fine Isaac. Busy there now. Long hunters coming and going. New folks moving in."

"I'm sure. Seems as if the frontier is experiencing growth."

"That it is. We'll have a bustling town back there soon."

"I expect so Reverend. Beautiful country all around."

"That it is. Beautiful." Reverend Sullivan looked at Anna and smiled.

"And I must ask Reverend. Have you seen Marybeth Wallace of late?" Anna's eyes sparkled at Isaac's words. He seemed to glow with the question.

"That I have Isaac. She is at church for every service and about the settlement daily."

"See that glow Liam?" Anna teased Isaac and looked at him with some measure of envy.

"I do. So that's what you mean Anna?"

"It is. And Isaac definitely has it."

"Stop it now you two. You are putting me in an awkward position here. I just asked because. . . .

"Because you are sweet on the Widow Wallace," Anna teased. "There is no need to deny it."

"No need. You are right. I do think highly of Marybeth."

"And from what I can determine Isaac, she is a fine woman. Not unlike your daughter here—a fine woman." Reverend Sullivan again looked at Anna with affection. "I can understand your interest in her. And I must add that she would also be fortunate. You are a fine man as well."

"Oh, thank you Reverend. I just try to live a decent life   231 under God's leading and do the best I can toward everybody I meet. I fall short, but my desire is to grow and be all I can be for God's glory."

"That is admirable."

"And he is the best man I know," Anna was quick with her conclusion. "No daughter could ask for a better father and no woman could ask for a better husband."

"Not so quick there girl. Nobody's said anything about a husband in all this."

"Not specifically, but it wouldn't surprise me if Marybeth Wallace didn't become Marybeth Walker before another year has come and gone. And I would welcome her into our home. It would be pleasing to have another woman around. Might ease my load of watching out for you *old man*." Anna put her arm around Isaac's shoulder and brushed across his scruffy beard. "Might even encourage you to stay a bit more presentable."

"Oh hush up there. No wedding plans for me right away. Too much to do around here for that. Reverend Sullivan, will you be staying the night?"

"Thank you, but no. I must head on back toward the settlement. Dark will catch me even if I leave immediately. And even though my horse will walk right back to the blockhouse and deliver me safely, I prefer not to ride in the black of night. I'm still not *that acquainted* with frontier ways." They all three laughed at Reverend Sullivan's admittance of uneasiness.

"Certainly Reverend, we understand. Can't be too careful out this way. A problem could arise, though there is little chance of that if you are going east. Anna and I will do our best to see you Sunday."

"Thank you Isaac. And thank you as always for your hospitality. Now if you two will excuse me, I'll head back. A long ride waits. Anna; Isaac." Reverend Sullivan tipped his hat and started toward his horse.

"Good to see you Liam. Isaac and I will plan to be there Sunday."

Anna turned to go inside, a smile on her lips but an uncertainty in her heart.

"A pleasant young man of God there Anna," Isaac

said as she stepped through the cabin door.

"He is Isaac. And make sure you don't ramble off and get lost before sundown. I'll have supper ready by then."

•   •   •

Travel for Jackson, Jule and Simon had been slow. Four days had passed since they left camp where the attack had occurred, and at least one more, perhaps two, remained before they would reach the Walker cabin. Although Jule's arm showed signs of improvement, Sun's wound was angry. Firey red spread through flesh around the jagged holes, both front and back. Fever was a constant companion, and Sun moaned at every bump encountered by the litter.

"Shorely are a' causin' me and Jule a mitesome lot of trouble a' takin' care of you Jackson." Simon attempted a good-natured laugh, but his effort at humor failed to amuse even himself. "What's today Jule?"

'Hain't too terrible shore. Monday, Tuesday? Just can't say for plumb certain."

"I'll reckon it's Monday. That'll make it Tuesday or Wednesday 'fore we get to the Walker place." Simon turned to Jule and spoke softly. "That boy back there ain't a' doin' none too spunky. I'm scared we a' gonna' lose him iffin we don't get him off this trail and take some better care of him. Maybe Miss Anna and Isaac can help us out iffin we can get him back there."

"Spect you's right Simon. He 'hain't a' lookin' none too healthful. Kinda' peeked and yeller. And them holes all red and such. And hot as campfire coals, he is. None too healthful." Jule fell silent for a few minutes as they crept slowly eastward.

"Been thinkin' Simon. 'Spect that Mr. Johnson saved my hide."

"'Spect you right 'bout that Jule. And mine too. He saved us both. Done alright, he did. 'Course, he's a' payin' heavy for it all. And iffin he makes it, 'spect he'll pay some more. Didn't seem to take no likin' to violence. Said that way back yonder when I first met up with him on the Wagon Road. I told him he might face such donis', but he said he wanted to   233 avoid 'em. Guess you can't avoid bad things all the time. Payin' heavy, he is."

"'Course me, I 'hain't never cared much for the feller. Kinda' smartsome and the like. Don't fit too regular out this a' way. Oughta' stayed in Boston I figger."

"Who'd a' saved your dirty hide iffin he'd a' stayed in Boston Jule?"

"'Hain't never give that no never mind. Reckon why he done it—saved my hide? He coulda' jest runned up there in the bushes and 'scaped from the ruckous. Why'd he do it?"

"Could be he's just a decent sorta' feller who ain't willin' to let his 'panions down. Could be he ain't bothered by triflin' things like you been bowed up 'bout since you stormed off to the creek that night back there at the Walker place. Could be the Good Lord figgered you's worth savin' and sent Mr. Johnson all the way from Boston to see to it. God done give you a second chance Jule. 'Spect you oughta' make the best of it."

Much unlike himself, Simon stopped talking and allowed his words to sink in, hoping Jule would reflect on them at length.

• • •

Boston

"Rebecca, I would like a word with you." William Clarkson turned from his work as Rebecca walked toward her father's office.

"I hope you want more than one word with me William Clarkson," Rebecca teased as she stopped and looked at him, her face radiant and eyes dancing in the morning light.

"Why yes, it was just a figure of speech. Rebecca Bomar, you cause me to say the silliest things. I can hardly speak in your presence. What is this hold you have?"

"It is a hold I don't intent to relinquish. Now settle down and talk. You *did* say you wanted a word with me."

"Yes, of course. I have been thinking. . . ."

234 "About me I hope!"

"About you. Naturally. And about me."

"That seems a fitting subject to think about—you and me."

"As I was saying; I have been thinking. I would like permission to court you, to see you at times other than when you come scurrying through here to visit your father. So, I am asking you for that permission."

"And I have been waiting for you to ask. But I must take some time to give this more thorough consideration. Let's see." Rebecca cradled her chin in her palm and glanced upward, her eyes dancing and a mischievous smile curving her lips. "All right; I have had enough time. Yes, you have my permission!"

"Oh Rebecca, I am. . . ."

"But you must ask my father."

"Your father?" William Clarkson felt a lump rise in his throat.

"Of course my father. This would hardly be proper without his blessing. His office is just up there." Rebecca gestured gently toward the top of the stairs and smiled.

"Well yes, I know where his office is. But now?"

"There will be no courting until you do. Now hop to it William. You are wasting my time."

"Are you going there now?"

"I had planned to, but I can wait."

"Perhaps you. . . . uh. . . . we. . . ."

"Not on your life William Clarkson. You will stroll right up to my father and ask him. You can make an appointment to see him later or you can do it now."

"But I'm working."

"And I am the boss's daughter. I give you permission to take a break."

"But first I must. . . ."

"Do what?"

"I must. . . ." William had no words. He stood with his head down and his face blushed red. Rebecca stood with hands on hips and stared.

"Shame on you. Afraid of my father. You have kept me   235

waiting long enough. I was beginning to wonder if you would ever ask. Now you go see my father, and if you survive that I fully expect you to come calling soon." Rebecca jabbed a petite finger into William's shoulder, smiled coyly, and whirled to go.

CHAPTER 28

Early October 1774 - The Frontier

Isaac Walker stood startled. Across the creek from the cabin he could see a disheveled and beleaguered Simon Keats and Jule Chillington. Behind them was a horse-drawn litter, the other mounts and pack animals following. Isaac could see a form lashed to the litter but was unable to determine details.

"Anna. Anna, come quickly. We need your help." Panic filled Isaac's voice as his words echoed through the pungent air of an early October morning. "Simon, what has happened? Are you all right? Is that Mr. Johnson on the litter?" Isaac's staccato of questions revealed his concern.

"Shawnees. They hit us at night in camp out on the edge of the Middle Ground." Simon's tone was filled with fatigue and worry.

"Well, are you and Jule all right?"

"I'm fine Isaac. Jule there got a nasty cut on his arm, but he's a' doin' better. But the boy, Mr. Johnson, he ain't a' healin' up none too good. 'Spect we may lose him iffin we can't do something purtty quick. Reckon you can help us?"

"We'll do our best. Let's get him on up to the cabin." 237

Anna had joined them and stood in shocked silence. She knelt beside the litter and brushed the hair back from Sun's sweat-soaked brow.

"Sun, can you hear me?" Jackson's eyes opened and he managed a whisper.

"Anna, I'm. . . ."

"Shhhh. Don't try to talk. Just lie still and let us get you to the cabin." Anna was heartsick.

Inside the cabin Anna heated a bucket of water on the hearth and Isaac used it to bathe Sun's face and wounds. "Looks bad," he offered. "We have to tame this wound if Sun is to survive. Simon, what did you and Jule do back there on the trail?"

"Ain't done nothin' 'cept put some rum on it there in camp five or six days back. 'Course, I burned the hole good with gun powder when I pulled that cane shaft outta' him. Didn't have nothin' else to work with Isaac."

"You did all you could. Guess I best head to the settlement and see if I can find something there. I'll ask the church folks to start praying for Mr. Johnson. Anna, can you and Simon handle this till I get back?" Anna simply stared at Sun and did not respond. "Do whatever you can. I won't be back till sometime in the night." Isaac walked out to saddle a horse.

"Sun." Anna spoke barely above a whisper as she continued to bathe his face and apply hot cloths to the wound in his chest and back. "Sun, don't leave us. Fight to live; please fight to live." Sun gave a faint indication that he heard and would comply with her request. The day would prove to be a long one.

"Reckon that's Isaac a' comin' back." Simon Keats roused from restless sleep beside the fireplace. Jule sat with Anna, who had stayed near Sun since his arrival on the litter. The cabin door opened to reveal Isaac and Reverend Sullivan.

"Got some alcohol and salve," Isaac announced. "How's he doing? Fetched Reverend Sullivan too."

"He is no better but at least still alive. I'm glad you are back. And hello Liam." Anna slumped in fatigue.

"Hello Anna. Sorry to be here on such a mission as this. Are you all right?" Anna nodded but said nothing.

238

"Reverend Sullivan, this is Jule Chillington." Isaac made the introduction as he extracted the medicines from his haversack. The two shook hands and then turned their attention back to Jackson.

"Anna, let me help you over to the fireplace. You are exhausted." Reverend Sullivan draped a blanket across Anna's shoulders, shoulders that were strong and filled with resolve but now appearing frail, vulnerable. "Isaac and I will see to Mr. Johnson." Liam coaxed Anna to a bench beside the warm fire.

"Thank you Liam," Anna managed to say, her voice weak and filled with the weight of worry.

"Reverend Sullivan, help me get some alcohol on these wounds." Isaac lifted Sun gently to expose his back where the arrow had entered. "We'll put some salve on too and some warm, clean bandages." Reverend Sullivan complied. "Not much more we can do after that but pray."

"And we will pray Isaac. Thank you for recognizing God in all this. He is the only real healer." Reverend Sullivan was pleased with Isaac's show of faith. "And daylight can't come soon enough."

Morning broke clear. A gentle autumn breeze stirred the countryside with refreshing newness. It rustled leaves on the hickories and oaks, causing them to dance and sparkle in the sunlight as mist snaked from the ground and lifted skyward. It was a spectacle like no other. Reverend Sullivan stepped onto the porch and took a deep breath, a breath now removed from the smell of injury and violence. "I love autumn," he said to himself.

"And so do I Liam." Anna opened the cabin door and stood beside him. "It is a marvelous blessing."

"Good morning Anna. Did you sleep any?"

"Very little. I dozed there by the fire, but it was hardly sleep. Did you?"

"No. Isaac and I tended Mr. Johnson."

"He is asleep I see." Anna had checked on Sun before she went outside.

"Yes. Soundly. And he needs the rest. So does Isaac. I'll see if I can get him to let me take care of Mr. Johnson for a while."

239

"Thank you Liam. If I know Isaac, he will stay right there beside Sun for as long as it takes." Anna looked at Reverend Sullivan and tears began to track her cheeks. For the first time in their relationship, Reverend Liam Sullivan gathered Anna in his arms and held her close. She felt the comfort of his embrace and allowed herself to relax in its warmth. She cried freely, as she had at her mother's graveside, sobs robbing her body of what little strength that remained.

"That's good Anna. Cry it out. It is all right to do so. I'm here with you; God is here with you." He brushed the hair that hung down on her shoulders and wiped away the tears that spilled from anxious eyes.

The cabin was soon alive with activity. Jule and Simon threw back their blankets and eased over to Isaac and Sun. "How's the boy a' doin'? Simon asked.

"Seems to be resting well. Let's not disturb him." Isaac spoke softly.

"And how you a' doin' Isaac?"

"I'm fine. Just a little tired. What about you Jule? That arm giving you any trouble?"

"Shorely is a mitesome touchy there Isaac, but I 'spect hit's a sum bettern' Mr. Johnson there. 'Sides, 'hani't nothin' so never mind as a knife blade in a arm gonna' git the likes of Jule Chillington down. Shorely 'hain't. You's a' lookin' at the bestest man on the frontier a' standin' right here 'fore you Isaac."

"Well thank you Jule. 'Bout time you recognized that I'm the foremost hunter and scout in these parts. And 'bout the handsomest too. Yessiree, 'bout time. I's been a' tellin' you that for nigh on five years now."

"Not 'chew you ole coot. I's talkin' 'bout my own self. I's the bestest."

"Don't you two get started. You'll disturb Mr. Johnson. Let's get out there on the porch so we won't wake him." Simon felt the urge to slap his leg and disrupt the hillsides with his familiar laughter, but he thought of Mr. Johnson and exercised restraint.

"Good idea Isaac. Jule here's a mitesome obnoxious, a' braggin' and all. Let's me and you get him outta' the way so's Mr. Johnson can rest and get all healed up and such." The three walked outside.

"How is everybody this morning?" Reverend Sullivan was light-hearted, jovial. He and Anna had only minutes earlier broken the embrace and stood looking at one another. Anna's eyes had begun to clear from their teary blur.

"We's good Reverned. 'Course Jule there's a' getting' all smart-some. Done started braggin' and a' struttin' 'round 'bout bein' the best man on the frontier. Shorely a mite troublesome in all his loud mouthin'. Me and Isaac had to get him from underfoot. Mr. Johnson in there needs his rest and can't nobody rest in the presence of such greatness as Jule thinks he is."

"And Mr. Johnson?" Anna's voice was a welcome change from Simon's rambling.

"Seems to be doing fairly well daughter. He is still sleeping, and the red around those wounds may be a little less severe this morning. We'll just keep doing what we are doing and pray for healing."

"Isaac, I want to relieve you; let me take care of Mr. Johnson so that you can rest."

"Thank you Reverend, but I won't hear of it. You have things to attend to back in the settlement. And besides, there is plenty of help here. Please feel free to go back in and see to other folks. Sunday services will be coming along soon. Don't feel obligated to stay here."

"Not at all. I will be happy to stay and do whatever I can."

"I know that, but it's not necessary. We'll be fine here. Just go on back if you need to, and be sure to ask the church folks to continue in prayer for Mr. Johnson."

"That I will do, but are you sure you don't need me to stay?"

"Of course you are welcome—now or anytime. But we can take care of things here."

"Well Isaac, I do need to make some visits. And I could use some time in study. So if you are certain that I. . . ."

"Certain Reverend."

"In that case, I'll head in. I will try to get back out here   241 early next week after Sunday's service. Is there anything I can get for you there in the settlement?"

"Not that I know of. We still have plenty of the medicine. Just take care of the other church folks and keep praying."

"Thank you Isaac. And I will be back as soon as I can." Reverend Sullivan shook hands with the men. He stepped beside Anna and put his arm around her shoulders. He took her hand in his and smiled. "Take care of Mr. Johnson all you. And you gentlemen take care of this young lady." He smiled at Anna and walked toward his horse.

"Shorely gonna' do that Reverend." Simon Keats chuckled under his breath and said to no one in particular, "Well, well. Looks like the courtin' is a' plumb takin' hold. Shorely looks like it."

• • •

Two Weeks Later

While Jackson was not completely healed, his recovery had been nothing short of miraculous. With his wounds no longer inflamed and his right arm in a sling fashioned from muslin, he had begun to move about the Walker homestead, Anna often with him.

Reverend Sullivan had checked on them all two days back, and Simon and Jule had gone back with him to the settlement.

"Anna, would you care to join me for a walk down by the creek, maybe even onto the trail beyond that?" Sun wore a clean long-hunter shirt and greatcoat, the right side of which was draped over his shoulder and arm. Though his leggings were stained, they were not the ragged pair he had on when he was brought in by Jule and Simon after the attack.

"It is a glorious day for a walk, but are you sure you are up to a trip like that?" Anna was pleased that he had asked her to join him.

"Certainly. I feel well. This sunshine and autumn air can only help. And the company of a lovely lady of course. That will be a medicine far superior to anything else." He smiled at Anna, affection showing in his face, the same face that was not long ago filled with fear and pain.

"Oh, your words again. Always filled with flowers." Anna shut the thought of her initial fondness for Sun from her mind. "I'll be happy to join you. Care for some jerk and a piece of fruit pie? And what about a cup for some water from the stream"

"Yes, and that is a good idea. We can sit by the ripples up there and eat. I'm ready when you are."

"I'll be right along. Let me get the food." Anna also took time to remove her apron and bonnet and loose her hair so that it hung freely to glint in the morning sun. "You will be careful not to stumble and fall, won't you?"

"I will. Put your mind at ease." Anna met him presently on the porch.

"You look radiant Anna Walker."

"No flattery. Let's just enjoy the walk and the gift of life. Especially your life. A second chance I would say. I was afraid we would lose you."

"That almost happened. There were times when I didn't know whether or not I was even alive. That is a strange thing. Dreamlike. And there were times when I could hear the voices of you and Isaac, and yes Simon, but could not respond. The strangest of all, however, was the voice of God." Anna and Sun walked alongside the creek.

"The voice of God? Tell me about that voice." They sat together beneath a big hickory.

"I believe it was God. A faint, soft voice, but very close. Not far away as I have always thought of God."

"And what did He say?"

"That would be difficult to determine, for it was not words. It was a presence, a feeling of acceptance, love. Maybe forgiveness."

"Forgiveness? Forgiveness for what?"

"A great many things I fear. But Anna, you must know that I killed two men. Me Anna. I killed them. Took two lives. I am sickened by the thought. How could I. . . . ?"

"How could you not? Evil sometimes shows its ugly face and we must fight it."

"But Anna, I killed those two Shawnees. They were   243

just men as I am. They were fighting what they perceived as evil. Maybe they had families—wives, children. Certainly they had parents or siblings. Someone is grieving what I did. God forgive me."

"He will Sun. And He will heal. Completely. The scars will remain and the hurt will surface, but God will heal. He has given you a second chance." Sun did his best to avert his face and refuse the tears freedom to flow, but he was unsuccessful.

"Sun, I am so very sorry," Anna said as he hung his head and gave himself permission to cry. She put a gentle hand on his shoulder. The breeze sent a strand of hair across her face and she shivered in the agony she shared with Jackson.

Eventually Sun stood, taking Anna's hand and assisting her up. He looked into the distance and then at Anna. "And I thought of you. On the trail and during the sickness, I thought of you."

"And I thought of you as well."

"But probably not in the same context as my thoughts."

"What do you mean? I don't understand."

"At some point in that ordeal, I came to think that God put you in my life."

"Perhaps He did. And perhaps He put you in my life as well. If I have had any influence on you that would point you toward God, He was and is the primary force in our meeting. I have prayed for as much."

"And have you prayed for something else regarding the two of us?"

"What do you mean something else?"

"Anna, I think God put you. . . ." He suddenly stopped speaking and pulled Anna to him with his one good arm. Her face touched his and she felt the trace of tears still moist on his cheeks. He then moved his lips so that they contacted hers and kissed her. Anna at first resisted but found herself lost in the moment, giving her own passion over to that he offered. Her heart raced, her faced flushed with a glow she had never known. Anna pushed away.

"No Sun. No. We can't."

244   "Oh Anna, yes we can. Come back. . . ."

"No. You don't understand. This is just too confusing. You see, Reverend Sullivan—Liam—and I. . . ."

"No Anna, please. Please don't tell me. . . ."

"Liam is courting me. We have become close of late. He is a man of God and wants to make a life with me. I just can't. . . ."

"Anna, no. Please, no."

"I am profoundly sorry Sun, but this is all confusing. Please try to understand, and please forgive me. I must go back to the cabin. Please don't mention this again." Anna turned and hurried away. Sun stared after her, hope draining from the very core of his being, a being that had scarcely survived his visit to the Middle Ground.

CHAPTER 29

"Shorely gotta' be him Isaac." Simon Keats spoke with conviction on the porch of the Walker cabin four days after Anna and Sun had talked beside the creek. "Said his name was Bain, Jackson Bain. Word woulda' been here sooner but his folks back there didn't know 'xactly where he was. Just knew he was on the frontier. Word sorta' drifted down the Wagon Road and spread out to the settlements." Reverend Sullivan stood with Simon.

"Yes I agree. This must be Mr. Johnson as you know him. The message came from his mother, a Mrs. Martha Bain. She is the wife of Squire Bain, a powerful businessman from Boston. I'm sure you have heard of him."

"Of course. I knew of the Bain family long before we moved out here. But this can't be our Mr. Johnson."

"'Fraid it is Isaac. Can't be nobody else; gotta' be him. Word is his paw done fell terrible ill and some bad things done happened to his sister and her younguns. Mr. Johnson shorely needs to go home and check on 'em, so his maw says. And where is Mr. Johnson anyhow?"

"He's out in the woods somewhere. Doing much better. Even slept rolled in his blanket down by the creek the last few nights. I guess he has the frontier blood in him after all."

"That might be so and might not be so. Don't reckon I'd specalate much on what's so with Mr. Johnson. But me and you's gotta' find him and fetch him back. 'Spect the Reverend would like to talk this over with Miss Anna."

"Yes, that would be good Simon. I'm sure she will be somewhat disillusioned by it all. Where is she Isaac?"

"Gone back over to the Jacobson's place, but she'll be along directly. Said she wouldn't stay long this time."

"If you two don't mind, I will wait here for her while you go look for Mr. Johnson—or Mr. Bain or whatever name he chooses to use." Reverend Sullivan's words contained a sharp bite.

"That is fine with me Reverend."

"Me too. Shorely don't want to get in the way of a little courtin' that might get squeezed in somewhere. Courtin's got a way of gettin' squeezed in to just 'bout every part of life. Come on Isaac. Me and you'll have Jackson hollered up in no time. Can't be far off. That shoulder's still troublesome I 'magine."

•   •   •

"His name is Bain, Anna. Simon and I are sure this is the same man. Even has the same first name—Jackson."

"No, this can't be. It is Mr. Johnson."

"That is what he told you, but the facts seem to support falsehood. We will have to wait for Isaac and Simon to get him back here, but I fear you will find he has deceived us all. He is, surely as night follows day, Jackson Bain, son of Squire and Martha Bain of Boston. I have known of them all my life."

"No Liam. Sun would not . . . ."

"I am very sorry Anna." Anna's lower lip quivered and her brow wrinkled, the look of dismay creeping from usually effervescent eyes.

•   •   •

"My father is ill?"

"Yes, critically I am afraid." Reverend Sullivan took no pleasure in delivering that message.

247

"And my sister and her children have been in an accident? Which sister? I have two."

"We were not told which one, but it is true that one—and her children—were the victims of a fire. No specifics on that. But your mother has sent word for you to come home as quickly as possible. I'm sorry that the message is so late arriving. Simon and I came the moment we got notice of this."

"Thank you Reverend. I must make plans to leave immediately."

"Reckon you in any condition to travel there boy? 'Spect it's gonna' be a tiresome journey. Boston's a long way from here." Simon maintained his faith in Jackson Bain. "I 'sppose I could tag along with you so's you ain't by yourself. What do you think of that? 'Course, I'd have to leave soon as I got you there. Got some business in one of the settlements east of here I'd like to tend to 'fore the new year."

"I would appreciate that, but it is not necessary."

"Plumb necs'sary iffin you need me boy. Simon Keats ain't gonna' abandon no friend."

"Am I your friend Simon?"

"Shorely boy. You a good a friend as a man ever had. Saved my hide out yonder a few weeks back. but you ain't gotta' save my hide 'fore I call you a friend. You just plumb rubbed off on me. 'Spect we made the best team to ever hit the frontier."

"I don't want to impose, but if you are sure you want to go, I welcome your company. This will be a dreary trip. I don't know what I will find when I get back to Boston."

"And your name?" Isaac was curious but not condemning.

"It is Bain—Jackson Bain. My father is Squire Bain, a well-known Boston businessman."

"We are familiar with the name Bain," Isaac noted. "Heard of his business endeavors all the way down to Pennsylvania long before we left."

"I am sorry about not telling you the entire story before now."

"And you should be." Anna stormed away and disappeared around the bend toward the creek.

"Guess she done got a mite upset with you there boy."

"As well she should be," Reverend Sullivan added. "You have deceived these good people. There was no cause for that."

"You are right Reverend; there was no cause. But no harm was intended."

"But harm has been done Mr. Johnson—uh, Mr. Bain. I will talk with Anna before I go back to the settlement."

"You do that. And since there is little need to go over this all again, I will gather my belongings and begin moving eastward. Simon, when can you be ready?"

"Always ready boy. I'm a' waitin' on you."

"Isaac, Reverend, may I speak with Anna alone?"

"I think my daughter would want to see you before you leave. She just may have an apology waiting."

"I need no apology. It is I who should apologize. And Reverend, do I have your permission to speak with Anna?"

"I suppose that is acceptable. I don't have to like it, but I think common courtesy requires it. And I will wait here and have a word with her myself after you leave." Sun thanked Isaac and Reverend Sullivan for their understanding and went down the trail after Anna.

•   •   •

"Leave me alone Sun." Anna didn't try to hide her tears or her anger. "Your name *is* Sun, isn't it?"

"Please Anna. I am sorry. I didn't intend to. . . ."

"To hurt me. To deceive me—and all the others. How could you do such a thing? You lied to us."

"Not a lie Anna.

"If it is not truth it is a lie. What else would you call it?"

"It was not a lie in the sense that I simply didn't divulge the entire truth."

"It was a lie. A relationship can't be built on a lie."

"A relationship?"

"Forget I even said that. How could you do such a thing as this?"

"Oh Anna. I am sorrowed by this. Allow me to explain when I say there was no intent of harm."

"I'm not sure you can explain that *Mr. Bain.*" Anna's emphasis on his name had the sting of a bee.

"Probably not, but allow me to try. I want you to understand my motives before I have to leave you behind."

"And never see me again?"

"I hope that is not the case, but it is entirely possible. I have no idea what I will find when I get home. So yes, and possibly never see you again."

"Is that what you want—to never see me again?"

"Not at all. I do want to see you again. I lo. . . ."

"Not now Jackson. Not now. Let's hear what you have to say regarding your lies."

"As you wish Anna. My father and I are estranged. His plan for me was to return from London and marry Rebecca Bomar, a life-long friend and daughter of another businessman in Boston. A beautiful and precious young woman, Rebecca, but I am not in love with her. I was to step into my father's business, blend it with that of Richard Bomar, and form the largest conglomerate in the East. But I could not do that. I wanted to come to the frontier, come to know myself a little better. Business would come after that. And marriage I suppose. But not to Rebecca Bomar. My love for her is not that type love."

"So you chose to lie?"

"No, I didn't *choose* to lie. I simply had reservations about giving out too much information. I didn't see that it mattered if I used the name Johnson. I figured I was just passing through. It wasn't a deliberate choice to be untruthful."

"But that is what it was—untruthful. And that makes it a lie."

"Yes, I suppose it does." Sun sighed in resignation.

"And I suppose you were never going to be honest with me regarding the situation with your father?"

"Not initially, I'm sorry to say. But after the attack and

my convalescence, I decided otherwise. I was going to tell you everything that day down by the creek."

"But instead of being truthful you gathered me up in your arms and kissed me, never considering whether I wanted that or not."

"Anna, that may have been the most truthful thing I have ever done. And perhaps I read you wrong, but I fully believed you wanted that as much as I."

"Truthful thing?"

"Yes, truthful. I tried to tell you then as I tried just now to tell you I lo. . . ."

"Stop it Jackson. I will not hear you. I have told you that Liam and I have grown close. He is an honest, Godly man. You could do worse than follow his leading."

"That I could Anna. My life has not always been headed in the direction I know is right. That has changed. Do you believe that?"

"And why should I? You deceived me."

"Yes, and for that I am sorry. But you ask why you should believe me now. You should believe me because I am being completely honest. I have met the same God you talk so freely about, the same God you tell me is a God of love, of forgiveness. I have asked Him for that forgiveness and I am asking you. The choice in that matter is yours."

"That it is. And I'll pray that God will help me forgive you and that He will forgive me for my unforgiveness."

"I must go Anna. Boston is a long way from here."

"Sun, please. Promise me something."

"That depends."

"Promise that you will do your part in reconciling with your family. I believe that is the starting point for you now. How your father or anyone else reacts is not your responsibility. Just be sure they know you are sincere in mending the break."

"I promise. And I promise to come here again as quickly as I can."

"So you say." Sun attempted to pull Anna close and hold her one last time before he left but she refused. "God be with you Jackson Bain." Anna whirled and ran toward the cabin.

· · ·

"They are gone Anna—Simon, Mr. Bain. Even Isaac said he would take a walk and leave us for a while." Reverend Sullivan smiled as he spoke softly to Anna.

"Sad Liam. I pray for Simon and especially for Mr. Bain. He is troubled."

"That he is, but he brought it on himself."

"Even if he did, that doesn't lessen the pain. In fact, it may make it worse. I will ask God to heal in that situation."

"Anna, is there something. . . . ?"

"I don't care to discuss anything at the moment. I'm sorry, but I just need to be alone." Liam reached for her hand and tried to pull her close. "Please Liam, not now. Please. I need some time alone."

CHAPTER 30

Late October - Boston

Robert Jamison assisted Cora into the house and seated her in a parlor chair. He returned to the carriage to get Mary Martha. As he lifted his daughter from the carriage seat, he thought of how frail and vulnerable she was. Even with hands still aching from the burns and already beginning to contort with scars, he considered Mary Martha's weight negligible. "We're home baby girl," he said softly. Mary Martha's tiny smile quickly morphed into a whimper as she tucked her face tightly against his chest. "It's all right little daughter. It's all right. I will take care of you."

"Alice. I want Alice." Mary Martha's voice was high pitched, pleading.

"We all do sweet one. We all do. I am so very sorry." Tears filled Robert's eyes; he hoped Mary Martha didn't notice.

• • •

On the Trail to Boston

"You done bettern' I figgered you would so far there boy. You still a' travelin' alright?"

"I'm fine Simon. Weary of this saddle, but fine."

"The shoulder there a' troublin' you?"

"I would be less than truthful if I said it wasn't, but it is healing. Hope to be out of this sling by the time we get to Boston."

"Reckon you prob'ly will. Still some time yet."

"Simon, I'm worried."

"Ain't 'sppoed to worry none. The Good Lord don't take kindly to His folks a' worryin;."

"No, I don't suppose He does. He is capable of worrying for us."

"*Cast your burdens on me* He tells us in the scriptures. 'Spect you'd best just do that and quit that worryin' you a' doin'."

"You are right, but I can't help but be concerned. What if my family won't welcome me back? What if they won't forgive me?"

"Don't 'spect that's a' gonna' happen boy. 'Spect they's a' gonna' be just like that feller in the Bible. You know that feller with the prod'gal son. That youngster went off a' ramblin' and got in all manner of troublesome spots. Wound up in a pig pen, he did. And what's his daddy do when the son comes a' walkin' back up to the house? Why, he starts a' dancin' and jumpin' 'round and runs down there to that boy and just 'bout hugs him plumb to death. Kills a fat bull yearlin' and puts on the biggest shindig you ever seen. Don't 'spect you got no never mind to worry 'bout your folks neither."

"I hope you are right. But my father is a hard man. He said I was not his son when I left Boston."

"Spect he's plumb sorry 'bout that by now. 'Spect he's a wishin' he hadn't a' done that, hadn't a' done a whole passel of other things he done too. Yessirreee, 'spect so. And 'sides, ain't nothin' you can do 'bout your paw. He's gotta' be the one to do all that decidin'. All you can do is tell him, and your maw too, that you love 'em both and that you's plumb sorry for a botherin' 'em in any way. And you gotta' mean it boy. Down deep there, you gotta' mean it."

"I will do that and I definitely mean it."

"Well stop all that worryin' and a' troublin' yourself. Turn it over to the Good Lord and rest easy."

"And what about Anna?"

"What 'bout Miss Anna there boy?"

"She is hurt, confused. I doubt she ever wants to see me again."

"Ain't so boy. She's a' sittin' there right now a' wonderin' when you's gonna' get back out that way."

"I'm not so sure Simon."

"I am. Shorely am. You forget you's a' talkin' to a man that knows womenfolk. Shorely do know 'em. And Miss Anna's head's just full of thinkin' 'bout Sun Bain."

"But I hurt her Simon."

"Shorely done that. Did you tell her you's plumb sorry 'bout it all?"

"I did."

"Well what's the worryin' 'bout? The Good Lord and time's all she needs and she's got 'em both aplenty."

"Not if Reverend Sullivan has his way about it."

"So now you's a' worryin' 'bout Reverend Sullivan?"

"Yes, I guess I am. He seems to have a solid hold on Anna."

"Don't think you gotta' worry none 'bout that. A fine young preacher he is, but don't hold no candle to Jackson Bain in Miss Anna's eyes."

"I wish I could be as sure of that as you Simon. You see, I love Anna Walker."

"Shorely know that boy. Been a' knowin' it since that first day me and you walked up to the Walker cabin. You's just a glowin' and such in the first few minutes there. And so was Miss Anna—a glowin'. Don't 'spect you oughta' worry none 'bout the Reverend, or 'bout Miss Anna neither. Just finish your business on up there in Boston, and when you done got it right and things done got more smoothsome, you rush back out yonder toward the Walker cabin. Scoop up Miss Anna in them strong arms you got, spout off some of them flowery words you so good with, and tell her how you feel, tell her the Good Lord done opened your eyes to the gift you 'bout to let slip right through them hands of yours. And mean it. No a' hidin' stuff she needs to know 'bout and no shenanigans. Got that boy?"

"Got it Simon!" 255

• • •

The Frontier

Liam pulled Anna close and kissed her cheek. "I enjoyed the visit today Anna."

"So did I. It was most pleasant. When will you be back out here?"

"Not until one day next week, after Sunday's service. Will you and Isaac be there for worship?"

"Yes. Isaac said we were going to the settlement Saturday and would spend the night and attend church."

"That is good news. I always look forward to Sunday service, and even more so when you are there." Anna smiled.

"And I rather enjoy the young preacher who presents the message." Liam felt vibrant, alive.

"You are more than kind. You inspire me to do my best."

"That is as it should be. I want to inspire you in your work."

"Consider me inspired Anna Walker."

"You leaving Reverend?" Isaac Walker poked his head out from a small shed near the house.

"Must go Isaac. I have sick folks to visit along the way. Best get started before darkness catches me. Oh, and Marybeth Wallace said to give you and Anna her regards."

"Thank you Reverend. And please do the same. Of course, Anna and I will be there this Sunday. I'll tell Marybeth hello myself."

"I'm sure he will," Anna said with a gentle smile.

"Yes, Anna said you two would be in the settlement. I look forward to seeing you again."

"As do we Reverend. You watch the trail and take care of yourself on your way back."

"I'll do that. Good day Isaac. And an especially good day to you Anna." Liam tipped his hat and stepped into the saddle. "I can hardly wait until Sunday." Anna was pleased.

CHAPTER 31

Boston - November 1

 Martha Bain saw Sun step from his horse and hurried to the door. She rushed outside and gathered him in her arms as if he were a little boy, the way she had longed to do for weeks. "Oh thank God. It is you Sun. Welcome home. I can't tell you how glad I am to see you. You are hurt Sun. What happened?"

"It is nothing of consequence at the moment mother. I'm just pleased to be home, to see you. And how are you? Cora and the children, how are they?"

"They are home, but I have bad news."

"Bad news?"

"Sun, I am terribly sorry to tell you this, but your little niece, Alice, died as a result of the injuries she sustained in the fire. I am so terribly sorry." Sun pushed Martha to arm's length and stood as if he were in a trance, his eyes fixed on his mother but seeming not to see.

"No mother. No. Don't tell me that. This can't be. Sweet little Alice. Gone?"

"I am afraid that is true. What a tragedy Sun. What a horrible loss." He again pulled Martha to him and began to sob, as did Martha. They remained in that posture for long minutes until Sun again released her and stepped back so that he could look into her eyes.

"What happened? All I heard was that there was a fire. Cora and Mary Martha?"

"They survived. Mary Martha has burns on her legs and feet. Cora is scarred badly. She will never look the same."

"Still beautiful though. She will always be beautiful."

"She will. Nothing can rob her of her beauty, her true beauty."

"And what happened? Tell me the details."

"They are few. Robert said he had gone outside the wagon after he and Cora got the children tucked in. He and Cora were sharing the wagon with the children. He went out to check on something and walked away, when suddenly there was an eruption of flames. He said it sounded as if gun powder ignited. Past that there is little to know about the fire. It destroyed two wagons of freight as well as the wagon they were traveling in. They lost everything. Most importantly little Alice."

"An intentional fire?"

"We don't want to believe that, but Robert thinks so."

"And Robert—how is he?"

"He was also burned when he tried to get Cora and the girls out. His hands and arms. But he is recovering. His hands are already beginning to twist and draw but he is doing well."

"I must see them immediately."

"Yes."

"And what about father; how is he? The message I received indicated he had fallen ill."

"Seriously I am afraid. He has lost use of his right side and his face is contorted. He simply lies there staring upward, basically unable to talk outside a few slurred words. I am not even sure how much of this he understands. Cora has not seen him since the fire."

"He is upstairs in the bedroom I assume."

"Yes. Would you like to see him?"

258

"Would he like to see me mother?"

"I can't answer that. I no longer know this man who was once the love of my life, the father of my children, the loving husband of my youth. Still, it is proper for you to see him."

"It is; you are right. I must see him. I must, at some point soon if I can't at the moment, apologize to him, attempt to reconcile. And apologize to you mother."

"Sun, you owe me no apology."

"Yes I do. I feel that I have been a contributor in father's condition, and that impacts you. Please know that I never intended. . . ."

"Of course you didn't. Never did I think such a thing. Please don't feel that you have anything to apologize for."

"Kind and gracious as I expected. Just like Simon said."

"Simon?"

"Yes, Simon Keats. Did I mention him in the letter? You did get my letter."

"Yes I did. And it gladdened my heart. And yes, you mentioned Simon Keats."

"He is down the street arranging lodging for a few days before he returns to the frontier settlements."

"He is here?"

"Yes, here in Boston. To be truthful, I am not sure I could have made the journey without him."

"Well please, you must collect him and bring him to meet us."

"I will do that, but now I need to see father and other members of my family. Shall I just go on up to his room?"

"That will be fine, but if you will allow I will go and announce you."

"Of course mother. And feel free to stay by my side if you wish."

"But do you wish?"

"I do. I would very much appreciate it. I will follow you." Martha turned to go inside and Sun spoke.

"Mother, permit me to tell you once again how very good it is to be home. And I want to tell you how very much I love you." Martha smiled devotedly. "And I must also tell you that I am not the man who left here in the   259 spring. I am new mother. God has made me new. I have met and accepted Him personally. I will share that story with you later."

"Oh my dear Sun. No more precious words have ever come to me. No other words could be more welcome to my ears. And yes, I want to hear every detail. But first, let's go see your father." Martha and Sun went inside and to the top of the stairs. Martha moved to the bedroom door and levered an ornate brass handle.

"Squire, you have a visitor." They stepped inside quietly. Squire made no attempt to look in their direction or to speak. "It is Sun. Jackson is home and here to see you." Sun walked to the bedside and looked down upon his father, a faint shadow of the towering giant Sun had left behind less than a year ago. The sight caused Sun to startle and step back momentarily. He then moved forward again and spoke.

"Hello father. It's Jackson. I have come home to see you." No response.

"How are you feeling? I hear you have been ill." Still nothing, save that hollow stare to which Martha had become accustomed.

"It is all right father. Don't try to speak. I just want you to know that I am here for you. It is good to see you father. And I want to tell you that. . . .That I. . . ." The words seemed frozen, rigid, refusing to emerge and touch this haunting room and this silent man. "I want to tell you that I love you father." Sun choked, tears again filling tired eyes that showed remorse and concern. "I love you." Martha's shoulders shook with her weeping.

"Perhaps we should go Sun," Martha managed to say between sobs. "We must let your father rest."

"Yes we probably should. I will be here for you father. And I will see you a bit later. Rest father. Rest." Martha and Sun went quietly from the room, the huge door proffering a vacant, ghostly sound as it closed the mystery of words not voiced from the remainder of the house. "Oh dear God," Sun whispered. "Can that be Squire Bain in there?"

•   •   •

"Jackson, welcome home." Robert Jamison spoke with affection, his countenance yet ravaged from the ordeal of the past weeks. "Please come in. Sorry, but I can't shake your hand." Robert lifted his own hands to reveal the horrid scars with which he must now contend. "And what happened to your arm?"

"Nothing of importance right now. I will tell you about it later. It is so very good to see you." Sun put his left arm around Robert's shoulders in uncharacteristic fashion. "I am so terribly sorry about all this. So terribly sorry. And sickened by it. I simply can't believe we have lost little. . . ."

"Thank you Sun. And so are we. All of us I fear will be a long time recovering from what has happened. And there will likely never be full recovery. The losses are just too great. Please, have a seat. I'll tell Cora and Mary Martha you are here." Robert ushered Sun into the parlor.

"Cora," Robert could be heard saying in the back of the house, "guess who is here."

"Yes Robert, I heard him. My dear brother has come home. Please, help me get to the parlor to see him." Robert supported his wife and guided her to the parlor. "Sun, you are here. Thank God above you are here." Sun stared in disbelief. Had he not been in her house, Sun was not sure he would have recognized his sister. Words failed him. Instead, he embraced Cora and held her. "It is all right Sun." Cora read his silence with full understanding. "It is all right. Robert, go get Mary Martha. She will want to see her uncle. And what happened to your arm?"

"Cora. Dear, dear Cora. Oh how I have missed you. And my arm is fine."

"And I have missed you more than I can say."

"I am so very sorry Cora."

"I know. I know." Cora attempted to pat her brother with affection, but her battered arms would hardly allow. "We are all sorry. We will heal. God is with us."

"He is. And He has been with me. I have a great deal to tell you in that regard when we have time to talk more. 261

For now, I just want to be near you, know that you are all right. And Mary Martha?"

"Here she comes now." Robert walked from the hall and into the room, presenting Mary Martha to her Uncle Jackson. Her feet and legs wore bandages.

"Well hello there little lady. You are more beautiful than when I left. Do you remember your Uncle Sun?" Mary Martha nodded slowly in the affirmative, the fear and pain of the incident that took her sister holding otherwise bright eyes in bondage. "How are you doing?"

"Fine," Mary Martha answered in a tiny, subdued voice.

"Mary Martha, let's put you and your mother here on the sofa." Robert put his daughter down gently and helped his wife get seated beside her. "Jackson, please sit and visit. We have much to talk about."

"That we do. And it can't all be said in one visit. This will require hours and hours of discussion."

"It certainly will," Cora added. Mary Martha sat silently, snuggled against her mother.

"I would like to hear what you have been doing since I left and what led up to this horrible incident. I have heard few details." Sun was hesitant to bring up the subject of the fire, but he wanted badly to get some specifics. "That is if you don't mind talking about it."

"Of course not," Cora said. "We all need to talk about it. This is as important to you as it is to us. I think you will understand as you hear more. Robert, please give Sun some additional information."

"Well, not long after you left, I felt that I needed to do something else with my life. Your father was good to us and provided abundantly, but I was not fulfilled, not satisfied. I would guess you understand that feeling Jackson."

"I do. I definitely do. And thank you."

"Cora and I talked it over at length and prayed about it, and I determined to leave the employ of your father and form my own business."

262   "You quit working for father?" Sun was taken aback.

"I did. Cora and I decided to begin a freight company and ship supplies to the frontier. That seemed a viable idea; the frontier is growing it seems."

"That it is. It is quite amazing out there. I will tell you more as time allows."

"Father Bain was not pleased, as you might imagine. In fact, he was angry, sullen. Told Mother Bain and Cora that he was being abandoned."

"But of course he wasn't." Cora's voice was filled with sadness. "I tried to talk with him but he wouldn't hear me. He kept saying he was being abandoned and that he would not tolerate such. It broke my heart."

"I am sure it did. And it broke mine that he wouldn't give his blessing when I left for the frontier. That trip was what I needed, what I had to do. I badly wanted father to understand and support me."

"I don't think he could Sun. He worked himself into such a condition that he quickly became someone none of us knew. Cassie, mother, me—we hardly recognized our own father and husband. His was a desperate and rather hasty fall to disaster."

"And what do you think of the situation now Cora? What about our father?"

"I fear it is too late. I fear we have lost him. Not only emotionally as a father and husband, but we are losing him physically. I don't see how he will come out of this. His time is short."

"Yes, so it seems. I am just glad I got home when I did. I fully intend to sit there by his bed and do all I can to reconcile, to tell him I care, to outline my business interests that developed while I was away. I only hope he can and will hear, but that is out of my control. I want things to be right and will do all I can to see to that end."

"And so do I Sun. I will join you in that effort. However, I hold out little hope."

"*Where hope is absent, faith remains.*" Sun spoke in soliloquy.

"What did you say Sun?" Cora was surprised by his words.

"Uh, I'm sorry. Just something someone out there on the frontier said."

"And I think that person was right."

"Wise beyond years. I am beginning to learn that those words are accurate."

"Your faith Sun?"

"It is growing. And I want to tell you about it. But let's allow Robert to continue with his story."

"Yes, let's. Robert." Cora nodded to her husband.

"Well, I secured teams and wagons. Even employed drivers. I went down to Philadelphia to set everything up; the freight was to leave from there. Then Cora and I decided to go along, at least part of the way, with that first shipment. Or rather I decided. Oh God, had I only not decided to do that."

"Now Robert," Cora interrupted, "the decision was made by both of us. I'll not have you blaming yourself."

"Yes, but. . . ."

"No but Robert. It was a shared decision. We did what we thought best. And we considered the children. The trip, as we saw it, would be interesting, educational."

"True. But had I not insisted. . . ."

"Now I insist. Stop doing this to yourself. You are in no way at fault. No more than I am or Jackson is or any of us are. This just happened. It was the human condition. Not always pleasant, the human condition."

"That it is not sister. Please Robert, continue with the details."

"We left Philadelphia with the freight wagons. It was a terrific journey. We bounced along the Great Wagon Road and laughed and talked and saw some grand country. The drivers slept each night around the campfire in their blankets. Cora, the children, and I made beds in our wagon. It was wonderful—until that night. . . ."

"I understand you think the fire might have been deliberately set." Sun was curious about that possibility.

"I can't say for sure, but after I left the wagon and walked away, I thought I heard something like flint striking steel and there was this *whoosh* like gun powder going off. The wagons were covered in flames within seconds. There was little I could do. Oh Sun, we have lost our daughter and our entire investment. What will we do?" Robert hung his head, revealing what Sun perceived as shame.

"I don't have a complete answer for that, but I do know that God and time will heal. It is not easy; few things are. But healing will come. Just focus on the important things now and those are your relationships - with your family and with God. You will heal. And you will survive this business loss."

"Perhaps." Robert spoke with doubt.

"You will. Be assured you will. And I find it interesting that you and I had the same idea."

"The same idea Sun?" Cora had a quizzical look on her face, evident even through the distortion caused by the flames.

"Yes. I saw a need on the frontier for freight, for shipments of goods. In fact, I am considering developing such a business. Seems you have beat me to it."

"I don't know about that. I have nothing to invest now."

"Let's not be concerned about investments at this point," Sun suggested. "Let's not be concerned about anything other than healing. And my first step in that is to talk to father. It is not something I look forward to, but I must do it—for myself if for no one else. God has led me to this. I must follow."

"You speak openly of God Sun." Cora found his obvious change encouraging but at the same time confusing. "I don't recall you. . . ."

"And you wouldn't for I didn't. But things are different now. I will be more than happy to share all that with you in time, but I must get back. Mother is waiting."

"Yes. Feel free. I know she wants you near. God bless you brother. I love you, and it is good to have you home."

"And I love you sister—and you Robert and Mary Martha. God bless you all as well. I will see you soon. And I must get over to see Cassie and Jonathan before I go back home."

CHAPTER 32

"Howdy there boy." Simon Keats was walking along the streets of Boston when he saw Sun doing the same. Two days has passed since their arrival.

"Well hello Simon. I was looking for you. I guess you found lodging with no problem."

"Shore, shore. Even folks in Boston come a' runnin' and a' invitin' when they see smartsome gentlemen such as Simon Keats 'bout town."

"People invited you to stay in their homes?"

"Well, can't say that's 'xactly what happened. I just sorta' walked in the Gage yonder and plopped some money down. But I shorely got lodgin' boy. Shorely do."

"That's good Simon. And you are doing all right?"

"Doin' just dandy boy. How's them folks of yours?"

"They are surviving. That is about all I could expect under the circumstances I suppose."

"Reckon you's prob'ly right. Shorely did go through a passel of tough times. Got some more to come I 'spect. But iffin they know the Good Lord, they'll be moren' alright in all this."

"They do, and they will. They have faith and strength. Simon, I want you to come home with me and meet my mother."

266   "And your paw too boy?"

"Well, I suppose that would be all right. But he doesn't seem to know anyone or try to communicate in any way. He simply lies there and stares at the ceiling. We are not sure that he is even aware of his surroundings. But we will try."

"Whatever you think best Sun. Simon Keats ain't one to impose or get in the way of family doin's."

"No imposition Simon. I have told mother about you and she wants to meet you while you are here. When do you plan to leave Boston and go back to the settlements?"

"A mite chillsome outside now. Still, 'spect I'll head out in a day or so. Need to get back out that a' way 'fore Christmas. Folks out there'll be a' wonderin' iffin they's got cause to celebrate iffin Simon Keats ain't amongst 'em. 'Course, most of 'em know why we celebrate anyhow. Shorely ain't 'cause of me or you or nobody else 'cept Jesus. He's shorely the one that's cause for celebratin'."

"As usual, you are correct. And I can tell you with certainty that this will be my first *real* Christmas."

"Shorely good to know boy. But then I ain't surprised by it none. You's a smartsome feller. Curious and a' wonderin' all time. No sir-reeee. Ain't no surprise that you done seen the truth. Glad for you boy. Shorely am."

"Thank you Simon. But I still have a long way to go."

"That's true, for shore. But you a' gonna' get there. Shorely as my name's Simon Keats, you a' gonna' get there. 'Spect Miss Anna'll help keep you on the straight and narrow." Sun looked away, a trace of sadness creasing his face at the mention of Anna Walker.

"I don't know about that. I'm not sure Anna will ever want to see me again."

"Shore she will. Ain't we done plumb talked this out back there when we's a' headin' in to Boston?"

"We did. But. . . ."

"Now boy hush up. Just you get your doin's done all proper like here at home and then you rush on back out there to Miss Anna. She'll be a' waitin' and proud you's back."

"I can only hope Simon—or at least have faith. And I

don't suppose your rush to get back out there is because of Nora Jean is it?"

"'Spect that might have something to do with it. I ain't bull headed like you; I ain't a' gonna' miss out again. No sirreeee. Simon Keats is a' headin' home. 'Sides, these Boston womenfolk done got me plumb tiresome a' chasin' me 'round."

"I have said it before and will say it again: Simon Keats, you are insufferable. But a likeable old rascal just the same. Now you come to meet my mother tomorrow, 10:00 a.m. on the dot." Sun gave Simon directions. "And you will have the noon meal with us."

"I ain't never been late for nothin' You just look out the winder and check the clock. You'll see me a' comin' right on time."

"I am sure I will. Look forward to it. And in the meantime, take care of yourself Simon. I don't think I could bear to lose one such as you."

"And you be shore to do the same. Ain't a' interested in a' losin' you neither. Done got too much 'vested in you as it is. Gotta' see you all growed up and a' settled down 'fore the Good Lord calls me. Look out that winder at 10:00. I'll be there."

• • •

"Cassie, Jonathan, Franklin—please, come in." Robert Jamison was gracious. "I'll tell Cora you are here."

"Thank you Robert. And how are Cora and Mary Martha today?" Cassie Richardson was anxious about her sister and niece.

"They are coming along well. Thank you."

"And you Robert?" Jonathan asked. "How are you?"

"I'm fine. These hands won't ever work as they once did, but I am fine. My primary concern now is for Cora and Mary Martha."

• • •

The Frontier

"Do you suppose they are there yet papa? Simon and Sun I mean. Do you think they are in Boston?"

"I would guess they are. Jackson was in no condition to make a long trip like that, but even moving at his slow pace I'm sure they are there."

"I have been praying for them."

"So have I Anna. Every day."

"I hope Sun can reconcile with his family."

"As do I. And tell me Anna. If he does and one day before too long comes riding back up here to the cabin, what will you do; what will you say?"

"He won't—come riding back. He won't."

"But if he does?"

"Liam is coming tomorrow Isaac."

"Good. I look forward to seeing him. We have fresh bear meat and I'll help you cook dinner."

"That's fine. I'm sure he would like that."

"You are growing fond of him, are you?"

"Yes, fond. At least he cares enough to ride in the dark to see me."

"These short days see to that. And the glow Anna?"

"Not like a spring sunrise, but there seems to be a little orange around the edges."

●   ●   ●

Boston

"Simon, this is my mother, Martha Bain. Mother, this is the most contrary fellow on the frontier, Simon Keats."

"Shorely glad to meet you Mrs. Bain. I been a' hearin' a bunch 'bout you folks, 'specially you."

"Well thank you Mr. Keats. I am sure my son exaggerated in his description of me. And very pleased to meet you, to have you with us."

"No ma'am. Ain't no 'xaggeratin' to it. Said you was a beautiful and gracious woman. Shorely right on that account Mrs. Bain. Shorely was."

"Goodness. You will have me thinking too highly of myself. Now please, come in. We have a 269 great many things to discuss. I want to hear about your travels with my son."

"You oughta' be right proud of that boy of yours. Right proud. He just plumb took to long huntin' and the frontier."

"I am proud. I was proud of him even before he left for the frontier. I have always been proud of him. And perhaps you can give me an accurate account of what happened to his shoulder."

"He ain't told you nothin' 'bout that yet?"

"Not much. He said there was an incident and that he was healing well." Sun sat uncomfortably beside Simon.

"Now Simon." Sun preferred to keep the particulars of the Shawnee attack quiet.

"Why, that boy of yours just plumb showed his upbringin'. Hadn't a' been for him, don't 'spect me and you would be a' havin' this here conversation."

"Jackson, what is this all about? What really happened out there?"

"Mother, it is of no concern now. I will be fine."

"Shorely is a concern too boy. Tell your maw what happened. We done discussed this whole truth thing 'fore we hardly got outta' the settlement back there. Now go on. Tell her the story."

"Simon, please. Not now."

"Yessireee now. Out with it boy. Your maw deserves the truth."

"Mother, I didn't want to worry you. You have more worry than one person can stand as it is."

"Sun, the truth. What happened? I know you are safe now and that is all that matters."

"I suppose you are right, but this is a painful story, and I fear the details will cause alarm."

"Alarm is something with which I have become familiar. Please continue."

"Yes, I shall. Mother, the frontier is grand. Simon and I made two trips, the first not far out from the Walker cabin and the second on out into the edge of the Middle Ground. One night three of us were camped—

270

Simon, Jule, and me. I will have to tell you more about Jule Chillington later. We suddenly found ourselves under attack."

"Attack? Sun no."

"Yes. Shawnees. I woke to find a warrior trying to kill Jule. I intervened. Then I was hit with an arrow."

"Oh God, Sun. You could have been killed."

"That's what them Shawnees was a' tryin' to do—kill us. But your boy there. . . ."

"Mother, I killed those Shawnees. Killed two men. Oh mother, I am grieved. This will haunt my life forever. I am so terribly sorry to tell you this, to admit to acting in a violent fashion." Martha Bain's face showed anguish.

"Dear God Sun. Killed two men. I. . . ."

"Weren't nothin' to do 'cept that ma'am. Sorry, but weren't nothin' else to do. The frontier's sorta' differentn' it is back here. Some warin' a mite strong poss'bility 'round every bend near 'bout. Hope that'll stop soon; gettin' better but still a mite touchy. Your boy there just done what he had to do. Saved all three of us, he did. Can't fault him there." Martha still sat aghast.

"Mother, I wish I could have avoided all that, but it happened. I am healing from the arrow wounds; the other will take a life time. Please, I didn't want to worry you."

"But what is a mother to do? Worry is normal."

"I am sure it is. Forgive me."

"You are forgiven—always forgiven. I love you Sun. And thank God you are safe."

"Yes, thank God. And I love you mother."

"Now you gettin' right down to the grit of this thing boy. 'Pologizin' and a' askin' for forgiveness. I'm proud of you. See, ain't so hard to 'pologize and be plumb honest. Only way to go boy. Only way. You talked to your paw yet?"

"I have seen him."

"You come clean with him yet?"

"I am not sure what he can understand, if he can even hear me."

"That don't make no never mind. You gotta' clean it all out for you moren' for him. You gotta' make it all whitern' snow on your part. Let the Good Lord take it from there. You hear me boy?"

"I hear you. Tomorrow will be the day. My father will have me to himself and I will, as you say, clean it all out."

"Promise boy?"

"I promise Simon."

"Well see to it then. Now iffin you folks will 'xcuse me, I best wander on out and make plans to get movin'. These old bones'll freeze plumb up at the base of a oak tree iffin I don't get outta' here 'fore winter bites hard."

"I'll not hear of you leaving at this moment," Martha Bain said with authority. "Didn't Sun invite you to have the noon meal with us?"

"That he did ma'am, but shorely don't want to trouble you folk none."

"Trouble? Goodness, it certainly is no trouble. The meal is prepared and waiting. And after all you have done for Sun. No, I will not hear of it. You are staying for the meal. Now come on you two. The food is ready." They moved to a huge mahogany dining table filled with a variety of food such as Simon had never seen.

"Mr. Keats, would you please give thanks?" Martha Bain looked first at Simon and then at her son. She sat with great dignity.

"Shorely be glad to ma'am. Shorely will." Simon put his hands together and bowed his head.

Lord, shorely do thank You for the day You done made for us, and shorely do thank You for this good lookin' food here. And Lord, thank You for the Bain family. Bless 'em Lord. Take care of 'em. And thank You for givin' me the chance to meet 'em, 'specially Jackson. He's a good and smartsome young feller, and shorely do 'ppreiate what You done in his life. You mighty good to us all. In Jesus name. Amen. Martha and Jackson looked up, their eyes showing a hint of tears.

"Thank you Mr. Keats."

"You welcome ma'am. And iffin you don't mind, it's just Simon. Don't need no mister."

"That it will be Simon. And thank you for taking care of my son."

"Weren't none of me. The Good Lord's the one a' takin' care."

"That is true. Still, I thank you. You were God's instrument. Now have some food before it gets cold."

"Shorely some fine victuals," Simon noted as they completed the meal. "Shorely was. Me and Jackson there didn't have nothin' like that out yonder in the Middle Ground. That boy of yours ain't much of a cook. 'Spect he'd a' plumb near starved iffin it hadn't a' been for me. Iffn any man knows how to cook salt meat and cornmeal, it's Simon Keats." Simon's laughter rumbled about the entire expanse of the Bain house.

"When do you plan to leave Simon?" Martha asked after the laughter subsided.

"Spect I'll mount up 'round daylight tomorrow. Long journey 'head of me."

"Tomorrow Simon?" Sun asked, a measure of sadness in his voice.

"Yeah, reckon so. Ain't nothin' I need to do here now and I want to get home. The frontier's a' callin'."

"And Nora Jean?"

"Shorely is boy. A' callin'."

"Simon, I want to thank you for everything you have done. You have meant more to me. . . ."

"Now don't go a' gettin' all sent'mental and such there boy. We's gonna' meet up a'gin soon. 'Sides, ain't no thank you needed in all this. Just a' seein' you get all straight and such and a' seein' you a' gettin' all growed up's moren' 'nough thank you. Now see to that big discussion with your paw—no latern' tomorrow."

"That I will Simon."

"Mr. Keats, Simon, thank you. And it was a pleasure having you in our home. Please, do come again."

"Thank you ma'am. 'Course, don't 'spect to be back in these parts no more. Just too tiresome to get here. But I'll be a' hearin' from you folks right reg'lar I 'magine. Jackson here's a' gonna' keep a' reportin' on the goin's on."

"That I will."

"Well, see that you do there boy. And good bye Mrs. Bain. Take care of this boy for me."

"I will do just that. And good bye to you. You are welcome here anytime. But before you go, wait a few minutes while I pack you some food that will keep on the trail."

"Thank you kindly ma'am. 'Spect I'll need it 'fore long out there. Huntin' ain't too good right along the trail this side of the frontier. Now Jackson, take care of your folks. And I ain't a' sayin' no good byes to you boy. I 'spect to see you a' ridin' toward the frontier 'fore the snow melts from the mountains and the buds start settin'. Shorely 'spect to see you."

"And that you will Simon. Now off with you. And Simon, take care of that old battered hide of yours."

• • •

"Cora, we are losing our father." Cassie Richardson was distraught.

"Yes, I fear you are right. This is all tragic."

"And Jackson."

"Jackson?"

"Yes. There is something not quite right with his return."

"I think you are wrong about that Cassie."

"Perhaps, but it all seems so strange, so. . . ."

"First, he had little choice. Word was delivered to him regarding the situation with his family here. There was nothing to do but come back."

"He should never have left."

"Cassie, please. Think of what you are saying. Jackson made it clear that he needed to go. . . ."

"Needed? What about our needs?"

"I don't see that as significant."

"It is. In fact, it was his leaving that caused father's illness."

"You can't mean that. Father allowed himself to fall into anger. He came to mistrust us all. That was not Jackson's fault."

274 "Maybe not, but he certainly contributed to it."

"Perhaps there is a measure of truth in that assumption Cassie, but it was all ultimately father's decision. He chose poorly." Jonathan Richardson had sat quietly to this point.

"And the business. I am the one who has had to take responsibility for it. Working and doing my best to suit what I thought your father would want. And now Jackson. . . ."

"Do you think Jackson has come back to take the business from you Jonathan?"

"What else can I think? I mean, it seems more than a coincidence. Now I must move from under the control of one Bain to the control of another." Cora felt hurt and anger emerge.

"Jonathan, Cassie, before we say things we will regret, I think we need to set all this aside for the moment. We have more important things to consider. Father for instance. And mother. Cassie, you just said that we are losing our father. I agree. And we need our strength to face that. God knows we have already faced tragedy. Let's not add to that and let's not fabricate situations that don't yet exist. We need to remain a family, a family dedicated to the wellbeing of all involved."

"You are right Cora. I'm sorry we brought this up," Cassie added. Jonathan sat without speaking, solemn and frowning.

"I understand Cassie." Cora was gentle, the anger subsiding. "And I ask you to give Jackson time. I fully believe you will see a new man, a man you have not known before. He has experienced change; has met God face to face. Give him time. Please, let's turn our attention to our parents. They need us—both of them need us."

CHAPTER 33

Jackson Bain knocked softly and pushed the big door open tentatively. "Father, it is Jackson. I'm coming in." Sun stepped inside and closed the door behind him, its eerie click causing Sun to halt momentarily. He walked to the bedside and gazed at his frail father, hardly recognizing him in this supine posture that spoke of weakness rather than strength as Sun had known him. "I want to talk to you." Sun pulled a chair up beside the bed and sat.

"How are you feeling?" There was no indication that his father heard or recognized him. "It is a beautiful day outside. Sunny, bright. Cold at nights now, but this is November in Boston." Sun attempted to brighten the mood but there was no response.

"Father, this may take some time and I hope I don't ramble or tire you too much. But I have some things that must be said." Jackson shuffled in the chair and tightened his courage.

"First, let me say I love you. I love you more than you can know, and I am profoundly sorry for all that has happened. I apologize for disappointing you by not coming immediately into the business when I returned from London, but I was simply unable to do that. I had to do something else. I had to go to the frontier. My prayer is that you can come to understand that." Sun looked into his father's eyes for some sign. There was none.

276 "The trip was one that opened my eyes and heart. I

discovered a great many things about myself. It was essential that I go. Most important in all this is that I discovered relationships. Deep relationships. And the deepest one I encountered was with God. I have come to know Him father. I hope you have as well.

"I was wounded father. Attacked by Shawnees. And while it grieves me to tell you this, I took the lives of those two who attacked. I am so very sorry. Forgive me. God has already and He is helping me heal. The physical wounds are healing even now, but the other pain will take more time. I hope you can understand.

"I met some extraordinary people in my travels. Simon Keats is one. He is quite amazing. Insightful, entertaining. A man of God. And there is Anna and Isaac Walker. A father and daughter. They live out near the Gap miles from the last settlement, and they let me see true contentment. They are to be admired. Poor and without resources that we think essential, they live a full life. That is what I want to do—live a full life.

"And I love Anna Walker father. I love her deeply. But I fear I have spoiled any chance that might have been with her. I deceived her and crushed her spirit. I have asked her to forgive me, but I hold little hope that I can rescue that relationship. Tragic, broken relationships. Why can't we see that before we shatter those around us?

"You might also be interested to know that I have begun to think seriously about business. You are a businessman; you should appreciate what I am considering. The frontier is growing. There are countless needs for goods and supplies out there. Service is anything but sure and timely, and I am giving thought to providing more and better service for what is sure to be an explosive expansion within a few years. Imagine that—your wayward son who rejected business is thinking about going into business! Spreading the Bain name westward. I wish you could share your thoughts and expertise with me.

"Father, I am a new man. I am more fully finding myself each day. God is leading and I want to follow. He has His work set before Him, but He is more than capable of accomplishing anything I will allow. I want to allow Him control—full and complete control.

"I ask you again to forgive me. And I ask you to forgive mother and Cora and Robert and all others who you think have wronged you. Forgiveness is essential if life is to have meaning. Consider it father. Please consider it." For the first time since Sun had entered Squire Bain's room, there appeared a flicker, a faint ray of cognizance.

"Father? You are hearing me, aren't you? You do recognize me and know what I am saying. Can you respond?" Sun reached under Squire's shoulders and lifted him slightly. With much effort and with his slurred speech coming is one-word sentences, Squire whispered:

"Is. . . . there. . . . redemption?"

"There is father. There is."

About the Author

Tony Kinton began writing for outdoor magazines more than 30 years ago. He remains active in that pursuit, with more than 2,000 articles and four books published, all pertaining to the outdoors. *Summer Lightning Distant Thunder* is his first Christian fiction.

Kinton has long been an avid reader, and his love for writing grew as a result. He earned graduate degrees in music and English and retired as an English composition and American literature instructor on the community college level. He and his wife Susan live in rural central Mississippi.